RECONSTRUCTING A
SHATTERED
EGYPTIAN ARMY

GENERAL MOHAMED FAWZI ACCEPTS HIS ASSIGNMENT AS EGYPT'S WAR MINISTER
FROM PRESIDENT GAMAL ABDEL NASSER IN 1968.

Rogers Photo Archive/Keystone Media. Photo courtesy of ArgentaImages™ and used with permission.

RECONSTRUCTING A ★★
SHATTERED
★★ EGYPTIAN ARMY

War Minister Gen. Mohamed Fawzi's
Memoirs, 1967–1971

Edited by Youssef H. Aboul-Enein

NAVAL INSTITUTE PRESS
ANNAPOLIS, MARYLAND

Naval Institute Press
291 Wood Road
Annapolis, MD 21402

Library of Congress Cataloging-in-Publication Data
Reconstructing a shattered Egyptian Army : War Minister Gen. Mohamed Fawzi's memoirs, 1967–1971 / edited by Youssef H. Aboul-Enein.
     pages cm
Includes bibliographical references and index.
  ISBN 978-1-61251-460-4 (hardcover : alk. paper) — ISBN 978-1-61251-459-8 (ebook) 1. Fawzi, Muhammad. 2. Generals—Egypt—Biography. 3. Fawzi, Muhammad. Harb al-thal-ath sanawat, 1967/1970. 4. Egypt. Jaysh—History. 5. Israel-Arab War, 1967. 6. Israel-Arab War, 1973. 7. Egypt—History, Military. 8. Arab-Israeli conflict—1967–1973. I. Aboul-Ene-in, Youssef H., editor. II. Title: War Minister Gen. Mohamed Fawzi's memoirs, 1967–1971.
  DT107.828.F39R43 2014
  355.00962'09046—dc23

                                                                        2014001600

♾ Print editions meet the requirements of ANSI/NISO z39.48-1992 (Permanence of Paper).
Printed in the United States of America.

22 21 20 19 18 17 16 15 14   9 8 7 6 5 4 3 2 1
First printing

THE DEDICATION OF THIS BOOK IS SIMPLE:

First, to Arlington National Cemetery Section 60;

Second, to my National Defense University students,
civilian as well as military—I learned as much from you as you did from me;

Finally, to Egyptians rediscovering their history—this I hope will be among the positive
by-products of Egypt's struggle for freedom in its Second Republic—
and to a final transition from an illiberal democracy.

CONTENTS

MAPS

PREFACE

*There is no longer a way out of our present situation
except by forging a road toward our objective,
violently and by force, over a sea of blood and
under a horizon blazing with fire.*

—GAMAL ABDEL NASSER—

THIS BOOK REPRESENTS A SINGULAR PASSION THAT HAS BEEN CENTRAL TO MY career in the U.S. military. Since the 1990s I have advocated the introduction of America's military leaders to Arabic works of military significance. Just as our predecessors in the U.S. armed forces obsessed over Russian tradition and culture during the Cold War, we must develop a deeper understanding of the Middle East from direct sources as we continue to wage war on al-Qaida and witness the complex aftermath of the Arab Spring. The memoir of General Mohamed Fawzi, Egypt's war minister from 1967 to 1971, was published in 1984, but even after his death in 2000, his work has not been translated for English-speaking readers. Many in the U.S. armed services have yet to be introduced to his ideas and perspectives, which laid the foundation for the 1973 Yom Kippur War. I was determined to change this by writing a series of essays for the U.S. Army's *Infantry Magazine* that would bring attention to the military thoughts of General Fawzi. This book presents my essays on Fawzi in a single volume, expanding on the original series and adding further source materials.

Fawzi is unique among Arab generals for his scathing critique of his own armed forces, and by critically examining what went wrong in 1967, he was able to slowly build the Egyptian armed forces to a level that enabled Anwar Sadat to consider an offensive in 1973. In his memoir Fawzi provided insight into the level of cooperation and military aid the Soviets provided Egypt after the 1967 Six-Day War (known in Arabic as *al-Naksah* [the setback] and not to be confused with the 1948 Arab-Israeli War, known as *al-Nakbah* [the catastrophe]). Did he lapse into conspiracy? Sure! Did he indulge in wishful thinking? Yes! Did he use the language of pan-Arabism on occasion? Of course! But he is no different than Soviet military theorists who couched their ideas in Marxist-Leninist rhetoric, and this rhetoric has not stopped serious American students of war from recognizing the occasional brilliance of General Alexander Svechin (1878–1938) or the fine tactics amid the brutality of Georgy Zhukov (1896–1974) or the brilliant synthesis of guerrilla and conventional tactics of Vo Nguyen Giap (1911–2013). Fawzi also leaves out details from his memoir, and the essays in this book attempt to draw the reader's attention to these gaps and omissions. As you are reading, consult the notes section for alternative views.

In 2006, while sitting at my desk in the Office of the Secretary of Defense at the Pentagon, I received a call from the British Library in London. The producer of the documentary series *20th Century Battlefields*, Stephen Douds, was asking me to act as military history consultant on the next installment in the series. He asked if I was the author of the collection of essays highlighting Egyptian generals in *Military Review* and *Infantry*. I said that indeed I had written essays based on the memoirs of Abdel-Moneim Riad and Saad el-Din el-Shazly. He then proceeded to tell me that Egyptian authorities would not cooperate with him and that my pieces represented the only way to get the Arab perspective for episode 8, featuring the 1973 Yom Kippur War. Thus began my involvement in the episode, which aired in 2007. It was eerie to see Peter and Dan Snow walking about the desert, opening their attaché case to reveal an interactive map, and bringing my words to life with animation. I paused and realized that only through my service in the American military, as a U.S. Navy officer who wrote and commented on the memoirs of Arab generals in U.S. Army journals, could I be sought by British producers of a military documentary. The right confluence of events had led to that phone call: my career in the Navy, the U.S. Army giving me my writing start as a junior officer, military and civilian mentors, and an armed service that has capitalized on my intellectual diversity before and after the events of September 11, 2001.

As director for North Africa and Egypt from 2003 to 2006 for the Office of the Secretary of Defense, I had the rare privilege of meeting many Arab and Egyptian generals. At social events we sometimes discussed and even disagreed about the various military leaders who played a role in the 1967 and 1973 Arab-Israeli wars.[1] Understanding generals like Fawzi helps us to understand the mind-set of many generals ruling Egypt today, as the country transitions from a failed First Republic to a hopefully brighter Second Republic. Members of Egypt's ruling Supreme Council of the Armed Forces (SCAF) have read Fawzi's memoir, as well as those of General Shazly and General Abdel-Ghani El-Gamasi.

Fawzi's memoir is an important source for the new generation of American military leaders. The United States will continue to be engaged in the Middle East for the foreseeable future, and educating America's military officers and decision makers about Arab military leaders is vital to cultivate a more comprehensive strategy for operations there. Immersion in direct Arabic sources will help American leaders to understand the language of, rationale for, and thinking about warfare from the Arab perspective. This immersion will also help us to comprehend the mechanics of the relationship among Egyptian leaders, the populace, and the armed forces that led to, for example, the removal of the elected president Mohamed Morsi from power by a populist-backed military in July 2013. I cannot emphasize enough the importance of incorporating Arabic works of political-military significance in the education of our future officers and civilian leaders who will shape America's policies toward the Middle East. The current Egyptian defense minister, General Abdel-Fatah al-Sisi, is himself a graduate of the U.S. Army War College, and he spent a year absorbing the ins and outs of U.S. national security policy formulation. Al-Sisi's 2006 thesis focused on democracy in the Middle East—four years before the events of the Arab Spring. The thesis centers on how democracy would work in the Middle East and tackles the concept of "freedom from religion" versus "freedom of religion."[2] Like al-Sisi, we Americans should spend time cultivating an in-depth understanding of our Arab allies. In addition to familiarizing ourselves with direct Arabic sources, we should implement a proposed exchange program whereby American field-grade officers with a certain score on the Arabic Defense Language Proficiency Test (DLPT) can spend a year auditing classes at Arab war colleges.

Following the fall of Hosni Mubarak in 2011, Egyptians are reinstating many generals, including Saad el-Din el-Shazly, Mohamed Fawzi, and Abdel-Ghani El-Gamasi, to their proper historic roles. For too long these men have been marginalized by Egyptian cronies of Mubarak in favor of a dictator who consumes all the glory, in murals, paintings, and the popular imagination. Only true students, Arab and non-Arab, of the Arab-Israeli conflict know about the ideas of these generals and Mubarak's role in the 1973 Yom Kippur War beyond the sound bites.

Further critical assessments of Fawzi's memoir have been included herein. These draw on many themes omitted by Fawzi but found in the memoirs of other Egyptian generals and political advisers, as well as accounts collected by American scholars. A list of books to enhance your understanding of Fawzi's memoir and the lead-up to the 1973 Arab-Israeli War is provided in appendix 1. Included in the appendix are two essays published in *Infantry* about Egyptian generals Saad el-Din el-Shazly and Abdel-Moneim Riad. Shazly played an important role in the 1973 Arab-Israeli War, and Riad played an integral part, along with Fawzi, in the reconstruction of Egyptian arms. Riad died in 1969 while inspecting defenses along the Suez Canal; he was the highest-ranking Egyptian officer to be killed in action. In the summer of 2013, as I write this preface, Egypt is undergoing violent turmoil, and it is my earnest hope that the country's diverse history will not go up in flames and that it can make that transition from an illiberal democracy to a more representative democracy that considers the diversity of all Egyptians. That Egypt reconciles itself to the reality that democracy does not mean majoritarianism. There is so much for the world to learn from and about Egypt.

ACKNOWLEDGMENTS

RARELY CAN A BOOK BE COMPLETED ALONE, AND I HAVE MANY PEOPLE TO THANK. First and foremost, let me thank Ms. Dorothy (Dori) Corley, who, as a recent Boston University graduate in international relations, edited every sentence of this series. It is not an exaggeration to say that her advice and improvements have left an imprint on this book. Dori also was a delight to have as a teaching assistant in my National Defense University graduate-level elective, Islam, Islamist Political Theory, and Militant Islamist Ideology: Understanding Nuance. My 2014 intern Ms. Rachel Rizzo of George Washington University was instrumental in the final indexing and proofing phases. I also need to thank Ms. Michelle Rowan, deputy editor of *Infantry*, and Mr. Russell Eno, editor of *Infantry*, for encouraging me to write this series and for giving me a voice in *Infantry* since I was a lieutenant. They understood my vision, as a junior naval officer, of training America's twenty-first-century military using direct Arabic sources. Appreciation also goes to my daughter, Maryam Katherine; my son, Omar Youssef; and my wife, Cheryl Anne, who endured me bringing General Mohamed Fawzi home every day in the form of papers, books, and discussions. Now that this collection has been published, I promise to relegate him to the classroom. My wife helped me make my publisher's deadline and made space in our home for papers, books, and maps. I am now under the gun to remove these papers and books, clearing space in our home.

In addition, the following libraries need to be mentioned. They provided not only a quiet place to read and write but also research material on Soviet weapons systems and Arabic military terms. These libraries include the John T. Hughes Library in Washington, D.C. (thanks to Gretchen Reynolds, who helped me track down the names of Soviet generals Fawzi mentions only by rank and last name in Arabic); the National Defense University Library in Washington, D.C. (particular thanks to Ms. Karen Cooper; Ms. Trish Bachman, Ms. Camille Majors, and Ms. Lily McGovern in the map room; and Mr. Mike McNulty); the Pentagon Library; the Library of Congress Middle East Reading Room; and the Blackwell Library at Salisbury University in Salisbury, Maryland. My appreciation goes to the librarian at Salisbury, Ms. Martha Zimmerman, and to Captain Christopher Ahlstrom,

Maryland Army National Guard, who is assistant professor of military science, for providing me additional documents while I was visiting my daughter, who is studying at the university. The John T. Hughes Library was instrumental in putting me in touch with former Soviet intelligence analysts who had a deep understanding of Soviet weapons systems; it is regrettable that we let this skill atrophy as the Cold War came to an end, even though Soviet-era military hardware proliferates in the twenty-first-century battle space. I must also mention the Army and Navy Club Library at Farragut Square, where I wrote chapter 4 using the desk Supreme Court Associate Justice Anthony Kennedy once used as he prepared for his Senate confirmation. I see why the justice picked this desk, as it is in an excellent and quiet corner of the library.

Fawzi's memoir contains very rudimentary and crudely drawn maps, so I would be remiss if I did not thank Lieutenant Colonel Raymond Hrinko, USA, of the Department of History at the U.S. Military Academy at West Point, for securing permission and providing maps 3 and 4. Mr. Matt Grace was instrumental in obtaining permission from ArgentaImages to use the 1968 photo of Fawzi formally receiving his charge as war minister from Nasser, which appears as the frontispiece of this book.

My parents continue to be a great source of inspiration. My father took me on tours of Egypt's military sites, from the military museum inside the Cairo Citadel to the battlefield at El-Alamein to the site in Alexandria where Napoleon's legions landed in 1798. This enabled me to conduct professional military education (PME) tours in some of these same sites, while I was specially detailed to the 24th Marine Expeditionary Unit (MEU) during Exercise Bright Star as a junior officer. My mother and my late maternal grandmother, Fawkia Ali Rushdi, imbued me with a highly attuned sense of the various political narratives of the Middle East. Yes, my mom and I still argue about Arab politics today, including the historic presidential debate on May 10, 2012—the first candidates' debate not only for Egypt but for the Arab world—and lately the removal of Mohamed Morsi from the presidency and what this portends for Egypt domestically and internationally.

Other relatives who inspired me to study the Arab-Israeli conflict are my two uncles, retired Egyptian general Gamil Haress and retired Egyptian judge Ahmed Kamal Al-Din. They provided me with oral histories that stimulated my thinking. General Haress is now in his nineties and spends his retirement from the Egyptian army among beautiful Arabian stallions, training equestrian riders at Cairo's historic Gezira Club; he is magnificent to watch with the ponies. Amid the eucalyptus trees and horses, the general (to me, Uncle Gamil) recounted how he walked the Sinai Desert toward the Suez Canal, barely surviving, suffering the effects of hunger and dehydration, lost, evading Israeli capture, until Bedouins guided him toward the canal during the 1967 Six-Day War. My family tells stories of how Uncle Gamil was nursed to health mentally and physically by my paternal great-uncle Fouad, then living in Suez, after spending days making his way back amid the Egyptian army's retreat. Judge Ahmed Kamal Al-Din, after years of practicing law, adjudicating cases, and rising to be a judicial adviser to the Majlis al-Dawla, or Council of State, recounted to me his experience working as a Suez Canal Authority lawyer, and in particular the impact the Arab-Israeli War had on people living in the city of Suez. As you will read, thousands of Egyptians relocated from the city to escape artillery duels and antiaircraft rounds. I could not help being affected by the story of this human side of warfare, and this led me to study warfare as a young child and then as an adult. I am privileged to be a member of the U.S. profession of arms, which among other things has enabled me to constantly think about aspects of warfare and America's national security.

I would be negligent if I did not thank Mr. Gary Greco, who retired from the Defense Department in 2012. Gary and I spent many mornings talking about Mohamed Fawzi, Gamal Abdel Nasser, Lyndon Johnson, and Leonid Brezhnev over coffee. It was one of those informal educations that comes from a lifetime in the service of the United States, both as a civilian and in the U.S. Army. The late Peter W. Rodman (d. 2008), as assistant secretary of defense for international security affairs, provided me, as a lieutenant and lieutenant commander, a ringside-seat education on the power words have to shape ideas in the interagency debate about America's national security. I also would like to thank my fellow instructors at the Industrial College of the Armed Forces, now called the Eisenhower School, specifically Mr. Gustav (Gus) Otto, Captain Chandler (Chan) Swallow, USN, and Captain John Meier, SC, USN, for listening to my constant talk about this project and offering their encouragement.

You will note that each chapter contains a foreword, and the author of each foreword has supported my efforts to bring to life Arabic works of military significance for U.S. military readers. Each has aided in my intellectual development, and I am grateful. In addition, Ms. Mara Karlin, at the time an intern at the Office of the Secretary of Defense, assisted in editing appendix 3 when it was published in *Infantry* in 2005. Lieutenant Colonel Thomas Veale, USA, not only cleared the entire series for publication but went beyond the call of duty as a Defense Intelligence Agency (DIA) public affairs officer by suggesting improvements in language. Vice Admiral Adam Robinson, MC, USN, the former Navy surgeon general, deserves special mention for convincing me to stay Navy, after a very rough first deployment to Liberia as a newly minted lieutenant. I count each senior officer, educator, and thinker who contributed a foreword to the Fawzi series as a cherished mentor. Finally, let me thank my copy editor, Julie Kimmel; my cartographer, Christopher Robinson, who brought my sketches of maps 1 and 2 to life; Lieutenant Commander Tom Cutler, director of professional publishing at the Naval Institute Press; and Emily Bakely, production editor at the Press, for helping me bring out this, my fourth book. Tom and I started with militant Islamist ideology, then tackled Iraqi political history and the Middle East in World War II, and now turn to General Mohamed Fawzi. He will likely ask me when we meet again, "What's next?"

★★★

ABBREVIATIONS

AA	antiair
AFB	air force base
APC	armored personnel carrier
ASU	Arab Socialist Union
ASW	antisubmarine warfare
BBC	British Broadcasting Corporation
CAS	close air support
CENTO	Central Treaty Organization
CIA	Central Intelligence Agency
COMINT	communication intelligence
CORDS	Civil Operations and Revolutionary Development Support
CPSU	Communist Party of the Soviet Union
DIA	Defense Intelligence Agency
DLPT	Defense Language Proficiency Test
DMI	director of military intelligence
EADF	Egyptian Air Defense Forces
EAF	Egyptian air force
EGIS	Egyptian General Intelligence Service
ELINT	electronic intelligence
EW	electronic warfare
FIS	Islamic Salvation Front
FLN	National Liberation Front (Algeria)
GID	General Intelligence Directorate
HE	high explosives
IAF	Israeli air force
IDF	Israeli Defense Forces
IFF	identification friend or foe
IO	information operations
ISAF	International Security Assistance Force
KM-8	Kilometer 8
KM-30	Kilometer 30
MEDO	Middle East Defense Organization
MEU	marine expeditionary unit

MLRS	multiple-launch rocket system
MP	military policeman
NATO	North Atlantic Treaty Organization
NCO	noncommissioned officer
NDP	National Democratic Party
NKVD	People's Commissariat for Internal Affairs (USSR)
PBI	President Bureau of Information
PHIBRON	amphibious squadron
PME	professional military education
POW	prisoner of war
RCC	Revolutionary Command Council
RPG	rocket-propelled grenade
SAM	surface-to-air missile
SCAF	Supreme Council of the Armed Forces
SEATO	Southeast Asia Treaty Organization
SF	special forces
TP	torpedo boat (Egyptian designation)
TRADOC	Training and Doctrine Command
UAR	United Arab Republic
UN	United Nations
UNEF	United Nations Emergency Force
USG	U.S. government
VHF	very high frequency

RECONSTRUCTING A
SHATTERED
EGYPTIAN ARMY

Introduction

People do not want words—
they want the sound of battle—the battle of destiny.

—GAMAL ABDEL NASSER—

T
he 1973 Arab-Israeli War saw many direct applications of a revolution in military warfare. In the years following the conflict, the U.S. military studied the war carefully, as Soviet hardware had worn down U.S.-supplied Israeli warplanes and tanks in the first forty-eight hours. The war was the first to see the extensive use of antitank wire-guided missiles, which equalized the playing field between the infantry and the tank. It pitted Soviet-designed air defense systems against American-made fighter jets. Egyptians, understanding they could never compete qualitatively with the Israeli air force, came up with a massive surface-to-air defense system to negate Israel's air advantage. In addition, the Egyptians and Syrians conducted an elaborate deception campaign that overwhelmed Israeli forces in the opening phase of the war. On October 6, 1973, at 1400 (Cairo time), two thousand artillery pieces opened up in surprise attack along the Egyptian side of the Suez Canal. Only a few thousand Israeli soldiers were on the other side to meet the tens of thousands of Egyptians who would cross the canal on boats and by bridging equipment amid the roar of the artillery.

This book provides an analysis of the memoir of General Mohamed Fawzi, who, as Egypt's war minister from 1967 to 1971, undertook the reforms, decisions, and personnel selection that established the architecture for the surprise attack on October 6, 1973. Fawzi offers an insider's glimpse into discussions with Gamal Abdel Nasser, the Soviets, Arab leaders, and Egyptian military as well as civilian leaders who pulled off something rare in military history: the reconstruction of a demoralized armed forces. Fawzi's memoir was published in 1984 and regrettably has never been made widely available in the English language. It is impossible to truly understand the 1973 Yom Kippur War (known to the Egyptians as the Ramadan War) without understanding Fawzi's structural reforms and the lessons he learned by directly observing Egyptian combat performance in the Yemen War (1962–1967), the 1967 Six-Day War, and the War of Attrition (1967–1970). Fawzi is scathingly critical of Egyptian arms, and this makes his ideas worth reading, as he examined failures at the tactical, strategic, and operational levels.

As a student of the National Defense University's Eisenhower School for National Security and Resource Strategy, I was often told that if serious thought is not given to the logistics and financing of national security, all ideas will be relegated to the realm of fantasy. This book goes beyond the 1973 surprise attack, the crossing of the canal (*al-ubur*) by 80,000 Egyptian troops, the tank battles, the surrounding of the Egyptian 3rd Army by the Israelis, and the redemption of Egyptian arms leading to the Camp David Accord and discusses, through Fawzi, how these combat units were formed, trained, financed, and integrated as part of a newly developed Egyptian national strategy. Fawzi's memoir was published as *Harb Thalathah Sanawat, 1967–1970: Muzakirat al-Fareeq al-Awal Mohamed Fawzi, Wazeer al-Harbiyah al-Asbaq* (The Three Years War, 1967–1970: The Memoir of General Mohamed Fawzi, the Former War Minister).[1] The book used for this critical examination is the 1990 fifth edition by Dar al-Mustaqbal Printing in Cairo. Fawzi's fifth edition contains a chapter on the outcomes and lessons of the War of Attrition, not included in previous editions. All Fawzi quotations are my translations taken from the 1990 fifth edition of his memoir.

This book takes you into Fawzi's world from 1967 to 1971, when he was rebuilding a shattered army logistically, educationally, and culturally. The book in your hands represents an analytic and abridged translation of Fawzi's memoir. The original memoir is 408 pages and presupposes an understanding of modern Egyptian and Middle East politics that must be explained to an uninitiated Western reader. I wanted the work to be accessible to as many members of the U.S. armed forces as possible, not just specialists in Middle East affairs. Also, the book distills from Fawzi's memoir only significant items useful to the military decision maker; I have chosen these items on the basis of my service in the education of fellow officers and civilians attending both the National Defense University and the National Intelligence University as an adjunct member of the faculty in both locations. Finally, I wanted to highlight Fawzi's omissions and expand on the fifteen essays that have appeared and will appear in *Infantry Magazine*; a book allows for a deeper exploration of Fawzi's thoughts, perspectives, and ideas as well as critiques of those ideas and comparisons with other archival materials from such sources as the U.S. State Department.

Incredibly, General Mohamed Fawzi is confused in English books with Egyptian foreign minister (1952–1964) and prime minister (1970–1972) Mahmoud Fawzi, most notably in David Kimche and Dan Bawly's *The Six Day War: Prologue and Aftermath*.[2] This oversight makes understanding the main Arab players of the Arab-Israeli wars that much more difficult for English-speaking readers. Anthony

Nutting's definitive biography of Nasser published in 1972 makes this same mistake, citing General Fawzi correctly on page 430 but incorrectly in the index.[3] This book provides a voice to the Arab perspective, first by clearing up the confusion between Mohamed (the general) and Mahmoud (the diplomat) Fawzi.

In a small way, Mohamed Fawzi is to Egypt what George B. McClellan—who trained, equipped, and drilled soldiers, providing an army with which Ulysses S. Grant and Abraham Lincoln could challenge the Confederacy—was to the Union. Fawzi pulled together an integrated, trained, and competent armed forces from the ashes of the crushing defeat of Egyptian arms in the 1967 Six-Day War. He set up the necessary military infrastructure, revised and crafted legislation, delegated authority, appointed service chiefs and field commanders, and operationalized conceptions from setting up a defensive line along the Suez Canal to gradually projecting military power in the War of Attrition. The reforms he implemented from 1967 to 1971 led to revisions in tactics, operations, and military planning that made possible the opening shots of the 1973 Yom Kippur War, over four decades ago. It was Fawzi who had to worry, for instance, about the level of education needed among the Egyptian enlisted and officers in order for them to understand the latest complex Soviet military hardware.

This book is an attempt to orient America's military readers to Arab military thinking at the strategic, operational, and tactical levels, something I have advocated as I approach my second decade of service in the U.S. armed forces. U.S. national security is dependent on a thorough appreciation of the perspectives, views, and perceptions of people in all areas of the world who have seen conflict or could see conflict in the future. Fawzi matters because the U.S. Army was influenced by the events of the 1973 Arab-Israeli War through General William Depuy, who formed Training and Doctrine Command (TRADOC) the same year, and through the evolution of the U.S. Army's AirLand Battle concept, which dominated American military doctrine until the late 1990s, when it was replaced by Full-Spectrum Dominance. Sergei Khrushchev, son of Soviet premier Nikita Khrushchev, wrote about the 1967 Six-Day War, "Neither long training nor modern equipment have taught the Arabs to conduct modern warfare."[4] This perspective is dangerous as it overlooks the preparations, thought, and innovations that Fawzi highlights in his memoir and may make one complacent in analysis and comfortable in an unpredictable world. One must never intellectually underestimate the capacity of a military to innovate, even in the face of past defeats. Changes in conditions, generations, and technology can enable any military to address perceived and real grievances with a creative use of force. Fawzi's account is extraordinary among military memoirs, as it demonstrates how an armed forces learns from failure. One often hears the adage, "one learns more from failure than success," whether in business or in the realm of military planning, exercises, and actual combat.

Today, the Egyptian armed forces are fighting an escalating battle against various movements sympathetic to al-Qaida in the Sinai Peninsula. Understanding the terrain and Fawzi's use of special forces (SF) in the Sinai can offer insight into how al-Qaida terrorist cells and Egyptian forces will confront each other in 2014 and beyond. In August 2013 Egypt and Israel conducted coordinated air strikes to take out terrorists attempting to launch rockets from Egypt into Israel in the Rafah border area. That same month two dozen Egyptian security personnel were killed in an ambush in the Sinai. We can only hope this level of cooperation between Israel and Egypt can be maintained to counter the transnational threat undermining Egyptian and regional security.

★★ **Chapter One** ★★

Deep Structural Problems Leading to
the 1967 Six-Day War Defeat

An opinion can be argued with; a conviction is best shot.
—T. E. Lawrence (of Arabia)—

Foreword by Lieutenant General Richard F. Natonski,
USMC (Ret.), former commander, U.S. Marine Corps Forces Command

Professional military education is a hallmark of the armed forces of the United States. From the time I entered the Marine Corps as a second lieutenant until I retired thirty-seven years later as a lieutenant general, education was a continuous process. During my career I had the opportunity to learn from my predecessors by walking their battlefields in the Pacific, Europe, Africa, North America, and the Middle East. This experience was invaluable during my combat tours. Understanding terrain is an important aspect of a military education; another is the ability to get inside the mind of fellow commanders and their decision-making processes. Commander Aboul-Enein has provided our current and future leaders with a treasure trove of information that educates and highlights Arabic works of military significance. This essay takes an intimate look at General Mohamed Fawzi, who offers a candid assessment of Egypt's failure in the 1967 Six-Day War and his interactions with President Gamal Abdel Nasser during the reconstruction of the Egyptian military after its crushing defeat. Readers will get a ringside seat to watch decisions that shaped military history in the Middle East. I applaud the U.S. Army *Infantry Magazine* for providing Commander Aboul-Enein a forum to educate our military leadership on Arab strategic, operational, and tactical thinking. This chapter offers us all an insight into the human terrain of the Middle East.

Introduction

In February 2000 former Egyptian general Mohamed Fawzi died in Cairo at the age of eighty-four. During his life he had held the titles of armed forces chief of staff and war minister under President Gamal Abdel Nasser and President

Anwar Sadat. He served as commandant of Egypt's military academy from 1957 until 1962, when he was sent to head Egypt's military mission in the Congo.[1] Fawzi had a ringside seat for the tactical, operational, and strategic decision making of the Egyptian armed forces from 1948 until his military career ended, with the death of Nasser in September 1970 and Fawzi's involvement a year later in a conspiracy to remove Sadat from power. He is best remembered in modern Arab military history as the lead architect of the rebuilding of the Egyptian armed forces after the demoralizing defeat of Egyptian arms in the 1967 Six-Day War (known in Arabic as *al-Naksah* [the setback] and closely tied to the 1948 Arab-Israeli War, *al-Nakbah* [the catastrophe], which ended with the creation of Israel and the displacement of Palestinians). In 1984 Fawzi published an extensive military memoir, *Harb Thalathah Sanawat, 1967–1970: Muzakirat al-Fareeq al-Awal Mohamed Fawzi, Wazeer al-Harbiyah al-Asbaq* (The Three Years War, 1967–1970: The Memoir of General Mohamed Fawzi, the Former War Minister). The version of the memoir used for this critical examination is the 1990 fifth edition by Dar al-Mustaqbal Printing in Cairo, which contains a chapter on the outcomes and lessons of the War of Attrition (1967–1970) not included in previous editions.

Nasser and Abdel-Hakim Amer: Triumph and Tragedy

Among the challenges Fawzi identified in his assessment of Egypt's defeat in the 1967 Six-Day War was dealing with the removal and forced retirement of officers on the active list from 1952 to 1967. In addition, at the time of the Six-Day War, Egyptian forces were already mired in the Yemen War (1962–1967), which framed Egyptian military thinking in favor of guerrilla warfare; conventional warfare skills had been left to atrophy. Another problem from Egypt's geostrategic perspective was a single-minded focus on merging the general commands of Syria and Egypt into the Unified Arab Command; the merger caused military training to be neglected in Egypt. Although these challenges were important factors in the Egyptian defeat, one of the most debilitating internal weaknesses was the unconstructive and nepotistic relationship between Nasser and his war minister, Field Marshal Abdel-Hakim Amer.

The Amer-Nasser relationship affected the quality of preparations for the 1967 Six-Day War. Through Fawzi's memoir, we discover that Amer was unable to accept countervailing views and developed a cult of personality loyal to him and not to the nation. This cult of personality proved fatal for Egypt. Over time, Nasser, at Amer's urging, concentrated most elements of Egypt's security institutions in Amer's hands. The Egyptian military assumed responsibility for civil security, with defending against external threats a lesser priority, and put ever more resources toward combatting internal threats and countercoups. The Egyptian army's popular image after the 1952 revolution began to erode as the military became a state within a state, a condition that still exists within today's Egyptian armed forces.

Fawzi writes, "The relationship between Nasser and Amer began to deteriorate in 1962." He presupposes that his reader is familiar with the Nasser-Amer relationship, which is part of modern Egyptian political lore. The story is a political tragedy of two officers who rose through the ranks together, planned the 1952 revolution, named one another's sons after the other, and led Egypt, with Amer rising from the rank of major to field marshal in a matter of a few years. Amassing power, Amer came into conflict with Nasser. He made a series of strategic blunders that Nasser initially overlooked because of their friendship. The Six-Day War was the final straw. Amer attempted a countercoup against Nasser that ended with the field marshal's suicide under suspicious circumstances.

Fawzi writes that what Western militaries term "effects-based planning" was lacking on a military-political level when Nasser, at the urging of Amer, decided to close the Gulf of Aqaba to Israeli shipping. Amer then deployed massive formations in the Sinai Peninsula on the eve of the 1967 Six-Day War. Fawzi writes, "There were no objectives outlined for these deployed forces, no operational instructions, leading to an improvisation of military plans. This improvisation led to a change of military plans no less than four times." A positive result of the 1967 war was that the crisis of power between Amer and Nasser was resolved once and for all, with Amer being discredited by the dismal performance of Egyptian arms.

A serious reconstruction of the Egyptian military could then begin under the guidance of Fawzi, who concentrated on linking the armed forces to civilian support, unifying civil and military authority, and developing Egypt's first coordinated national strategy. Fawzi advocated for the integration of Egypt's defense establishment within the cabinet. The first chapters of his memoir imply that Egypt was attempting to reattach one element of power—the military—to other elements of national power. The Egyptian High Command after the 1967 war used the buzzwords *consolidation*, *confrontation*, and *combat* to shape the thinking for the development of operational and strategic planning for the 1973 Yom Kippur War.

Amer's Presidential Decrees: Enhancing Power and Undermining Civilian Oversight

To say that Amer merely used street protests to get his way would be a grave mistake, and Fawzi's memoir provides an analysis of the deeper strategies Amer used to consolidate power in his hands: "He [Amer] used his influence, charm, and friendship with Nasser to get him to sign Presidential Decree 2878/1962, which made the deputy supreme commander of the armed forces responsible to the president and Presidential Council for all affairs of the armed forces, both military and administrative. By linking the president and Presidential Council, Amer marginalized the Presidential Council, as Amer felt he could directly appeal to Nasser. This meant Amer retained in effect the status quo where he continued to be solely responsible for promotions, personnel assignments, and military equipage." He would remain Egypt's second-most powerful man after Nasser and perceived heir apparent to the Egyptian leader.

Fawzi describes how in 1964 Presidential Decree 117/1964 concentrated the powers of the war minister in the hands of the deputy supreme commander, who at the time was Amer. This decree allowed Amer to control the army budget, and with this power he created a funding site for the military administration of Gaza, which enabled him to hide funds. In 1966 Presidential Decree 1956/1966 attempted to diminish the independence and powers of the war minister position. Amer responded to this decree by appointing his deputy, Shams Badran, as war minister. Appointing Badran, an Amer sycophant, enabled Amer to ignore the 1964 constitution, as well as the 1966 presidential decree, and make the war minister subordinate to him. Amer would once again avoid being legislatively or constitutionally restrained, maintaining his own center of power around his personage.

Of all the decrees Amer pushed through in an attempt to concentrate power in his hands, Fawzi considers Presidential Decree 367/1966 the most dangerous because

> it gave War Minister Shams Badran [and thereby an Amer protégé and lackey]
> - the portfolio for military secrecy;
> - administration of military courts [in 1966 Military Decree 25 stipulated that if a civilian got into a dispute with a military member, it would be resolved by military tribunal];
> - administration of military intelligence;
> - [responsibility for] morale and welfare of the armed forces;
> - oversight of budgetary affairs;
> - [responsibility for] customs and coastal defense;
> - [responsibility for] military industries;
> - oversight of the procurement offices in Moscow and Cologne, Germany;
> - [responsibility for] census for the draft;

+ linkage between the Office of the War Minister and EGIS [the Egyptian General Intelligence Service, the civilian intelligence agency];
+ oversight of military districts [Egypt was divided into military districts that could be described as states within the state].

Using this decree and the pretext that the nation would benefit from military leadership expertise, Amer and Badran took over key industries. They appointed military officers to key ambassadorships, usurping the job of the foreign ministry, and began maintaining a presence in Egyptian high schools and universities in order to oversee the political indoctrination of the youth. Amer distanced Nasser from the military apparatus and began eroding the president's authority as supreme commander. It is unclear why Nasser signed these decrees knowing that his power would be eroded. One explanation is that he could not say no to his best friend.

As an example of Amer's power, Fawzi writes that "Nasser attempted to have me remove his [Amer's] cronies," and cites a 1960 incident whereby "Nasser decided to travel to an Arab summit meeting in Casablanca on board the presidential yacht *Hurriyah* [Freedom]. The presidential yacht was to be escorted by two Egyptian naval destroyers, but to Nasser's embarrassment, both destroyers could not complete the mission because of malfunctions and had to put in to Algiers for repairs. Nasser called for the relief of his naval chief, but Amer ignored these calls."

As more of Egypt's civil life, including the census, customs, and public transportation, was placed under military oversight, less attention was paid to offensive and defensive combat competencies. Adding to this was Amer's program of providing military officers priority housing, giving away automobiles, and raising pay, despite the economic strains these actions were placing on Egypt. Fawzi comments, "This new substrata of society, the military, had a detrimental impact by placing the entire nation on a war footing. In addition, military leaders became inward looking and therefore were not looking to plan and train for projecting offensive power outside of Egypt's borders. It also made no difference that Egypt was provided the latest Soviet combat weaponry because its leaders under Amer were not interested in combat effectiveness [and training with new weapons systems], but instead in making the most of the opportunity to personally enrich themselves."

After the 1967 war, Fawzi was provided access to Amer's papers and classified safes, in which he found a classified Egyptian Military Headquarters document. The document was a plan by Shams Badran to create a secret cabal composed entirely of Badran's military cadet class of 1948. This secret cell informed on the loyalty of fellow officers to Badran himself and to Field Marshal Amer. The document shows the extent of division within the Egyptian army on the eve of the Six-Day War.

Regional and Internal Challenges

Fawzi writes, "The symptoms for the crippling defeat of the 1967 Arab-Israeli War began not with the mass retreat of the Egyptian army or the decimation of the Egyptian air force within an hour, but years before." Regional, external, and internal dynamics brought about the conditions for Egypt's defeat. According to Fawzi, "The defeat manifested itself in the hidden conflict between Nasser and Amer over final control of the Egyptian armed forces." Both Nasser and Amer failed to fully anticipate regional responses to growing Egyptian influence from the Israelis, Arab monarchies who feared pan-Arabism, Cold War competition, and the Europeans' efforts to maintain their last colonial possessions. Fawzi writes that "these pressures caused the breakup of the union of Egypt and Syria, or the United Arab Republic (UAR)," which existed from 1958 to 1961. His memoir also reveals Nasser's decision making regarding Egypt's involvement in the quagmire of the Yemen War.

The 1956 Suez War was the debut of the Cold War superpowers—the United States and the Soviet Union—in the affairs of the Arab world. This crisis signaled the eclipse of the traditional colonial powers in the region, Britain and France. The Soviets pursued a policy of supporting national liberation movements and undermining colonial influence in the Middle East. As colonial oversight diminished, attempts were made to fill the vacuum, leading to coups in Egypt (1952) and Iraq (1958), to the Algerian War of Independence from France (1954–1962), and to attempted coups in Morocco and Saudi Arabia. Fawzi writes that Nasser began to gradually drift into the Soviet orbit, yet he wanted to retain independence from the superpowers. Working with India's Jawaharlal Nehru, he was an architect of the Nonaligned Movement, and he tried to upset President Dwight Eisenhower's creation in 1954 of the Middle East Defense Organization (MEDO).

Nasser viewed the United States as entering the colonial void left by Britain and France. The United States failed to appreciate how MEDO collected Arab traditional monarchies, such as Jordan and Iraq, against newly formed Arab nationalist governments in Egypt and Syria, which had unified around the UAR. Washington, however, was trying to establish stability in the region by rolling back what it saw as Soviet influence. Despite the open debates that led to the long-standing American policy of Soviet containment, there is no indication Nasser ever discussed this policy or Egypt's role in the emerging Cold War global architecture. The United States cut funding for the Aswan High Dam after Egypt signed a massive arms deal in 1955 with Czechoslovakia. As a result Nasser increased his ties with the Soviets, who took up funding the dam. Given increased economic and military assistance from Moscow, Nasser had difficulty maintaining Egypt's policy of non-alignment. Meanwhile, America's popularity was at its height in Egypt after the 1956 Suez

War. The Egyptian people believed the United States had caused the withdrawal of British, French, and Israeli forces from the Sinai in the aftermath of the Suez War.

Ultimately, America's popularity was eroded among Arabs generally, and Egyptians specifically, because of increasing American support for Israel as well as for Arab monarchies, rivals of Nasser's pan-Arabism. Although Israel and Arab monarchies were hostile to one another, they both saw the danger in Nasser's progressive regime. Fawzi saw himself and Egypt "as locked in a struggle to preserve and spread pan-Arabism against forces that wanted to roll this ideology back." Nasser did not understand that he needed to balance Egyptian national independence with Soviet encroachment or appreciate that pan-Arabism was judged by American policy makers only in the wider context of containment, and this led the Egyptian leader ever closer to Moscow. He declared a new subset of pan-Arabist ideology, Arab Socialism, and supported national liberation movements in Asia, Africa, and Latin America.

Africa, the Arab League, and National Liberation Movements: Pulling Egypt in Different Directions

In 1962 Fawzi was commandant of Egypt's War College and tasked with representing Egypt in what Nasser's generals called the Combined African High Command. The joint command was an attempt to operationalize Nasser's ideas of pan-Arabism and pan-Africanism, which feature prominently in his book *Egypt's Liberation: The Philosophy of the Revolution.*[2] Although published in both English and Arabic in the 1950s, there is no indication that either Eisenhower's or John F. Kennedy's Defense Departments read or analyzed this work. Fawzi writes, "Egypt provided expertise, training, and coordination for this joint African force. Military officers in many African states, many newly independent, would train in Egyptian war colleges and military academies."

Nasser wanted to capitalize on this wave of independence sweeping Africa and ordered an Egyptian paratroop division to deploy to the newly independent and highly unstable Congo to bolster President Patrice Lumumba. The Belgians, in what is described as the worst and cruelest example of European colonialism, had left the Congo with virtually no local Congolese institutions, and predictably the nation descended into chaos after independence. Ironically, under Sadat, Egypt sent troops once again to the Congo to bolster the Mobutu regime, as part of a multi-national anti-communist coalition.

Egyptian military leaders, bolstered by Nasser's anti-imperial and anticolonial rhetoric, also deployed a tank regiment to Iraq to aid in its confrontation with British forces over Kuwait in 1961. Egypt provided a conduit for Soviet military advisers, facilitating the disbursement of aid, training, and logistics to Algeria, Sudan, and Somalia, much as the United States used Pakistan as a conduit for several Afghan mujahideen groups fighting the Soviets. In fact, the Soviets used Egypt as a conduit for supporting several national liberation movements in Africa and the Middle East. The Cold War in the Middle East would harden into a competition between the so-called progressive Arab countries—Egypt, Syria, Iraq, Algeria, and Yemen—and traditional monarchies—Saudi Arabia, the Gulf States, Jordan, Iran, and Morocco. The United States and the United Kingdom stood behind traditional monarchies, and the Soviets behind progressive Arab states.[3]

The League of Arab States, or Arab League, created in 1945, underwent a sociopolitical reengineering by Nasser with the creation within the organization of the Unified Arab Command. Although this group may have seemed menacing to American policy makers at the time, the United States failed to understand the mechanics and problems of coordination the command created for its members. Fawzi reveals that attempts at creating an Arab defense collective "caused Egypt's leaders to neglect defining any national security policies for Egypt. There were no questions on how Egypt's security fit within the collective security of differing Arab states." Fawzi criticizes Nasser and Amer, as well as Egypt's General Staff, for "failing to tie together the economic, political, and military aspects of a unified Arab security pact. Instead, the General Staff focused on operations, tactics, and formations, and completely lost sight of a military designed to advance national geopolitical objectives." According to Fawzi, "There was no Arab comprehension of national security that drove or even kept together any Arab collective defense arrangement."

Seminal Events Leading to Egyptian Strategic Disadvantage in the 1967 War

Before the 1967 Six-Day War, several seminal events involving the failure of the UAR shaped the regional strategic landscape to Egypt's disadvantage. According to Fawzi,

> The union between Egypt and Syria was a euphoric moment for Arab nationalists and Nasser personally, but after the euphoria there were massive disruptions in the merging of Egyptian and Syrian ministries in Cairo and Damascus. These disruptions made the coordination and execution of policy unwieldy. The UAR saw Amer as deputy leader of Syria, leading him to devote less time to military affairs while retaining his defense portfolio. Other problems became apparent months into the union, when Syrian Abdel-Rahim Sirraj became UAR interior

minister. Sirraj and Amer clashed continuously, and Syrians objected to Egyptian moves to dominate Syria's defense and security institutions, and to impose Egyptian military and police methods on Syria. Economically, Egypt poured tens of millions of pounds in loans and aid into Syria.

Combining and bureaucratizing the military was a contentious affair, as Egypt attempted to meld Egyptian and Syrian combat formations into one. Aside from the imbalance of forces between Egypt and Syria, no thought was given to morale or unit cohesion cultivated over time. Egyptians were heavy-handed in implementing control over Syrian military personnel, and I spent three months out of the year as chief of staff for the Military Academy, inspecting and overseeing the academy in Damascus. Egypt was ahead in air defense, naval systems, and technical units compared to Syria. Another contentious aspect of merging the two armed forces was the imposition of Egyptian military intelligence personnel instilling revolutionary discipline on the Syrian troops.

Amer began assuming more powers and his cronies began marginalizing the Syrians in their own country. The Syrian military intelligence [2nd Bureaux] and Egyptian military intelligence conspired and conducted counterplots against one another. Political cells that resented Egyptian dominance in the union began forming within the Syrian army. Communists, Socialists, and Baathists coalesced and plotted around anti-Egyptian feeling.

Egyptian officers abused their positions in Syria, putting personal enrichment above the successful project of making unification with Egypt and Syria work. Critics of the UAR scored propaganda points and dominated the airwaves to talk of a separation between Egypt and Syria. The date of the *infisaal* [separation] came on September 28, 1961. It was successfully completed by a small clique of Syrian colonels who ran the office of Field Marshal Amer in Damascus. The coup against Amer took less than two hours, and with the threat of violence, Egyptian top officers of Amer's staff and their families were surrounded. Nasser, fearing his close friend would be captured or killed, ordered the organization of an Egyptian paratroop regiment and naval assets to land in the Syrian port of Latakia. Based on faulty intelligence that the Latakia barracks were pro-union, this Egyptian contingent was taken into custody upon disembarking into the port.

During the following weeks and into October 1961, Egyptian military personnel and their families in Syria were exchanged for Syrian military personnel and their families in Egypt. Nasser's humiliation caused by Amer's mismanagement of Syria culminated in the Shatura Conference in Lebanon that formally dissolved the UAR. Events of the UAR would have a direct bearing on Nasser's strategic thinking when it came to providing military aid to Yemeni colonel Abdullah Sallal in September 1962, a decision that would escalate into a five-year quagmire for Egypt, known as the Yemen War.

Conclusion

Egypt's defeat in the 1967 Six-Day War began long before the war even began owing to regional, internal, and external challenges. Included in those dynamics was the deteriorating relationship between Nasser and Amer, as Amer gradually extracted more and more power from the president. Amer's hunger for power led him to catastrophically mismanage Egypt's relationship with Syria, causing the eventual split of the UAR. The dissolution of the UAR had a detrimental impact on the thinking of Egyptian leaders before the 1967 war began. For one, Nasser had a chance to rid himself of Field Marshal Amer, but instead he allowed him to continue on despite the UAR debacle and even to amass power and preside over the most significant failure of Egyptian arms in the country's modern history.[4]

The Cold War in the Middle East forced Egypt's leadership to focus efforts on defending the country from outside disruptions while also keeping an eye on internal affairs. External and internal complications culminated in Egypt entering the 1962 Yemen War (discussed in the next chapter). Although internal security was of paramount importance to Nasser, international affairs could not be neglected by Egyptian leaders. U.S. State Department archives reveal the distrust Nasser and his inner circle held for the United States, which would be exacerbated by the Yemen War.[5]

★★ **Chapter Two** ★★

The Impact of the Yemen Guerrilla War
on Egyptian Military Thinking

We used to wonder where war lived,
what it was that made it so vile. And now we realize that we
know where it lives, that it is inside ourselves.

—ALBERT CAMUS—

Foreword by Lieutenant General Walter E. Gaskin, USMC,
deputy chairman of the Military Committee,
North Atlantic Treaty Organization

As the United States cultivates a new generation of warrior-diplomats, it is vital that we continue to explore regional perspectives of strategic interest. The events of the Arab Spring have ushered in a period of great change that will affect political as well as military relationships for some time. The 2011 Egyptian Revolution and the assumption of power by the Supreme Council of the Armed Forces (SCAF) have led to many questions about the thinking of the two dozen officers constituting this ruling body. Part of understanding this generation of senior officers is comprehending not only the psychological impact of the devastating Six-Day War but the influence of events in Yemen prior to 1967 that shaped the thinking of operational and strategic leadership. In this series Commander Aboul-Enein introduces readers to General Mohamed Fawzi's views on the impact of the 1962 Yemen War on Egyptian military thinking. For five years 60,000–70,000 Egyptian combat forces found themselves entrenched in a quagmire in Yemen. For those making policy in Egypt, such as President Nasser and Field Marshal Amer, the war in Yemen sharpened Egyptian combat effectiveness. Fawzi instead argues that the opposite was the case, and that leaders such as Nasser and Amer deluded themselves into a false sense of security. In Yemen, Egyptian units were engaged in fighting a guerrilla war, not a conventional war against a qualitatively formidable Israeli war machine. Fawzi makes a compelling argument that the Yemen War had eroded Egyptian combat effectiveness by 1967 on the eve of war with Israel. Commander Aboul-Enein has done much to educate soldiers, sailors, marines, and airmen both in classrooms and in his published writings.

I applaud *Infantry* for giving Commander Aboul-Enein's work a forum; the magazine is helping him in his quest to educate us all using direct Arabic source materials of military significance. This is vital in cultivating the intellectual capital of our most strategic asset: our active, reserve, and civilian personnel.

Introduction

The previous chapter examined the strategic dynamics among the Egyptian leader Gamal Abdel Nasser; his deputy supreme commander and de facto war minister, Field Marshal Abdel-Hakim Amer; and the vortex of pan-Arabism coupled with the greater competition between the Soviet Union and the United States. Causes of Egypt's brutal defeat in the 1967 Six-Day War can be traced back to the Yemen War of 1962–1967. Although the war had some positive outcomes for Yemen, Egypt suffered most of the negative outcomes, according to Fawzi, and this only further harmed Egypt when it came to preparing for the 1967 war. Egyptian leadership attempted to prepare for the 1967 war by creating strategies such as the Unified Arab Command and Plan Qahir (Conqueror), but as General Fawzi explains in his memoir, these efforts proved futile.

The Yemen War: Fawzi's Perspective

Colonel Abdullah Sallal, commander of the royal guard, and a cabal of Yemeni officers staged an effective coup in September 1962—with one mistake. They failed to capture or kill Imam Muhammad al-Badr of Yemen. The imam retreated to Yemen's northern mountains and waged a war with the support of Saudi Arabia to recapture his rule over the country. From Nasser, Sallal requested Egyptian intervention in Yemen to keep his Republican coup alive. According to Fawzi's memoir, "Nasser, eager to regain Egyptian prestige after the UAR fiasco, sent Anwar Sadat on a fact-finding mission to Yemen to assess the needs of the Yemeni Revolutionary Command Council and Sallal. Sadat formed a military coordination and assessment group, composed of two colonels and one lieutenant colonel, within Yemen's military headquarters." Why the group was so small and included no flag officers remains a mystery. It is likely that Nasser wanted an assessment without input from Amer and so sent Sadat, who chose his own officers. Fawzi writes, "Sadat wired an immediate request to Nasser for a Saaqa [special forces] battalion, one wing of close-air-support [CAS] fighter-bombers, and aerial reconnaissance airframes."

Cairo had to plan for a two-thousand-kilometer support route from Egypt to Yemen, yet Egypt's aerial capabilities were limited. According to Fawzi,

Brigadier General Ahmed Nuh suggested outfitting PK-11 jet trainers with missiles. Among the options discussed was outfitting the PK-11 airframe with Oerlikon air-to-surface missiles. This plane was put together locally in Egypt and could be transported in pieces to San'aa, loaded on an Antonov-12 [AN-12] or Ilyushin-14 [IL-14] along with 500-pound bombs. The Egyptian air force [EAF] conducted a round-the-clock effort, landing AN-12 and IL-14 transports in San'aa carrying troops, supplies, planes, and parts. In the first week, Egyptian troop levels stood at a thousand with initial Egyptian estimates that they could suppress the Yemeni Royalist insurgency in three months.

This time line was wildly optimistic, and Fawzi adds, "The Egyptian General Staff did not even possess topographical maps of Yemen. The skirmish at Sirwah made Egyptian generals realize the reality of the situation when all members of a special forces team were wiped out, and First Lieutenant Nabil al-Waqqad became Egypt's first casualty in Yemen. Royalists organized tribes to oppose the Sallal Revolution, and anti-Nasserists, like Saudi Arabia and Israel, saw an opportunity to draw Egypt deeper into a quagmire."

Fawzi does not describe in detail the external groups that meddled in Egypt's intervention in Yemen, such as Arab monarchies fearful of Nasser's influence or the Israelis, who sought to contain Egyptian military power. He does, however, specifically mention the Central Intelligence Agency (CIA) and Saudi Arabia. Although Saudi support for the Royalists and Egyptian military incursions into Saudi Arabia are well documented, Fawzi's mention of the CIA contains no backing and appears to be more of a conspiracy theory. However, his suspicion is understandable as both Fawzi and Nasser were aware of the CIA-backed coups in Iran (Mohammad Mossadegh in 1951) and Guatemala (Jacobo Arbenz in 1954), as well as attempts to undermine Nasser himself orchestrated under CIA director Allen Dulles.[1] What the two Egyptians failed to appreciate is the change of administration in the United States and the election of John F. Kennedy, who appreciated the nuanced differences between nationalism and communism.[2]

Another factor was the impact the Bay of Pigs fiasco had in shaking up America's national security establishment, beginning with the resignation of Allen Dulles. If anything, Robert Komer, President Kennedy's senior adviser on the Middle East in the National Security Council who came from the CIA, crafted a balanced approach toward Nasser and Saudi Arabia's King Faisal. In his biography of Komer, Frank Leith Jones includes an excellent chapter that places Fawzi's claims of direct CIA involvement in the Yemen War in better context. Komer crafted a policy that included balancing Soviet competition, ensuring Middle East energy supplies, and preventing the conflict from spilling into Saudi territory, while recognizing the centrality of Egypt within the Arab world.[3]

As Egyptian SF became overwhelmed, additional combat forces were sent to Yemen. The escalation, according to Fawzi, included thirteen divisions; seven SF battalions; one armored division; ten artillery battalions, plus technical, medical, and administrative units to support this force; seventeen MiG-15s; one destroyer; two frigates, two sea-borne troop carriers; and one minesweeper.

Fawzi reveals the depth of Nasser's frustration, which was reminiscent of Lyndon Johnson's agony over Vietnam:

> By 1964 Egyptian general Anwar al-Qadi commanded 70,000 troops in Yemen. Although large, this force maintained control of only the triangle of T'az, San'aa, and the port of Hodeida. Nasser's frustration led him to replace al-Qadi with Field Marshal Abdel-Mohsen Murtaji. The new field marshal brought with him a division of Yemeni regulars trained in Egypt. Murtaji changed tactics, deploying the Yemeni division along the border with Saudi Arabia and the border with Oman. The new commander in chief for Yemen asked and was given both political and military powers, a first for the highly bureaucratized and control-obsessed Egyptian military. Murtaji also combined Egyptian forces with Yemeni units on joint search-and-destroy missions against Royalist insurgents.
>
> Egypt's conventional tactical mind-set was always pitted against guerrilla tactics, and Egyptian intelligence could never get a real understanding of Yemeni Royalist factions, the size of their forces, or their evolving capabilities. Egyptian military planners tried to understand and categorize Yemeni fighting methods, but ambushes, hit-and-run attacks, and guerrilla deployments followed no predictable logic.

Fawzi lamented, "Egypt never used its five-year war in Yemen to adopt, develop, or cultivate counterinsurgency tactics, which could have proved useful in the 1967 war." He attributes this lack of development to the "Egyptian pride of being seen by the world as a modern and conventional fighting force, which therefore caused Egypt not to focus on the type of war being fought in Yemen."

Fawzi comments on the Egyptian forces' indiscipline in firing artillery and arms. They fired their weapons with the objective of reassuring Egyptian combat units in the field, not of hitting their targets. News footage of these ferocious artillery barrages was shown in Egypt's major cities as propaganda; little did the people know it was merely for show. The largest expense during the Yemen War was replacing spent ammunition, missiles, and bombs.

Murtaji instituted what Western military historians call an "enclave system." Those areas held by Egyptian forces were furnished with an Egyptian—not a Yemeni—military governor, which made the Egyptians appear as an occupying force. According to Fawzi, "By 1965 Murtaji's system led to Egypt being effectively in charge of Yemen and diminished Yemeni Republicans in the eyes of the Yemeni people." Egypt provided economic and development aid to Yemen, paving roads, building schools, and developing the port of Hodeida, but it was considered an occupational force by ever-increasing segments of the Yemeni populace.

The Egyptians attempted to reframe the conflict as an anticolonial struggle and launched Operation Saladin, sponsoring Yemeni insurgents against the British Crown Colony at Aden. They were experimenting with pacification programs three to four years before Robert Komer designed the Civil Operations and Revolutionary Development Support (CORDS) program in 1966. CORDS was designed to protect the civilian population of South Vietnam from the Vietcong, and like Egypt's attempts in Yemen, the program suffered under a dependent local regime and over-reliance on external aid. There is no indication that the United States studied the failed attempts of Egyptian pacification programs in Yemen.[4]

The Positive and Negative Effects of the Yemen War on Egyptian War Strategy

In the summer of 1965, the Egyptians agreed to the Jeddah Accords, but it would take two years for Egypt to pull its forces out of Yemen. The accords, named for the seaport city where the peace talks were held, recognized the Yemen Arab Republic in return for the evacuation of Egyptian forces from Yemen. The reason for the two-year delay, as described by Fawzi, was that "the Republican Yemenis did not want Egyptian forces to leave without first stabilizing the country." He goes on to write, "The last Egyptian infantry division departed Yemen in March 1967. As they withdrew, Yemeni SF protested in front of Egyptian headquarters in San'aa, and an exchange of small-arms fire ensued. Except for this incident, the withdrawal occurred gradually and with the oversight of Moroccan and Sudanese military observers." However, Nasser left behind an insurgency in Aden that would later win power and create the first Marxist Arab state in South Yemen in 1968. The split between the North and South would persist until 1990. In 1990 the two regions of Yemen merged, but the legacy of the Yemen War endured until 1994, when Marxist Yemeni leaders, unhappy with targeting by militant Islamists, attempted to secede. A yearlong war of secession unified the country by force. The Socialist secessionist movement is still active in parts of southern Yemen, and along with the radical Shiite Houthi rebellion in the North, al-Qaida in the Arabian Peninsula, and the Arab Spring protests, it represents one of the many challenges facing Yemen today.

According to Fawzi, the strategic successes of the Yemen War for Egypt were as follows:

- The war opened the eyes of the globe to Yemen's underdevelopment. The imam of Yemen ruled the country in a medieval fashion. For instance, only he was allowed to own a radio, and the country possessed little in the way of hospitals, schools, or industry.
- The war ended British colonialism in Aden.
- It created a strategic Arab progressive state in the Arabian Peninsula.
- It changed the strategic calculus of Western oil and gas companies in the region.
- It oriented Yemen on the national liberation orbit and within the Soviet sphere of influence.
- It stabilized the Republic of Yemen.

Each of these perceived strategic successes is debatable, and Fawzi also outlines the arguments of the Egyptian opposition to the Yemen War:

- The war created economic strain in Egypt, particularly in 1964 and 1965.
- The combat fatigue of units returning to Egypt had a direct impact on the outcome of the 1967 Six-Day War.
- Disease, combat injuries, nonbattle injuries, and combat stress left Egyptian troops needing a lifetime of care.
- Using military decorations and promotions to lift morale rather than to recognize combat performance became a mainstay in Egyptian military culture.

Fawzi also pointed out that during the war the Egyptian media described skirmishes with guerrillas as major battles. In hindsight, he wrote, "Egyptian media should have called these counterguerrilla operations and not military or combat operations." Conventional combat operations involve a known, two-dimensional adversary, not a multidimensional, asymmetric, faceless adversary. The Yemeni Royalist insurgents fought primarily with small arms because tribal armies lacked armor, tanks, planes, and artillery. According to Fawzi, "Egyptian military planners in Yemen wrote to Cairo that Yemen was an ideal proving ground for practical combat training. The training was *tadreeb damawi* [bloodied training]." Fawzi found the planners' assertion delusional. The Yemen War did not provide the level of training needed to fight the Israeli Defense Forces (IDF), that is, a modernized conventional force. Fawzi laments that the Yemen War led Egypt to abandon joint operational or combined arms training; instead, the army began to dominate the fighting. Aerial defense and offense were neglected, and "for five years no aerial defense training occurred. Sinai defenses were completely neglected as an area for future military operations. The only positive outcome for the Egyptian military was that it forced it to take seriously the use of artillery in guerrilla operations, logistical planning, and vehicle wear and tear rates in actual combat." This kind of deep tactical and operational assessment and self-criticism rarely appears in memoirs by Arab generals; thus Fawzi is a unique read in this genre.

Furthermore, Fawzi wonders what the Egyptian army learned in Yemen, if it learned anything at all. Tactical and operational lessons learned by the Egyptian army seemed to include the following: "minimal coordination among the branches of the military was the norm, senior personnel could enrich themselves at the expense of military objectives, war involved a massive waste of military equipment, and hardware did not need to be maintained." Fawzi adds, "Officer cliques began to develop as a consequence of the war. The cliques had a total contempt for Nasser and politicians in Cairo, leading to a further solidification of the cult of Field Marshal Amer. The corruption among Amer and his cadres in Yemen was later dealt with by cashiering Amer's military secretary, Ali Shafiq Safwat, in 1966. That same year the armed forces chief of operations produced a report revealing that the war in Yemen was stretching the armed forces to the point that the defense of Egypt's front with Israel was becoming compromised." As the army chief of staff at the time, Fawzi endorsed this report, and in August 1967, weeks after the Six-Day War, he discovered "the report in Amer's safe within the Defense Ministry, unread and unanalyzed."

The Unified Arab Command:
Neither a Unified Command nor a Unified Army

Fawzi asserts,

> The Unified Arab Command created in 1964 was neither a unified command nor a unified army. Egyptian general Ali Amer [no relation to Field Marshal Abdel-Hakim Amer] was appointed commander of the Unified Arab Command to coordinate the defensive and offensive actions of the Arab armies of Jordan, Egypt, and Syria, the three front-line states in a state of war with Israel, as well as to align the efforts of second-tier supporting Arab states, like Saudi Arabia, Iraq, and Libya. An Arab Defense Council was agreed upon as consisting of senior

officers from Arab League nations. Plans were drawn up for defensive military action leveraging the armed efforts of all Arab nations against Israel. The eastern front (Syria and Jordan) would be supported militarily by Iraq and Saudi Arabia. The southern front (Egypt) would be militarily supported by Algeria, Libya, and Sudan. Egyptian air defense general Abdel-Moneim Riad was appointed chief of staff of the Unified Arab Command. Riad was not among Abdel-Hakim Amer's clique and was dispatched to a forward command in Amman, Jordan, composed of several Egyptian special forces battalions. On the eve of the 1967 war, the Unified Arab Command headquartered in Amman, Jordan, possessed no real unified divisions, units, or armies.

These unified plans against Israel were on paper only, and no real integration of forces or order of battle was implemented, much less discussed, according to Fawzi. In 1966 Egypt and Syria agreed in principle to a unified military command structure, but they never moved beyond agreeing to defensive plans. These discussions involved Fawzi, who represented Egypt, and General Ahmed Suweidan, the commander in chief of Syria's armed forces. According to one defensive plan, either Egypt's or Syria's air force would react in the event that the Israelis destroyed the other country's air force. In hindsight Fawzi writes, "The concept of a Unified Arab Command was wishful thinking and could never succeed, as no Arab nation's general staff would relinquish command and control to another nation."

The Unified Arab Command plans of 1964 and 1966 are significant. In them lay the seeds for Egypt's and Syria's simultaneous attacks in the 1973 Yom Kippur War, a coordinated assault that began at 1400 hours on October 6, 1973. The plans also reveal the level of concern senior Arab military planners had for their offensive and defensive air forces. They were aware of Israel's potential to deal an initial knockout blow to the EAF and hoped to make available a retaliatory strike option from the air forces of Arab League member states as well as allowing for a dispersal of Arab offensive warplanes.

Options for the Egyptian General Staff, 1955–1966

To coordinate Egypt's growing influence in the third world and African anticolonial movements, the military needed to be responsive. However, Egyptian military planners could not provide Nasser with options to project Egyptian offensive military power in the region or even deter Israel until the 1955 Czech arms deal, as Egypt lacked the technology to create a comprehensive offensive plan against Israel. This changed with Egypt's acquisition of advanced Soviet military hardware.

Fawzi writes, "The availability of these weapons led to a host of planning options for Egypt, leading to a change in doctrine by 1958." First, Egypt provided support to Algeria's National Liberation Front (FLN) and deployed Egyptian forces to the Congo to bolster Patrice Lumumba's newly independent country.[5] Second, by 1964 Egypt had laid the foundation for Plan Qahir, a response to Israel's diverting the Jordan River to inhibit Jordanian use of its waters.

Plan Qahir

Qahir was a comprehensive plan for a total war that integrated civil and military institutions in a collective effort against the Israelis. Although it ultimately did not work and the Egyptians faced a crushing defeat in 1967, Qahir was the Egyptians' earliest attempt to integrate tactical, operational, and strategic planning, at least on paper.

Plan Qahir had its beginnings in 1956. The plan, as described by Fawzi, was

a layered defense to prevent Israeli combat units from reaching the Suez Canal Zone and to wear down Israeli forces in the Sinai Peninsula. The plan was to use geography and terrain to mire Israeli forces. Artillery kill zones were assessed and bottlenecks determined from which the EAF would bomb and strafe. Next to UN [United Nations] forces would be an Egyptian combat layer of armored reconnaissance, border guards, and special forces units. By 1966 Plan Qahir would have a naval and air force counterpart [the air force plan was code-named Fahd, or "Leopard"]. The Operations Section of the Egyptian Chief of Staff laid out and scripted Plan Qahir, assigning orders of battle and areas of operation within the Sinai from the Suez Canal Zone to the thin layer of UNEF [United Nations Emergency Force] troops manning the Egyptian-Israeli border. War Game Faris [Mounted Knight] was conducted in February 1967, and the Third Infantry Group was used in this exercise, which was the earliest rehearsal of Plan Qahir. It revealed major problems to Egyptian commanders: preparation of the theater of operation, logistics, poor maps, and poorer map navigation skills. The Egyptian air force and navy provided token assets for the exercise. Plan Qahir divided the Sinai between the Giddi and Mitla Passes, with Gaza left primarily to the Palestinian National Army, reinforced with Egyptian advisers, equipment, and officers. Egyptians concentrated their forces along the few access roads linking the Sinai from East to West.

Despite the availability of Plan Qahir, which was at least partially exercised and familiar to the upper-level commanders, Amer decided to completely ignore Qahir and improvise orders.

Fawzi appreciated that improvised orders worked well at the theater and tactical level when the commander had a unified command and understood the battle space. But they were a disaster at the strategic level, causing conflicting and competing chains of command. According to Fawzi, Amer not only created these conditions but also visited the Sinai front only for parade inspections, not for evaluations of field combat capabilities.

Plan Qahir's Failed Implementation in the 1967 War

The Egyptian General Staff faced a myriad of tactical and operational problems in implementing Plan Qahir. Among the challenges Fawzi highlights are the following:

- reinforcing airports and providing protection to airfields
- creating and sustaining crossing bridges along the Suez Canal (when Qahir was created, Egypt still retained the Sinai and needed to protect crossing points from Israeli aerial strikes)
- identifying wells and setting up over sixty water tanks to aid forces traversing the Sinai
- creating a secure integrated communications link from headquarters in Ismailiyah, along the Suez Canal, and into the Sinai

The Egyptian constitution provided no clear lines of responsibility for undertaking the massive projects involved in Qahir. It placed all responsibility for military preparations with the National Defense Council, but within this council no one took ownership of a particular operational problem.

In 1966 the Ministry for Military Manufacturing was created to produce war matériel, such as ammunition and artillery shells, locally. Egypt had ambitions to eventually produce long-range missiles and imported German scientists to jump-start this project. Egypt also entered into an agreement with India to produce jet fighters, in which Egypt would produce the fighter's engine and the Indians would produce its body. Fawzi writes, "All of these projects failed, as they were undertaken by impulse, and no real studies on sustainment, economics, or personnel were made." Fawzi overlooks the effective Mossad operations directed against German scientists involved in Egypt's missile program.[6]

Fawzi writes, "The Egyptian reserve mobilization plan was a success on paper only, no practice or drill was conducted to test mobilization before the 1967 war.

A crippling reason for the utter defeat of Egyptian arms in 1967 was that although Plan Qahir was perhaps the only coherent military plan of action, Field Marshal Amer had discarded the plan. He instead chose to improvise, sending bodies into the Sinai without any planning, much less with mission statements for these units." Fawzi singles out May 14, 1967, as "the day Amer began to simply improvise military tactics, and the trickledown effect of this would be confusion and paralysis among the command and staff. Trained units were mixed with units needing training, diluting the efficiency of crack army units." In one case, "an entire infantry unit [that] was called up had not completed drills since 1956, during the Suez Crisis. More than a few field commanders first met while in the area of operation or in call-up processing areas. Command and control for the 1967 war was not conducted using the General Staff but was a war run by Amer through his secretariat and its chief, Shams Badran."

Lacking true military specialists, the war digressed to the point that forces had to anticipate Amer's whims and command decisions. Fawzi, army chief of staff at the time, writes, "The General Staff was completely bypassed. Shams Badran would issue orders to the field without coordinating with the army chief of staff. When the EAF chief referred to hardened shelters for jet fighters as useless tombs, Badran countermanded the chief's advice to Field Marshal Amer that hardened shelters for jet fighters were worthless and tactically left planes vulnerable to surprise attack. In the midst of the 1967 Six-Day War, Amer realized Shams Badran's secretariat was inadequate and placed other military officers to process his military orders." However, doing this during the thick of battle would only compound Egypt's failure of arms.

Regarding the military strategy of the 1967 war, Fawzi provides military readers an excellent lesson in the breakdown of unity of command, the problems with constant improvisation, and the difficulty of getting an institution, such as a field army, to respond rapidly to changes. If Egypt had fully implemented Plan Qahir, it may have had a better and more consistent grasp on its military strategy throughout the 1967 war. At a minimum Plan Qahir, which was entirely defensive, involved retreating, regrouping, and holding the line at the Giddi, Mitla, and Khatmiya Passes in the Sinai, instead of at the Suez Canal Zone; controlling these passes meant denying Israeli forces control of the entire Sinai Peninsula. After 1967 it was up to Fawzi to transform Plan Qahir from a defensive into a defensive and graduated combined-arms offensive plan.

Conclusion

Fawzi provides insight into how the Yemen War left Egypt unprepared for the 1967 Six-Day War. Although the war with Yemen provided several benefits to Yemen,

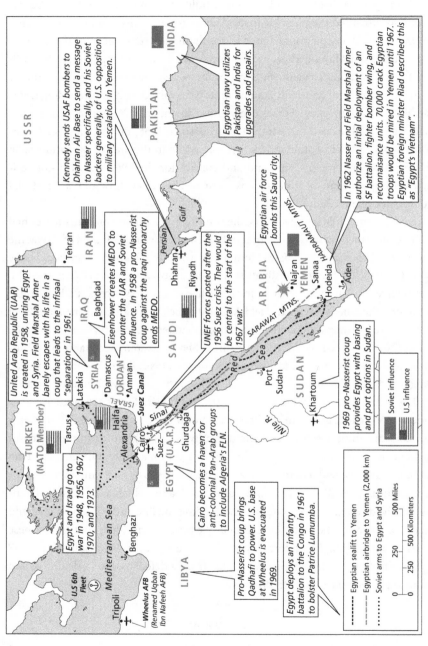

MAP 1. FAWZI'S WORLD: SUPERPOWER AND REGIONAL DYNAMICS, 1950S TO 1970S

Map created by Christopher Robinson.

such as national stabilization and world recognition, it was more detrimental to Egypt. Egypt suffered economically throughout the five long years of the war and lost many supplies and artillery to the fighting in Yemen. Egypt's lack of supplies and exhausted armed forces proved to be a huge disadvantage as the 1967 war drew closer. Although the country's leaders attempted to strengthen its military strategies by creating Plan Qahir, the failed implementation of the plan caused the entire effort to be ineffectual. Along with its failed military strategy, Egypt's lack of both trained personnel and consistent leadership ultimately caused its defeat in the 1967 war, as will be discussed in the following chapters.

In 2013 Jesse Ferris wrote a refreshing history of the 1962–1967 Yemen War titled *Nasser's Gamble*. What makes Ferris' work exemplary is his use of Arabic sources, including not only Fawzi's memoir but interviews with the general conducted by Egyptian historian Abdullah Imam. In one interview Fawzi recounted how his driver, an enlisted soldier, begged the general for a deployment to the Yemeni combat zone so that he would qualify for additional pay for his family. Ferris also includes Fawzi's observation that units coming from Yemen and redeploying to the Sinai in 1967 came with personal baggage; officers, for example, deployed in the field with refrigerators because they did not trust government storage.[7] Such was the level of material corruption endemic in the post-1967 Egyptian military. Reviewing declassified government archives provides further understanding of Nasser's dilemma, and comparisons of America in Vietnam with Egypt in Yemen—both quagmires—were not lost on Cairo.[8]

Chapter Three

Mistakes Made in the Preparation of Egyptian Combat Formations for the 1967 Six-Day War

Force and Fraud are in war the two cardinal virtues.
—Thomas Hobbes—

Foreword by the late Major General Joseph D. Brown IV, USAF, commandant of the Industrial College of the Armed Forces and the Eisenhower School, National Defense University[1]

In this third essay on Egyptian general Mohamed Fawzi, Commander Aboul-Enein, an adjunct faculty member at the Industrial College of the Armed Forces, continues his in-depth look at the development of the Egyptian army and how the poor preparation of the Egyptian armed forces contributed to their resounding defeat in the 1967 Six-Day War. This conflict has shaped not only a generation of Israelis but a generation of Arabs; its repercussions still reverberate today. Commander Aboul-Enein offers an Arab perspective on events, and it is my pleasure to introduce this chapter highlighting General Mohamed Fawzi's memoir. The memoir, summarized in English for the first time, offers a candid critique of the Egyptian armed forces' strategic, operational, and tactical performance before the 1967 Six-Day War. Commander Aboul-Enein provides a unique perspective directly from historic Arabic sources, allowing us to better comprehend the decision-making processes that led to Egypt's 1967 defeat. It is important that America's military leaders understand a conflict from various perspectives, and this chapter provides that opportunity.

At the National Defense University, we strive to provide America's senior military and civilian leaders an education grounded in the complexities of a globalized world. Commander Aboul-Enein's course on Islam, Islamist Political Theory, and Militant Islamist Ideology contributes to that goal by immersing students in the nuances of Islam and its differing ideologies. In addition, using his personal knowledge of the region, Commander Aboul-Enein has been instrumental in helping students understand the changes brought about by recent events in the Mideast, referred to by some as the "Arab Spring." His writings, such as the one you are about to read, continue his efforts to ensure the most comprehensive education possible for our military and civilian leadership in this complex and constantly changing region of the world. I applaud the U.S. Army *Infantry Magazine* for providing Commander Aboul-Enein a forum for this multipart work and look forward to the debate and discussion it will produce.

Introduction

As tensions with Israel escalated throughout the latter half of the 1960s, Egypt attempted to prepare for war yet was unsuccessful. Fawzi details the country's unpreparedness owing to its lack of military training, the chaos in Egypt's leadership, and Israel's ability to formulate a precise and successful military strategy. It becomes evident in Fawzi's memoir that Egypt was doomed to lose the 1967 war against Israel, that internal and external complications finally culminated in Israel's swift victory in June 1967.

The Absence of Adequate and Essential Training for the 1967 War

Fawzi writes, "Consistent and hard training is the measure of competence of any armed forces." His memoir shows an appreciation of the way training helps integrate reserve and active units through peacetime exercises and military education. Placing combat units in various tactical and operational exercises tests readiness as well as command and control. Fawzi notes, "Amer delegated responsibility for the training of the armed forces but never followed up or held anyone accountable for training the Egyptian military." As army chief of staff, Fawzi commissioned a report detailing the need to create training requirements for each rank of soldier up to officer. This training, he writes, "should be coupled with units and divisional training, and eventually reach the level of combined services training." In his memoir he laments, "The report was endorsed by Amer and sent to the Military Training Department for execution. However, it was never followed up with or acted upon. Instead, training commenced each calendar year at the unit level, culminating with a massive multidivisional exercise in May, but even this was scaled down from 1965 to 1967." Egyptian planners deluded themselves that the Yemen War represented a live training field for Egyptian combat arms. Fawzi argues, "The Yemen War, a guerrilla war, was not an adequate substitute for preparing for a conventional war with the Israelis." The Yemen War and the war with Israel represented two different tactical, operational, and strategic environments.

From 1964 to 1967, combat units in Egypt were exercised mainly in defensive warfare, and Fawzi compares this to developing a human Maginot line: "[Combat] units were not properly trained for offensive warfare, and from 1965 to 1966, not one Egyptian tank fired a shot in a combined armor and infantry exercise. Only 11 percent of fuel allocated for training was used in the training year of 1965–1966. Amer had the opportunity to notice this fact when he visited frontline units deployed in the Sinai and Suez Canal. He visited the units three times between 1962 and 1967, yet he failed to alter anything." Fawzi notes that exercise reports from this period were written to please senior leaders, not to shed light on the army's weaknesses. He adds, "Some reports contained Arab nationalist and socialist slogans, as if field commanders were being evaluated for political loyalty and not for combat effectiveness."

Another Achilles' heel of Egyptian combat arms was illiteracy. Fawzi notes, "Only 9 percent of personnel within the army had high school diplomas, 18 percent in the navy, and 21 percent in the air force. Those who joined the armed forces with a high school education completed high school with a barely passing grade [the equivalent of a D in an American grade system]." Fawzi expressed concern about the quality of education of Egyptian soldiers in an age of increasingly complex weapons systems. One argument against having a better educated force was that educated and technically trained personnel would be a security risk to the Egyptian regime.

Fawzi writes, "The armed forces before the 1967 war had no motto, mission statement, or general objectives. Complicating matters was the 2-million-man National Guard, an Egyptian popular army at the time. Within all forces was a shortage of medical, technical, and logistical units. The Egyptian air force showed acute shortcomings in trained pilots. New planes simply went into storage." Fawzi mentions that an entire wing of Sukhoi-7 fighters remained in their crates and that there was no armed forces inspector general office before 1967. In addition, there was a 40 percent shortage of men, 30 percent shortage in small arms, 45 percent shortage in tanks, 24 percent shortage in artillery, and 70 percent shortage in transport capabilities.

Without adequate training or supplies, the Egyptians entered into the Six-Day War at an obvious disadvantage to Israel. Fawzi observes,

> Before June 5, 1967, the start of the Six-Day War, the Egyptian air force had 260 planes and 150 pilots concentrated in ten air bases, with four of these bases in the Sinai and three in the Suez Canal Zone. The remaining fighters and bombers were concentrated along the Nile delta and within Egypt proper. Seventy-four Sukhoi bombers and twenty-one MiG fighters remained in crates or under construction. Most Egyptian

air bases had only one runway, and many of the fighters and bombers were parked on the runway and had barely been flown owing to the shortage of technicians and maintenance personnel. Air defense consisted of twenty-seven SA-1s and SA-2s and a hundred 85- and 37-mm antiair [AA] batteries. Only six antiair guns were allocated to protect ground formations, and all SAM [surface-to-air missile] batteries were assigned to protect urban centers.

Egyptian naval assets before the Six-Day War consisted of eighty warships, including destroyers, frigates, minesweepers, submarines, troop carriers, and torpedo boats. These were mainly concentrated in Alexandria, and 50 percent of these naval assets were not ready to deploy. The Yemen War had absorbed a frigate, a troop carrier, and a minesweeper. No maritime reconnaissance capability existed.

Failure of Arms Training

According to Fawzi, "Failure to train officers and troops on new Soviet equipment ran deep. Some units had not trained on weapons of any kind since the 1956 Suez Crisis. Reserve units, [particularly] the one used to concentrate forces in the Sinai, had severe shortages of weapons, equipment, and radios. Units that did train were only able to conduct one type of operation. For instance, the 11th Infantry Division had been trained since 1966 to defend Arish and could not conduct any improvised offensive operation or counterattack. Of 120,000 reserve units called up on May 15, only 80,000 responded at all." Fawzi points out that there was no rehearsal of forces to prepare for an Israeli attack. Forces were deployed and moved haphazardly. For example,

> The 14th Infantry Division moved from Cairo to Jebel Libni on May 18, and when they began to set up a perimeter, the entire division was moved again, this time to Sheikh Zuwaid on May 27 and then finally to al-Husnah on June 2. They moved four times and five hundred kilometers before the outbreak of the war. The First Light Infantry Battalion moved twice and 150 kilometers, and the 141st Armored Division was recalled from Yemen and, with no reacclimatization, redeployed to Jebel Libni, reaching this sector on June 4 and entering the combat zone the first day of the Six-Day War on June 5.

Chaos of Command

Fawzi's memoir offers a clear analysis of the chaos of Field Marshal Amer's command architecture:

> On May 16 Amer appointed Field Marshal Abdel-Mohsen Murtaji as theater commander of the Sinai-Israel front. At the time Murtaji was army chief of staff and commander in chief for ground forces. The problem was that there was no concept or organization for the theater commander within the Egyptian chain of command until Amer appointed Murtaji. To make matters worse, between May and June 5, 1967, Amer replaced twelve field commanders and field chiefs of staff. Amer compromised with Nasser on a mass military demonstration and felt that no actual combat operations would take place; he therefore went about concentrating as many combat units as possible into the Sinai. Amer conceptualized 10,000 officers, 130,000 regulars, and 80,000 reserve troops. The Egyptian military chief focused on numbers and not coordination, counterattack, or even static defense.

Superpower Maneuvers

On May 26 the U.S. ambassador to Egypt delivered a message from President Lyndon Johnson to Nasser urging Egypt not to initiate hostilities. The Johnson administration extended an invitation to Vice President Zakariyah Moheiddine to travel to Washington, D.C., for talks on the emerging crisis.[2] The Soviet ambassador to Egypt requested an 0300 meeting with Nasser to deliver a message from the Soviet premier urging Egypt not to initiate hostilities. French premier Charles de Gaulle announced a French policy of support would be based on who was the aggressor.

During this time, Fawzi notes, War Minister Badran was in Moscow to present Egypt's case for closing the Aqaba Gulf and to elicit political leverage against Israel. Soviet defense minister Marshal Andrei Grechko, who served in this position from 1967 to 1976, expressed solidarity with Egypt. Badran interpreted Grechko's enthusiasm to mean that the Soviets would directly intervene on the side of Egypt. According to Fawzi, "Nasser, Badran, and Amer discussed Badran's Moscow trip and the meaning of Grechko's farewell pledge of solidarity. The Grechko farewell solidarity pledge had a direct bearing on statements by Nasser and his subordinates after May 26 to Egypt's detriment. Nasser had delayed speeches to Parliament, the Arab Lawyer's Association, the Arab Labor Association, and the press until he heard from Badran [about] his trip to Moscow." Fawzi adds, "After getting the Grechko pledge, Nasser hardened his rhetoric, announcing, 'The Soviet Union stands with us in this battle and will not allow any nation to interfere.' Badran reassured the cabinet, the Council of Ministers, saying, 'If the American Mediterranean Fleet enters the war on the side of Israel, our Tu-16s and torpedo boats can destroy America's largest carriers.'"

The tempo of enthusiasm and wishful thinking compelled Jordan's King Hussein to visit Cairo on May 31. Fawzi writes, "Nasser was bolstered psychologically by all the frontline Arab states surrounding Israel and preparing for hostilities. There were statements of support from Jordan, Lebanon, and Syria, with pledges of aid, troops, equipment, and financial support from Kuwait, Iraq, and Algeria, who announced intentions to send forces to Egypt. Sudan sent a token ground force, while both Kuwait and Iraq sent small contingents of air and ground forces to Jordan. Egyptian leaders focused on the euphoria of support and not actual capabilities of forces sent or pledged."

War Plans

Fawzi offers one of the most intimate accounts of Nasser and Amer's discussions about Egyptian troop deployments. He writes,

> As early as 1965, while awaiting the return of battle-hardened forces from Yemen to Egypt's Port Tawfik, they [Nasser and Amer] entertained the idea of redeploying combat-tested forces returning from Yemen to Suez and Sharm el-Sheikh. Nasser saw the redeployment as political language that would shake the world, but it was decided that these forces needed to have time to reacclimatize to Egyptian society after over a year or more of guerrilla warfare. In 1966, while Amer was visiting Pakistan, he sent an encrypted message to Nasser urging the deployment of rested units from Yemen into the Sinai. He added that this should be accompanied by Nasser's threatening the closure of the Tiran Strait. This encrypted note began a series of actions that would end with the 1967 debacle.

Fawzi adds,

> The leadership in Egypt, pressed by Nasser, wanted a withdrawal of the United Nations Emergency Force from the Sinai. Nasser announced publicly his intention about UNEF forces when Israeli prime minister Levi Eshkol made threatening remarks against Syria. In addition, the Syrian defense minister informed Amer of a buildup of eleven to

thirteen Israeli divisions along the Syrian border. The Egyptian armed forces were surprised by a May 14, 1967, general order for mobilization at 1100 [local]. At 1200 [local] orders were given that began move-ment of forces to the Sinai, to be completed within seventy-two hours. This sent Egyptian staff planners into chaos; as such, a mobilization was not trained or planned for until the order was issued on May 14. Adding to the chaos of deployment was that the orders were issued from Amer's Secretariat Office and not the National Defense Council. Rumors flew as no direction was forthcoming from Amer. One pow-erful rumor among [Egypt's] generals was that the deployment was more of a demonstration on behalf of Syria and to honor the 1966 Joint Defense Pact.

There was widespread delusion that no combat would occur while the UNEF was evicted and that Egypt could gain control of the Aqaba Gulf without a war.

Fawzi was dispatched to Damascus on May 14 to evaluate the extent of Israeli deployments on the Syrian border and to examine Soviet intelligence provided to the Syrians. He writes, "There was no indication of an Israeli troop concentration when I toured the Golan Heights or even when I evaluated Soviet photo reconnais-sance taken on May 12 and 13." On May 15 Fawzi returned to Cairo and reported his findings to Field Marshal Amer. Before Nasser issued his order to deploy forces to the Sinai, Fawzi estimates, "only one-tenth of Egypt's infantry and armor was deployed in the Sinai, representing one corps and one armored division."

Amer, according to Fawzi,

ordered the concentration of ground forces in the Sinai on May 15 to be completed within forty-eight hours. Upon arrival in the Sinai, combat units were not given follow-up orders, and so the General Staff relied on Plan Qahir, approved in 1966. However, the problem was that only part of Egyptian combat units had trained for this plan. The result was mass formations concentrated in terrain they were not prepared for with no orders. An initial 3,595 officers and 66,675 troops were thrown into the Sinai without training, preparation, or orders.

On May 16, 1967, Amer sent a letter under my signature to the UNEF commander, Indian general Indar Jit Rikhye, demanding the withdrawal of his forces from the Sinai. The next day General Rikhye informed Amer that he was unable to withdraw the UNEF unless ordered by the UN Secretary General U Thant via the Egyptian foreign minister.[3]

Incredibly, on May 18 the UN secretary general ordered the withdrawal of the UNEF. Fawzi recounts his message to General Rikhye but does so nonchalantly. His memoir does not contain the text of the message or additional details about how the international community would react to Egypt's withdrawal demand. Fawzi fails to discuss the strategic impact of this momentous day, which would ultimately trigger the Six-Day War.

Rikhye's account fills in the gaps. According to Rikhye, this was the text of Fawzi's May 16 letter:

> Commander UNEF (Gaza)
>
> To your information, I gave my instructions to all UAR armed forces to be ready for action against Israel, the moment it might carry out any aggressive action against any other Arab country. Due to these instructions our troops are already concentrated in Sinai on our eastern border. For the sake of complete security of all U.N. troops which install OP's [observation posts] along our borders, I request that you issue your orders to withdraw all these troops immediately. I have given my instructions to our commander of the Eastern Zone concerning this subject. Inform back the fulfillment of this request.
>
> Yours,
> Farik Awal (M. Fawzy)
> C.O.S. of UAR[4]

When General Rikhye told Fawzi's representative, Brigadier General Ez-el-Din Mokhtar, that he could not fulfill Fawzi's request unless ordered by the UN secretary general, the Egyptian chain of command seemed surprised. Nasser had assumed that the matter could be handled from general to general and that the Egyptian Foreign Ministry would not be involved in the decision.[5] Instead, Egyptian foreign minister Mahmoud Riad would have to send the UN a formal demarche. As mentioned previously, U Thant eventually ordered the removal of UN forces from the Sinai.

Rikhye thought that Fawzi's initial letter, as engineered by Nasser and Amer, was the Egyptian president's attempt to bolster his credibility among Arab leaders with inflated threats. Having made the move, Nasser could have deescalated through the demarche channel provided by the Egyptian foreign minister. However, to lessen the threat would have meant an intolerable loss of face for Nasser among the Arab leaders.[6] Fawzi's note was for public consumption domestically and regionally, but his rhetoric would backfire internationally when taken in conjunction with Egypt's other aggressive maneuvers, such as closing the Tiran Strait and concentrating forces along the Sinai. General Rikhye regretted that he did not travel to Cairo immediately after receiving Fawzi's letter. He thought that the Egyptians might have been open to negotiations, since they were genuinely surprised that the UN would have to be involved in the decision to withdraw forces.[7] Clearly, had U Thant been more assertive, history would have been different.

Fawzi omits from his memoir any indication of what he felt when charged by Amer with writing the initial formal letter to the UNEF commander. It seems he realized the significance of this order only in hindsight. But did Fawzi in fact realize that his action would escalate the conflict from a defensive demonstration short of war to an offensive maneuver requiring a retaliatory Israeli strike? This question remains unanswered. As for Fawzi himself, can we hold him responsible? Field Marshal Amer had reduced Fawzi's authority as chief of staff to the extent that the position was almost meaningless because Nasser, not Amer, had appointed him to the post.[8] Incredibly, Amer gave no consideration to the November 4, 1966, agreement between Syria and Egypt that committed each country to the defense of the other; according to this agreement, Fawzi would be in command of joint military operations.[9] The personal trumped the practical in Egypt's politicized armed forces.

On May 18 Egypt began a hodgepodge deployment into the Sinai, and Nasser convened a meeting with his military chiefs. Nasser was considering blockading the Gulf of Aqaba, and in his memoir Fawzi wonders "whether Nasser's gambit to close the gulf was a nationalist or national objective." Fawzi argues, "Nasser's strategic thinking was influenced not by national but by nationalist goals. This meant that it was shaped not by the interests of Egypt but by those of Egypt and the wider pan-Arab national movement that Nasser felt he embodied." Fawzi and the deputy chief of operations briefed Nasser on the feasibility of an Aqaba Gulf blockade. They concluded that the drawdown of combat forces in Yemen, which required naval assets to move troops and equipment, coupled with the protection of the Sinai and Mediterranean coasts, made a total blockade unfeasible.

The May 18 General Staff meeting with Nasser resulted in Egyptian plans to conduct a mass combined arms demonstration, but not an outright offensive against Israel. A battalion of paratroopers, artillery, border guards, and mechanized armor was sent into the Sinai. Logistical units were pulled from other formations and placed around this newly created four-battalion combined-arms force. Added to this force was a 130-mm coastal artillery unit, a MiG-19 wing stationed at Ghardaga Air Base, and warplanes with a naval task force of two transports, one destroyer, one frigate, and several Styx-missile boats and mine-laying boats. Fawzi writes that communication among sea, air, and land combat units and headquarters was poor. Complicating matters was that field commanders' orders were countermanded by higher headquarters of ground, air, and naval assets in Cairo and Alexandria.

Fawzi writes,

> The political decision to close the Aqaba Gulf occurred on May 17, 1967, and was timed to coordinate with the visit of UN General Secretary U Thant. Nasser publicly asserted that Aqaba was closed to Israeli shipping and all nations shipping strategic materials to Israel. Even as Nasser made these assertions, both he and Amer affirmed the concept of freedom of the seas and navigation. However, on May 22 Egyptian naval ships were ordered to intercept and search cargo-bound ships entering the Tiran Strait. Amer and Nasser had different tactical visions, with Nasser opting for a military demonstration and Amer wanting a gradual military escalation. Their debate also focused on control versus closure of the Tiran Strait. No final operational or tactical guidance was issued, and as a result the commanding general of the Sharm el-Sheikh sector asked for rules of engagement to enforce Nasser's public order of conducting the blockage of the Aqaba Gulf.

Fawzi lists the questions coming from field commanders in the Sinai regarding how to react and redeploy and what rules of engagement would result from Nasser's closure of the Tiran Strait. Questions flooding to Cairo about enforcement of the blockade included the following:

- Should the Sinai field commanders engage foreign or Israeli merchant shipping or both?
- Should Egyptian shore batteries and naval assets engage foreign shipping for cargo-bound ships to Israel?
- Are oil tankers bound for Israel permitted?
- If merchant ships are escorted by destroyer escorts, are the Egyptian naval and air forces to engage the warships?
- If Israeli merchant ships are reflagged, are the Egyptian naval and air forces to engage them?
- Are the Egyptian naval and air forces to engage leased merchant ships bound for Israel?

These questions and more descended on Amer's office between May 20 and 23. Nasser issued a public declaration to close the Aqaba Gulf on May 23. That same day classified orders from Amer's office (not the General Staff) were given to intercept all cargo vessels bound for the Israeli port of Eilat. These vessels were to be given warning shots, and if they did not respond, they were to be sunk. If escorted by warships, they were not to be intercepted, even if the warships flew Israeli flags. On June 2 the United Kingdom, Australia, Israel, and the United States joined together to assert freedom of navigation and declared that they would challenge the blockade. The stage was set for a massive showdown that, to a minor degree, mirrored the Cuban Missile Crisis, when the United States threatened to intercept Soviet ships bound for Cuba. Yet the example of Cuba was never once discussed in Fawzi's memoir.

Fawzi writes of Nasser's historic visit to Bir Gifgafa and Inchass Air Bases on May 22. During this visit Nasser spent extensive time discussing national policy with the pilots and wider armed forces. This level of interaction between an Arab leader and the ranks was unprecedented in modern Arab history. Inchass Air Base contained the largest concentrations of MiG-21 fighters in Egypt, just as Pearl Harbor contained the largest concentrations of U.S. warplanes in the Pacific before the Japanese attack in 1941. Nasser was joined there by Amer and Air Marshal Sidqui Mahmoud. The pilots conducted a scramble drill for the Egyptian leader, after which Nasser discussed the political situations with his pilots. Oddly, in his remarks he never mentioned a conflict with Israel. The Egyptian leader thought he could take Israel, the United States, and the Soviet Union to the brink but never considered the tipping point that might lead to an Israeli strike.

According to Fawzi, "That week Amer ordered the 7th Infantry Group and 14th Armored Division to Rafah in Gaza. The 113th Infantry Division in Kunteila was deployed defensively with no thought of maneuver. Added to this was an improvised force led by Major General Saad el-Din el-Shazly that combined special forces, infantry, and armored brigades. It was deployed between Rafah and Sheikh Zuweid in order to harass communication lines for forces crossing the Sinai from Gaza. The tactical problem was that combining these different brigades and getting them integrated in the field would take practice and repeated exercises," something the Egyptians did not do until the eve of the Six-Day War. In the United States, it takes months of predeployment work-ups to integrate the staff of a new amphibious squadron (PHIBRON) with a marine expeditionary unit (MEU). Some of these work-ups are conducted shoreside in the expeditionary warfare training group as tabletop exercises, and others are conducted under way.

Intelligence Reports' Effect on the Psychology of the Egyptian Leadership

Fawzi discusses fifteen intelligence reports that shaped the thinking of Egypt's military and political leadership. His analysis offers lessons on how reports are psychologically and cognitively processed. Following are Fawzi's comments on the three most important documents in forming the views of Egypt's leaders:

> May 15: An intelligence report reveals a concentration of Israeli combat formations along the Syrian border, between five and seven divisions. This turned out to be false, shaped by Syrian and Soviet desires to pressure the Israelis after the trouncing Syrian air forces had taken earlier that month at the hands of the Israelis.

> May 17: Civilian morale in Israel is in a low state. This was a fallacy.

> May 18: Overestimation of Israeli units devoted to the Egyptian front. One takes the Syrian deployment of Israeli forces with six infantry divisions, an armored division, and one tank battalion. This far exceeded Israel's ground order of battle, yet Egyptian planners wanted to accept that Israeli forces existed on both the Egyptian and Syrian borders.

Fawzi discusses the conferences convened to discuss these intelligence reports: "The May 15 conference began at 2030 and focused on reinforcing Gaza and the southern Sinai sector of Kunteila. The debates zeroed in on the limited roads that bisected the Sinai from west to east. The General Staff discussions began with the chief of military operations, who discussed the need for aerial strikes into Israel. Amer interjected and ordered such discussions to be suppressed. The General Staff was incensed at limiting Egyptian options, particularly since Amer signed the aerial strike portion of an Egyptian offensive against Israel, called Plan Asad [Lion]."

Fawzi also highlights the May 28 conference convened at 2100 to discuss the defense and blockade of the Aqaba Gulf: "At this meeting Zakariyah Moheiddine [a member of the revolutionary Free Officers] was designated chief of civil defense. Moheiddine was the Egyptian vice president and scheduled to meet American president Lyndon Johnson the first week of June. Amer's ability to give orders to Egypt's vice president demonstrates the power Amer had within Nasser's government. In addition, Amer issued countermanding orders that the defense of the Sinai would be phased and gradual, and plans for an Egyptian counterstrike should the Israelis attack first were stood down."

On June 2, 1967, a meeting between Nasser and the General Staff convened. Fawzi considers this to be the most important meeting, writing:

> Nasser ended the discussion declaring that Israel would strike first on June 4 or 5. The General Staff focused on developing a counterstrike

package with Air Marshal Sidqui Mahmoud estimating that Egypt could sustain a 20 percent loss from an Israeli first strike. The Egyptian air marshal briefed other chiefs on the possibility that the Egyptian air force would be wiped out and advocated weighing the benefits of an Egyptian first strike versus world opinion. Nasser chose to focus on the 20 percent loss rate as being an adequate price for going to war with Israel and by extension with the United States. On June 3 Sidqui and Amer discussed moving fighter planes to the rear [Egypt proper versus the Sinai] and the need to disperse air assets. Sidqui argued that moving fighter planes from the Sinai to Egypt proper would demoralize the pilots. They discussed the issue of the Egyptian air force ability to absorb a first strike. The discussions between the two then focused on Amer's itinerary on June 5, 1967, to visit combat units in the Sinai. He was scheduled to arrive between 0800 and 0900 at the Bir Tamada Airfield, where many senior officers would be on hand to greet Amer. That morning Israel attacked Egypt. Amer and his senior aides were on their way to the Sinai in a military plane as Israeli jets roared toward the Mediterranean to loop around into Egypt and the Sinai, conducting one of the most decisive aerial attacks in military history.

Egyptian Combat Readiness on the Eve of the 1967 Arab-Israeli War

According to Fawzi, in the twenty-one days leading to June 5, 1967, the Egyptian army was not in any state of readiness for war:

On June 5, 1967, General Tawfik Abdel-Nabi, the military attaché to Pakistan, arrived to take command of a specialized antitank battalion. His new battalion consisted of no heavy armor, no mechanized armor, and not even vehicles necessary for the unit to conduct its assigned mission. The weapons were so paltry that they could not be called an antitank battalion or even certify that the battalion was ready for combat. From Yemen the first elements of the 18th Infantry Corps began to arrive. Field Marshal Murtaji and his field commander in the Sinai, General Salah Mohsen, spent the morning focused on Amer's itinerary. Sixteen communications battalions needed for the deployed Egyptian infantry corps and reserves remained behind the west bank of the Suez Canal on the Egyptian side and therefore had not been set up to communicate in the field.

Civil Control of the Military

According to Fawzi, one of the internal challenges to regaining Egyptian military morale after the humiliating defeat of 1967 was the armed forces' subordination to Egypt's political officials. Fawzi writes, "In addition, the armed forces needed to be aligned to the National Pact, a document committing the entire Egyptian population to pan-Arabism, Arab socialism, and the removal of class distinctions. For this to work the Revolutionary Command Council [RCC] needed to transition its power to the parliamentary system." The RCC, in place since the 1952 coup and made up of members of the Free Officers, was busy pursuing power and self-interest, which undermined the readiness of the armed forces.

In 1968 Fawzi met with Nasser several times to draft legislation placing the armed forces under civil authority. Fawzi recounts hours of discussion with Nasser and reveals that the Egyptian leader had considered the delineation of responsibilities and the issue of civil control of the military before the 1967 war, after the 1961 dissolution of Egypt's union with Syria. Fawzi notes that Nasser "wanted a military decoupled from policymaking and placed under the control of a civil minister. This is what led Nasser to create the Majlis al-Riasaa [Presidential Council] in 1962. It was supposed to make policy recommendations to the president and then implement approved recommendations. This body would also draft legislation for proposals to Parliament, in addition to implementing presidential directives." Nasser spoke to Fawzi about how the 1958 provisional constitution evolved into the 1964 constitution that created the Majlis al-Umma (People's Assembly). He admitted to Fawzi that all these reforms were diluted by Field Marshal Amer, who refused to answer to the People's Assembly.

Fawzi recounts an incident Nasser described to him: "Amer stormed out of a 1962 Presidential Council meeting in which it was proposed that military promotions of colonel and above be endorsed by the council. He tendered his resignation and retreated to Mersa Matruh, a Mediterranean Sea resort, while his military supporters protested in front of the armed forces headquarters." The division between Nasser and Amer should have been apparent to the Egyptian president then, but the personal ties between the two men and the power bases they had amassed made it difficult for Nasser to act.

Intelligence and Warning Messages
before June 5, 1967

Fawzi offers insight into Arab intelligence and warnings about the impending the Six-Day War:

The Egyptian War Ministry in Cairo received two warnings from military intelligence in Arish from Lieutenant Colonel Ibrahim Salama, who dispatched a message of an Israeli attack at 0700 on June 5, 1967. It reached the General Staff at 0940. The second warning message came from General Abdel-Moneim Riad in Jordan. At the time he [Riad] acted as forward commander and Egyptian representative to the Jordanian General Staff in Amman, part of the conceptual Unified Arab Command. This message was a result of the Jordanian listening post in Ajloun, where it began to detect Israeli movements at 0400 and where it then sent warnings to Egyptian posts in Arish. The Egyptian intelligence officers did not forward this 0400 message urgently, issuing it at 0700. This nonurgency meant the message arrived at the General Staff at 0940; the Israeli attack began at 0800. Frontline ground units in the Sinai did not grasp it was an Israeli attack until 0830, when Israeli jets were bombing and strafing their positions.

Fawzi estimates that 85 percent of the EAF was wiped out in four hours. He offers conspiracy theories popular among Egyptians of the time to make sense of the depth of the defeat. For example, he writes that the Israeli "attack was conducted and supplemented by the U.S. Navy Sixth Fleet, which provided air cover for Israeli assets, allowing the bulk of the Israeli air force [IAF] to attack Egypt." This is a slightly better conspiracy theory than Nasser's public declarations after the 1967 war, which asserted that American warplanes attacked Egypt. Fawzi believes that the Israelis planned and trained for the 1967 airstrike a decade earlier; it took that long to perfect the action. In this case Fawzi is likely deflecting Israeli successes by attributing battlefield ground and air victories to American support and even to direct intervention by U.S. forces.

The Aerial Attack

Fawzi writes that the Israeli aerial attack was divided into two main thrusts: "Each would contain a combination of approximately eighty fighter jets and bombers. The first attack group concentrated on the Sinai, with a focus on radar installations, Suez Canal air bases, and mainly four Sinai airfields. The second attack group focused on the rest of Egypt, with a focus on Cairo airfields." Fawzi's memoir is full of tactical criticism of Egyptian arms and questions that reveal an Egyptian military mind that spent years pondering the 1967 war:

- Why didn't Egyptian commanders immediately enact Plan Fahd to get a few Egyptian warplanes aloft? Fawzi discovered that the Egyptian warplanes were not armed and fueled, but he does not explain why not. He likely realized that because Nasser was concerned more with internal coups than with external threats, he did not see the need to maintain the warplanes in any state of readiness.

♦ How did the Israelis know of the few planes that escaped Cairo airfields during the attack and landed at Luxor air base? Luxor did not house any warplanes and, according to Fawzi, was not in the initial Israeli attack plans. He does not mention his sources for this information but instead implies that the Israelis had precise intelligence. He makes no allowances for electronic reconnaissance on planes or Israeli pilots' ability to make independent judgments regarding fleeing Egyptian jet fighters.

♦ Why were orders not given to disperse the EAF to Jeddah, Saudi Arabia; Uzma Air Base in Libya; or Khartoum Airfield in Sudan? Fawzi writes, "The single initiative of a wing commander allowed a wing of Antonov-12 bombers to leave Cairo Air Base for Khartoum in order to escape the Israeli air assault."

Fawzi writes that the Israelis further subdivided their two attacks into two waves: "One released bombs and fired missiles, and the second saturated the air bases with heavy machine-gun fire." He was highly impressed with Israeli antirunway cluster bombs, which Egyptian units experienced for the first time in 1967. He writes, "They created holes four to six meters wide and three meters deep, rendering the runways unusable." He laments that most Egyptian airfields consisted of one main runway, and to make matters worse, there were no real Egyptian technical units dedicated to repair runways.

Fawzi breaks down the Israeli air attack into forty-five minutes: "twenty minutes to target, five minutes to attack, and twenty minutes to return to refuel and reload." He writes, "The Israelis were able to reload and refuel in seven to ten minutes. They sacrificed dispersal [of warplanes] for a concentration of air assets [over Egyptian air space] and an offensive strike policy with no real threat of effective retaliation."

Fawzi spends a couple of pages commenting on the bombing and strafing of the U.S. Navy surveillance ship USS *Liberty* (AGTR-5). He thought that the American naval surveillance ship was "electronically jamming the Egyptian radar and aiding Israeli fighter-bombers by vectoring them to Egyptian targets. . . . The USS *Liberty* was key to Israeli air success." However, the IAF's misidentification of the USS *Liberty* resulted in the death of 34 and injury of 171 U.S. Navy sailors. While the Israelis focused on their attack on the USS *Liberty*, the diversion of the

U.S. Navy surveillance ship allowed thirty Egyptian fighters to be sent aloft, twelve were shot down by the Israelis, and the rest withdrew to the closest haven.

Fawzi's focus on the Israelis' mistaken identification and targeting of the USS *Liberty* is not uncommon among Egyptians wanting to write a more direct and active role for the United States in the Six-Day War. Fawzi could not believe that the Egyptians could be defeated so badly by the Israelis alone, without the direct intervention of the United States. Nasser even gave a speech during the 1967 war claiming American warplanes were attacking along with Israeli planes.

Mobilizing Egypt for Total War

Fawzi thought deeply about mobilizing Egypt for total war after the 1967 war. He wanted to prepare the theater of warfare not just along the Suez Canal but throughout the country for defense and to support the efforts of frontline units. He thought that concentrating on a national effort would restore morale. Fawzi writes, "The Egyptian General Staff saw shortcomings in the educational level of Egyptian soldiers and began to comprehend that a higher level of education was needed to integrate complex Soviet weapons systems into the Egyptian order of battle. There was a renewed focus to draft or recruit high school and college graduates. Egyptian military leaders discussed the need to abandon parade armies and make a serious attempt to absorb advanced Soviet weaponry and doctrine."

According to Fawzi, the shipment of SA-3, 6, and 7 SAMs led to

> a deep discussion of electronic warfare [EW] for the first time among the General Staff and the first thoughts of creating an elaborate defense umbrella along the Suez Canal. Plan 200 would be a tabletop exercise and eventual plan for the liberation of the Sinai in twelve days. It is the constant update of this plan that would find Egyptian military planners obsessing with countering the F-4 Phantom and A-4 Skyhawk, which the United States had provided Israel. On June 30, 1970, the Egyptians tested the SA missile system on Israeli F-4s probing the Suez Canal and claimed hits.

Egyptians believed that the Rogers Plan, the cease-fire brokered between Israel and Egypt after the War of Attrition, named after U.S. Secretary of State William Rogers (d. 2001), was designed to limit the impact of the loss of American-made F-4s in the Israeli encounter with the Soviet SA missile-defense system. But Fawzi's memoir shows he had a real respect for the American warplane. In 1979 Egypt acquired the F-4E Phantom equipped with Sidewinder, Maverick, and Sparrow missiles as part of the Peace Pharaoh Program.[10] Israel was the largest foreign operator of the F-4E, receiving the first delivery of the warplane in 1969 under the Peace Echo Program.[11] It remained in Israeli service until 2004.[12]

Scholar J. C. Hurewitz writes that the F-4 Phantom and A-4 Skyhawk were central to Nasser and Fawzi's discussions with the Soviets. According to him, within four months of September 1969, the IAF had placed the F-4 and A-4 into service, and this led to the "Sovietation" of Egypt's air defense in 1970.[13] Moscow did not provide the SA-3 AA system to North Vietnam but assured Washington that its deployment of SA systems was designed to protect Cairo, Alexandria, and the Aswan High Dam.[14] This was a deception—the Soviets deployed more SA AA systems than they let on. They also introduced their latest MiG-21J to the Egyptians to counter the American advanced jet fighters.

The United States used the F-4 and A-4 as one of several bargaining chips to drive the parties to a negotiated settlement. The jet fighter was mainly utilized as leverage with the Israelis, with shipments to Israel ceasing in 1971 and resuming in 1972 on the basis of constructive and destructive interactions between Egyptians and Israelis along the Suez Canal.[15] Of course, the Suez Canal, like Berlin, Cuba, North Korea, Vietnam, and Afghanistan, would become one of several epicenters of overt Cold War confrontation between the Soviets and the United States.[16]

Conclusion

Fawzi provides a clear analysis of why Egypt was so gravely unprepared for war against Israel in 1967. Whether the Americans aided Israel during the war or not, Egypt was unprepared for combat owing to a lack of training, equipment, artillery, and sound leadership. Although Egyptian military and political leaders attempted to create detailed war plans and strategies, such as Plan Qahir, the failed implementation of these plans left Egypt susceptible to Israeli attack and rapid defeat. Also, the gradual deterioration of the relationship between Nasser and Amer, as Amer gained evermore power, left a void in the Egyptian leadership. Egypt's halfhearted attempts at strategic planning did not stand a chance next to Israel's decade of detailed and sound planning. Most important, no single event caused Egypt to lose the Six-Day War; rather, several events over several decades ultimately left Egypt weak and unable to defend itself.

★★ **Chapter Four** ★★

The Collapse of the Egyptian Armed Forces
The 1967 Six-Day War

Cold wars cannot be conducted by hot heads.
—WALTER LIPPMANN—

Foreword by George Mitroka, director,
Denial and Deception Advanced Studies Program,
National Intelligence University

At the National Intelligence University we conduct a one-year graduate-level study program that develops expertise and in-depth knowledge in understanding and countering adversary denial and deception tactics, techniques, and procedures directed toward the United States. Nothing is more important to countering foreign denial and deception than understanding the mind of our adversaries—and even allies—who conduct deliberate attempts at deception. To penetrate the mind, one must cultivate empathy. To do this one must read what our adversaries are reading and writing for their consumption. This requires careful examination of their narratives, histories, and perspectives from a non-Western point of view.

To this end, we are glad to count Commander Aboul-Enein as one of our speakers during the phase of our program that explores the Arab mind. He has been instrumental in teaching, speaking, and writing about the Middle East for years. His current project brings to life the memoir of General Mohamed Fawzi for America's military readers for the first time and is exactly what is needed to elicit thoughtful examination of non-Western viewpoints in order to cultivate the future generation of leaders. While this essay may not involve deliberate deception directly, it does explore General Fawzi's mind-set as he, and other senior Egyptian military leaders, dealt with the seemingly irrational decisions made by Field Marshal Abdel-Hakim Amer at a most critical point during the 1967 Six-Day War. However, beyond the devastating operational impacts the decisions had on the battlefield for the Egyptians, these events add perspective to how and foreshadow why the deep friendship between president and strongman Gamal Abdel Nasser and Field Marshal Amer would lead others to betrayal, an attempted military coup, and,

46

ultimately, suicide. The U.S. Army *Infantry Magazine* is to be commended for providing Commander Aboul-Enein a forum for his long-term project of bringing Arabic works of military significance to America's military readership. I look forward to the discussion this series will generate and, more important, the learning that will take place in America's military classrooms that choose to use this series to educate students on the Middle East generally and the Arab-Israeli wars specifically.

Introduction

Egypt's defeat in the 1967 Six-Day War was characterized on the battlefield by disorganization and a lack of communication between the leadership and units in the field. Adding to the confusion was Field Marshal Amer's deteriorating mental state, which caused him to make questionable decisions, the most notable being the decision to rapidly withdraw from battle. The order to withdraw was given without clear parameters or instruction and caused chaos and uncertainty.

However, what really stands out in General Fawzi's memoir is the clash of two different military doctrines. From the Egyptian perspective, the armed forces were designed primarily to preserve the 1952 revolution, which meant that the military focused more on internal dissention within the ranks and less on projecting its power. Since President Nasser had attained power through a bloodless military coup in 1952, the RCC had obsessed about threats coming from within the military, and this obsession remains to this day. The Israelis and their military do not worry about military coups and can therefore focus more clearly on defending Israel and projecting Israeli military power.

General Fawzi's memoir also illustrates the collapse of a command structure amid an effective, modern, and rapid military onslaught. This chapter discusses Amer's actions and the crumbling of the Sinai front as a result of lack of initiative and the inability to improvise without approval from higher authority. General Fawzi carefully studied the Six-Day War and used the information he gleaned to reconstruct the Egyptian armed forces for the next phase of the Arab-Israeli conflict, the War of Attrition and the 1973 Yom Kippur War.

The Battles

Fawzi indulges conspiratorial narratives that need to be examined, since he rose to command all the Egyptian forces. His views were not uncommon among Egypt's officer corps. He writes, "The CIA informed Israel that Egypt had no offensive plans, or even counterstrike plans, which emboldened the Israelis to attack in 1967. The planned visit by Egyptian vice president Zakariyah Moheiddine to Washington, D.C., on June 3, 1967, at the invitation of President Johnson was a ruse that lulled Nasser into a false sense of security that the Israelis would not initiate hostilities." A declassified collection of CIA literature published by the agency's Center for the Study of Intelligence includes an article written by agency historian David Robarge titled "CIA Analysis of the 1967 Arab-Israeli War: Getting It Right." In Robarge's article Lyndon Johnson justifies his decision not to airlift military supplies or even publicly support Israel, telling Israeli foreign minister Abba Ebban, "All of our intelligence people are unanimous that if the UAR attacks, you will whip the hell out of them." The CIA assessment at the time indicated that "Israel could almost certainly attain air supremacy over the Sinai Peninsula in less than twenty-four hours after taking the initiative."[1] It appears that in the lead-up to the Six-Day War, CIA assessments of Egyptian and Syrian capabilities were used to reassure the Israelis that Nasser's war machine was hollow in order to dissuade Tel Aviv from conducting a first strike and thereby deescalate tensions.

Fawzi also overlooks that Johnson was the first president to use the Washington-Moscow hotline, which was established in 1963 in the aftermath of the Cuban Missile Crisis to avoid another tense situation between the United States and the Soviets. The 1967 Six-Day War saw a dozen exchanges between Johnson and Soviet premier Alexei Kosygin to contain the Arab-Israeli crisis. Communication began on June 5 with Kosygin expressing concern about possible U.S. intervention and included a June 8 hotline exchange between Johnson and Kosygin explaining that the USS *Liberty* incident was conducted by Israeli warplanes to avoid misunderstandings or miscalculations caused by the proximity of the U.S. Sixth Fleet and units from the Soviet Black Sea Fleet.[2] Once the president was briefed on the accidental Israeli attack on the USS *Liberty* on June 8, he wanted to quickly assure Moscow—that same day—that the Soviets would not even be considered a suspect in the attack and thereby decrease any added tensions between warships currently operating in close proximity to one another in the eastern Mediterranean.[3]

At 1100 on June 5, 1967, Fawzi was directed to ask Syrian chief of staff Ahmed Suweidan to execute Plan Rasheed, an attack on Israel from Syria meant as reciprocation for an Israeli attack on Egypt (the plan also included an alternative for a case in which Syria was attacked first). The Syrian general ignored Fawzi's entreaty but placated him by saying, "We shall try, Sir!" In Jordan, Egyptian general Abdel-Moneim Riad also requested Syrian intervention as part of the newly formed Arab Command, but he was also ignored by Damascus.

Fawzi describes the gradual decline in communications from the front in great detail. The panicked reports from the field that Field Marshal Amer and his war minister, Shams Badran, received at the start of the attack steadily declined as the

IAF tore into Egyptian formations. Tuning into foreign broadcasts, Amer learned of the magnitude of the losses, and this triggered a nervous breakdown in Egypt's top military leader.

Fawzi recounts, "The battle began at 1450 June 5 and ended at 2230 June 6. First reports of an IDF mechanized advance were at Khan Younis at 0900, with armor duels with the Egyptian 7th Infantry Division. At 1840 the IDF, using only 20 tanks and air support, isolated the Egyptian 7th Division at Rafah. Umm Qatef was subdued by the Israelis in two days. The Egyptian 2nd Infantry Group repelled two Israeli attempts to take Quseimah." Fawzi adds that Quseimah was taken only after Egyptians retreated from the town. He cites this and the Battle of Kunteila as examples of Egyptian arms holding their own despite a lack of air dominance.

According to Fawzi, the Battle of Kunteila began at 1300 June 5 with heavy Israeli saturation fire from mechanized artillery. The First Egyptian Artillery Division responded in kind, and according to Fawzi, the Egyptians gave chase to the Israeli harassing units. Fawzi admits that this attack was a feint designed to occupy the First Egyptian Artillery Division while the main Israeli ground thrust attacked the city of Arish. He writes, "The Battle of Arish began at 1500 June 5 and was met by the Egyptian 14th Armored Division, reinforced with an infantry battalion. In command was General Nasr al-Deeb, who attempted to close with the Israelis following the Soviet tactic of hugging an enemy to negate superior air or artillery firepower. Al-Deeb radioed for Egyptian air support, which, unknown to him, was already wiped out." Fawzi writes that al-Deeb is remembered because "he had briefed his sector prior to the start of the war and made an uncannily accurate prediction of how the Israelis would take Arish and Umm Qatef."

Fawzi continues,

> The Egyptian field headquarters in Sinai developed a plan involving the creation of a defensive line between Jebel Libni and Bir Tamada, enabling the reinforcement of the defense of Kunteila. Simultaneously, a plan was developed to defend the canal zone by General Sadek Sharaf. There was a problem with a lack of reliable communications to transmit orders to the 1st Armored Division, the 113th Infantry Division, the 4th Armored Group, and the 6th Infantry Group. The 4th Armored Division received orders at 0740 on June 7 to defend the Giddi and Mitla Passes until an order to withdraw was issued. In the mind of General Salah Mohsen, the order psychologically caused him not to plan for a counterstrike and to limit his options to only the order to defend or withdraw. What resulted was that the 2nd Armored Division fought Israeli units at the Giddi Pass, the 3rd Armored Division fought

along the Ismailiyah Road, and the 6th Mechanized Division fought at the entrance to the Mitla Pass. Jordan and Syria finally began an air attack on Israel on June 7, to which the Israelis responded with punishing attacks that decimated 80 percent of Jordan's air force and 50 percent of Syria's air force.

The Withdrawal

No issue is as controversial in modern Egyptian military history as are the details of how, when, and who gave the order to withdraw from the Sinai during the Six-Day War. Fawzi writes,

> The first inkling to withdraw occurred at 0550 on June 6. Amer sent a message from his command center in Cairo to the commander of combat forces in Sharm el-Sheikh to withdraw east of the Suez Canal. At noon on June 6, he [Amer] requested that I plan for a withdrawal and do so in twenty minutes. I attempted to reason with Amer, but Amer's mental state was not conducive to discussion or debate. I then summoned General Anwar al-Qadi, operations chief, and his deputy, General Tilhami to plan this impromptu withdrawal. We discussed the inconceivability of the order, because from our perspective all forces, except for the Egyptian 7th Infantry Group, were holding their ground. When we attempted to brief Field Marshal Amer, annotating key locations in the Sinai and saying a phased retreat to salvage as many men and as much equipment as possible would take four days, Amer cut off the briefer and in a raised [incredulous] voice said, "I've given the order already. Four days and three nights, Fawzi!" Amer then went into his sleeping quarters and suffered a nervous breakdown in front of me and the two generals.

A few hours later, Fawzi learned that Amer had ordered a withdrawal via Ismailiyah directly through Suez Canal Command. The order included a retreat of forces from Arish with their personal weapons only and a stipulation that the withdrawal be completed overnight. Fawzi and the General Staff were stunned and outraged at having been cut out of such a significant order. More important, the order meant that the retreat would be a rout, that many Egyptians would die in the uncoordinated and chaotic withdrawal. Fawzi describes the military reaction best: "The Arish commander abandoned his position based on Amer's order without informing higher command in the Sinai. Amer's order defies every military convention and compromises the safety of soldiers in the field. Without orders, even in a withdrawal, pandemonium sets in and, in this case, thousands of tons of equipment were lost." Fawzi was concerned that friendly fire could occur as some soldiers stumbled on each other in retreat, accidentally firing their weapons, and others, who had not yet received Amer's withdrawal order (which reached different units at different times), decided the retreating soldiers were cowards and deserved to be shot.

Fawzi writes,

> General Murtaji, Sinai front commander, was informed verbally by a military policeman [MP] and not given written orders to withdraw. When Murtaji asked where the order originated from, the MP replied that it was from the field marshal. Astonishingly, Murtaji took this verbal order at face value and withdrew with his staff to Ismailiyah, instead of remaining at his post to command an orderly retreat. Murtaji did not bother to inform higher headquarters in Cairo, the General Staff, or his field commanders in the Sinai of his withdrawal. General Salah Mohsen's desire to create a shielding force for the retreating units was undermined by Amer's order and the cascading effect that led to chaos on the battlefield.

Fawzi details Amer's erratic orders with this time line:

- 1130—Amer issues order to withdraw to a second defensive line in the Sinai.
- 1530—Amer orders 4th Armored Division counterstrike to lift the siege of Quseimah.
- 1600—Amer orders all forces to the west of the Suez Canal.
- 1630—Amer orders Fawzi to lay out a withdrawal plan in twenty minutes.

He continues,

> The erratic nature of his orders and his subversion of the chain of command in issuing his orders led field commanders to rely on MPs and military intelligence officers for orders. Rumor and confusion were the order of the day. Since commanders were not given a withdrawal point to muster, they relied on rumors, and thousands descended on barracks in Cairo to Deversoir on the canal and even to the city of Ismailiyah. In one instance an MP corporal was directing whole brigades and

battalions along Road 6 to Ismailiyah. A major arranged a flight for administrative personnel of his unit from the Sinai to Cairo West Air Base, while the remainder of his unit was scurrying on the ground from the Sinai back toward the Suez Canal. A rumor to destroy air bases and equipment circulated, which Fawzi had to stop. In one evening an estimated 120,000 troops were stampeding toward the Suez Canal.

Fawzi writes that it "took one week, from June 7 to 14, for 100,000 Egyptian soldiers to make their way out of the Sinai, with thousands showing up at their homes and villages before reporting to their base."

During this pandemonium,

Amer was in a state of nervous collapse, locked in his bedroom with his minister of war, Shams Badran, acting as his door guard, when these two men should have been giving orders. Shams Badran alternated between Amer's bedroom and phone calls to Nasser, the Soviet ambassador, and the Soviet foreign minister. Amazingly, at this late stage and after issuing his chaotic order, he [Amer] asked General Anwar al-Qadi, the operations chief, to take command of the 4th Armored Division and defend the Giddi and Mitla Passes. The Soviet military attaché was beside himself at Cairo headquarters that Egyptian units were ordered to retreat instead of standing and fighting. He finally yelled, "Why didn't you just let the Egyptian combat units fight and demonstrate their valor?" Moscow could have replenished the air losses, and on June 10, the fifth day of the war, forty MiG fighters arrived via Algeria. They had been ready to be delivered to Cairo as early as June 7.

Fawzi continues,

Nasser and Amer had a [heated] exchange early during the war, in which Nasser said, "You could've asked my opinion about a withdrawal, and now you ask my opinion about defending the passes?!" Amer issued the withdrawal order June 6, which was followed by a formal message. On the morning of June 7, Amer sent me on a fool's errand to stop the withdrawal of the 4th Armored Division. I traveled from Cairo and arrived al-Gala'a Military Base at Ismailiyah only to find the entire Sinai field command there. I informed Field Marshal Murtaji about Amer's new orders regarding the 4th Armored Division, but Murtaji did not take these orders seriously and angrily said that with no air cover the entire Sinai would be lost.

Some Egyptian historians believe that Nasser approved the withdrawal order and later developed a narrative to blame and discredit Amer. The war was lost in Murtaji's mind even before it ended on June 11.

On returning to Cairo from the Sinai, Fawzi saw "hundreds of new T-55 tanks being abandoned, their crews walking toward the canal." He came across General Emad Thabit, chief of armor administration, and pleaded with him to rescue the new tanks, but he was unsuccessful. Fawzi then attempted to persuade Egyptian artillery units to fire on and around the new tanks so that they would not fall intact into Israeli hands, but Egyptian crews were too afraid, telling Fawzi this would only attract Israeli air strikes.

To make matters worse, Fawzi recalls, "Egyptian combat engineers were given orders to destroy all canal crossings, except one, by 1300 hours on June 7." This only accelerated the stampede and rout of Egyptian combat formations heading from the Sinai toward the Suez Canal. When Fawzi returned to the Operations Center at Nasr City in Cairo, he "found officers in a state of resignation, shock, and defeat. Amer's order to withdraw all forces from the Sinai in one night deprived the Egyptian army of a chance to fight and defend the homeland. It also led to chaos and the abandonment of thousands of tons of equipment. Under the watchful eye of Egyptian MPs and intelligence officers, engineers from Ismailiyah blew the last bridge over the canal on June 8." They began to close the canal for international shipping by scuttling a dozen ships along it. The Suez Canal would not reopen for international shipping for another eight years. The closure of the canal would ultimately be devastating to Egypt's economy and to global shipping generally, for ships now had to traverse around South Africa to reach European markets.

Out of hundreds of tanks, Fawzi writes, "forty-seven reached the canal by diligent disciplined crews but were left in the Sinai side of the canal because the bridges were being destroyed. Some tank crews bravely turned around and went back to use their tanks as transports for more troops. General Ahmed Ismail was assigned commander of the eastern zone on June 11, 1967," and with his help Fawzi would have to pick up the pieces of the shattered Egyptian armed forces, learn what went wrong, and use these lessons to craft the rudiments of a massive offensive campaign that would become the seeds of the 1973 Yom Kippur War.

The Cost

Fawzi's memoir offers the first Egyptian assessment of the 1967 Six-Day War, and it is best to let his numbers speak for themselves:

Personnel lost:
- Air force: 4%

- Navy: no loss
- Army: 17%

Equipment lost:

- Air force: 85%
- Navy: no loss
- Army: 85%

Warplanes lost:

- Heavy bombers: 100%
- Light bombers: 100%
- Heavy and light jet fighters: 85%

Fawzi writes, "Determining who was missing or killed in action in the Sinai in 1967 was not easy, and some individuals designated missing were not determined as killed in action until 1971." Egypt would work with the Red Cross to attain Israeli cooperation in accounting for Egyptian war dead and missing. Fawzi estimates that "13,600 were killed and 3,799 taken prisoner, with 9,800 classified as missing in action until 1971, when they were designated killed in action. After the war it was determined that an armored group organized around 200 tanks had 12 destroyed and 188 abandoned; only 6 percent [of all personnel in armored units] stayed with their equipment and refused to give them up." Overall, the losses were devastating for Egyptian forces.

Conclusion

The causes of Egypt's defeat in the 1967 Six-Day War that manifested before the start of hostilities are several and include regional, external, and internal issues, such as Field Marshal Amer's erratic personality and quest for power. However, during the war itself a lack of communication and Amer's sudden decision to withdraw troops within a day were the primary factors in Egypt's loss. Although Egypt was gravely unprepared to fight against Israel, it lost its chance to defend itself when Amer abruptly ordered a withdrawal, which led to even more destruction and chaos than the war itself. With the confluence of all the aforementioned factors, Egypt's defeat was unpreventable. The United States, mired in Vietnam, did not want to commit additional forces to the Middle East, and in many ways Egyptian military incompetence coupled with Israel's decisive victory and Washington's management of the Soviets prevented an overstretched United States from committing to a more active involvement in the Middle East. The 1967 Six-Day War and the 1973 Yom Kippur

War were two instances of Cold War brinksmanship that caught the United States vulnerable in committing ground troops owing to its simultaneous involvement in Vietnam. This is worth pondering as twenty-first-century American leaders debate the extent of U.S. military commitment in Syria versus Libya and troop levels after the withdrawal of combat units in Afghanistan.[4]

Chapter Five

Challenges to Civil Authority

The military don't start wars. The politicians start wars.
—GENERAL WILLIAM WESTMORELAND—

Foreword by Ed Mornston, former director, Defense Combating Terrorism Center

We all share in the complex responsibility of protecting the national security of the United States. This responsibility means above all cultivating the intellectual capital of our men and women charged with the various facets of protecting our national interests around the world. America's long-term involvement in the Middle East necessitates that we explore direct Arabic sources, not only the writings of our adversaries, but of countries whose stability is deemed essential to the United States and the international community. Egypt is such a country. Not only is it the most populous country in the Arab world, but it has within it the strategic sea-lane of communication, the Suez Canal, linking Europe to Asia. Egypt is also one of the epicenters of the 2011 Arab Spring, and its people toppled the thirty-year Hosni Mubarak regime in eighteen days. However, Egypt currently faces a myriad of challenges and as of this writing is ruled by the SCAF, nineteen senior generals who have now pushed the country's presidential election to 2013, much to the disappointment of various factions within Egypt. (Note: Since this introduction was written, events have overtaken this decision. There was a presidential election in 2012, and the elected president, Mohamed Morsi, was ousted in 2013. The SCAF has since returned to influence in Egyptian politics.) To begin to comprehend the men who make up the SCAF, we must rediscover Egyptian military history, for these are military leaders shaped by wars with Israel and the way Egyptian rulers responded to the pressures of war. General Mohamed Fawzi's memoir offers a unique perspective on how civil-military rule was challenged in the aftermath of the 1967 Six-Day War. It provides details on how Egypt's strongman Nasser dealt with the challenge of his war minister, Field Marshal Amer, and segments frustrated by the humiliating events of the 1967 war. Commander Aboul-Enein has done us all a service by making Fawzi's memoir, originally published in the 1980s, available for English-speaking readers. He has worked hard to educate our combat forces and personnel using direct Arabic sources to enable us to make better decisions pertaining to the region. I also wish to offer my compliments to *Infantry* for providing Commander Aboul-Enein a forum. This effort reminds me of Colonel Hal Moore's innovative tactics in 1965, at the time called Air Mobility, which he tested in the Battle of the Ia Drang Valley. Colonel Moore immersed himself in the mind of the North Vietnamese, even reading materials in French. Close to five decades later, this generation must be able to access Arabic, Pashto, Urdu, and Dari works of military significance.

Introduction

Understanding the fragility of civil-military affairs in Arab regimes is an important component in assessing stability and instability. The Arab Spring demonstrated the centrality of the armed forces in countries such as Egypt, Tunisia, and Syria. Yet both Egypt's and Tunisia's armies have handled the protests differently, and in the case of Egypt, the army currently governs the country through the SCAF. This chapter provides General Fawzi's fascinating insight into the relationship between Nasser and his armed forces chief and best friend, Field Marshal Abdel-Hakim Amer. Specifically, it highlights the struggle between the two over control of Egypt during the instability created in the aftermath of the Six-Day War. Throughout the war Amer's quest for power and simultaneously deteriorating mental state inhibited communication between the leadership and those on the front line. In turn, this lack of communication was one of the largest contributing factors to Egypt's imminent loss.

Much has been written about Nasser and Amer's relationship in the Arabic language, including an Al Jazeera documentary on the war minister's attempt to stay in power and challenge the president after the Six-Day War. However, little is available in the English language beyond a few paragraphs on the subject. Perhaps the book that best discusses the struggle between Amer and Nasser is Michael Oren's *Six Days of War: June 1967 and the Making of the Modern Middle East.*[1]

This chapter offers English-language readers General Fawzi's perspective on the Nasser-Amer relationship. It covers his direct involvement in preventing an attempted coup by Amer and his military clique in the aftermath of the June 1967 war. One can argue that the obsession with internal security, coups, and counter-coups has in many ways undermined the ability of Egypt's military to project power.

President Nasser and the Isolation of Field Marshal Amer

Nasser took an extraordinary step for an Arab leader on June 10, 1967, in what some have called a politically staged event. He appeared on Egyptian television and took responsibility for the military disaster of the 1967 war. He ended his speech by saying that he would step down as Egypt's president. Soon after the televised event, hundreds took to the streets of Cairo pleading that he not resign. These hundreds grew to thousands. Initially, hundreds of pro-Nasser operatives whipped up the crowd, but the tens of thousands who joined the demonstration were the product of a genuine sense of solidarity. Before the end of June 10, Nasser used this populist momentum to announce the removal of Amer from all military and government positions, but despite this maneuver, he was not out of danger.

Unlike Egypt's service chiefs, Amer did not tender his resignation; instead, he ignored the announcement of his removal from military office. The discredited field marshal wondered why the people wanted Nasser, and not both him and Nasser. Amer stewed over why the Egyptian armed forces did not call for him to stay, such were his delusions and inability to accept the new realities after the 1967 debacle. Amer resigned in order to fight his internal critics, manage Nasser, and make plans to face the wrath of public opinion alone. He refused to relinquish the post of war minister, and loyalist among the officer corps along with his long-cultivated base of support refused to accept this resignation as commander in chief. Officers with elements of their units rallied around their wounded chief. The chorus of support for the wounded Egyptian and pan-Arab leader radiated to other Arab countries. Having managed Egyptian public emotion, Nasser, with Fawzi at his side, turned to the serious threats coming from the clique of Egyptian military officers loyal to Field Marshal Amer.

Field Marshal Amer's Inner Circle

Fawzi writes that perhaps

> one of the most dangerous aspects of the 1967 Six-Day War was 0900 on June 11, 1967. On that date and time, over fifty brigade- and battalion-level commanders convened in the Egyptian armed forces headquarters in Nasr City, Cairo. These officers, each in control of upward of three hundred men, demanded that Amer lead and resume his command of the armed forces. Demonstrating outside the head-quarters, these officers chanted, "No Commander, Except the Field Marshal." Twelve armored vehicles of the military police surrounded Egyptian armed forces [headquarters], with the intent of keeping Field Marshal Amer and these fifty officers in place. At Nasser's residence at Manshiah al-Bakri, in Heliopolis, a suburb of Cairo, a group of pro-Amer field-grade officers surrounded the president's residence.

General Fawzi threatened this mob of officers with courts-martial if they did not disperse. They left Nasser's residence and made their way to Amer's residence, forming a personal guard around the field marshal's home in Giza. On June 11 armed officers roamed the streets of Cairo, coalescing either around Amer or around Nasser through his newly appointed armed forces commander in chief, Fawzi (Nasser had appointed Fawzi to this position that morning). The delicate and tense situation was brought about by Amer's refusal to accept defeat and relinquish his position as war minister.

Amazingly, Nasser not only decided to confront Amer on June 11 but also, according to Fawzi, "allowed military supplies to reach forces camped out near his home in Giza." The friendship between Nasser and Amer was too deep, and the president would agonize over the decision to move against the man who had been by his side since they were junior officers and who had undertaken the 1952 revolution to topple the monarchy of King Farouk with him. Fawzi briefed a pained Nasser and kept him updated on the growing challenge Amer posed to his authority.

General Fawzi in Charge

On June 11 at 1430, Radio Cairo announced Nasser's appointment of General Mohamed Fawzi as Egypt's armed forces commander in chief. At 1900 on that same day, Fawzi went to Nasser's home to discuss replacements of officers of every rank from field marshal to brigadier general. Fawzi writes that he "recommended the governor of Aswan Province and former air force officer, Madkoor Aboul-Eez, as commander of the Egyptian air force. General Abdel-Moneim Riad was personally recommended by me as armed forces chief of staff, and the decision to appoint Amin Howeidy as war minister rested with me, as Nasser and I had narrowed it to two names, and the decision hinged upon whom I could work with best."

Fawzi and Nasser then discussed which presidential decrees urged by Amer should be rescinded immediately. The two focused on canceling decrees dealing with the military budget and providing the war minister unquestioned signature authority and control over the budget, without oversight by the National Security Committee. Law 25 of 1966, which provided the military authority to adjudicate soldiers, was canceled. Fawzi and Nasser also agreed to make the military budget more transparent to the Egyptian bureaucracy and thereby the people. This was a strategic move by Nasser and Fawzi, as Amer's power was derived from his being a founder of the 1952 RCC, his deep friendship with Nasser, and the cult of personality he had developed within the armed forces. Amer treated the armed forces, which had been instrumental in conducting the revolution of 1952, as his personal fiefdom. He viewed the army as the only institution capable of enacting national change and began to see Nasser as standing in the way of progress. The showdown between Nasser and Amer was, by necessity, one of the most difficult events of Nasser's presidency. The debate on the role of the military in Egypt's polity remains one of the country's central issues to this day.

Field Marshal Amer's Armed Fortress

Fawzi writes,

> Amer's villa in the Cairo suburb of Giza was transformed into an armed fortress with four officers loyal to Amer commanding 260 soldiers from a military police contingent. This army presence was supplemented with about thirty villagers and relatives from Amer's village in El-Minia, who acted as personal guards. Amer's protégé Shams Badran used his own network of cronies, along with a few cashiered senior military officers, to form a competing center of power to salvage Amer. Badran contacted journalists, diplomats, industrialists, and members of Egypt Majlis al-Umma to lobby on Amer's behalf and to pressure Nasser to keep the field marshal. On the evening of June 11, policemen failed to evict this troop presence from Amer's villa, and there were exchanges of gunfire.

General Fawzi telephoned Amer, and his memoir features this exchange:

> Amer: *Remove your troops and security men, I have [the] firepower to meet them round for round, Fawzi!*
>
> Fawzi: *This is a situation unbecoming [a] field marshal and against the law! It was Jalal Hureidi [from the Interior Ministry] who placed these men and opened fire.*
>
> Amer hung up.

Fawzi adds, "Amazingly, Amer left Giza for Istal, his village in the city of El-Minia. Joining him was a large entourage of cashiered officers." The general notes that it took a while for Nasser to realize that Amer could be removed only by force and that an opposition front and political threat to Nasser was growing with each passing hour.

Coup against Nasser

Fawzi reveals that at this time Amer's protégé Shams Badran plotted

> a military coup against Nasser using the Eastern Front Army, headquartered in the Suez Canal town of Ismailiyah under the command

of General Ahmed Ismail. The army would be supplemented by Saaqa units still assessed to be loyal to Amer in the Cairo air base of Inchass, some fighter pilots, and the 4th Mechanized Armored Division. All of Egypt's security apparatuses kept Nasser informed of various aspects of this conspiracy and included

+ Amn al-Dawla [National Security Department],
+ Mukhabarat al-Amma [General Intelligence Directorate],
+ Mukhabarat Harbi [Military Intelligence],
+ Mabahith Amma [Internal Investigation Service], and
+ Harass al-Riyasa [Presidential Security].

Intelligence gathered from the various security branches revealed that the plot was to take place during the three days Nasser was attending the Arab League Summit in Khartoum from August 27 to 29, 1967. The plot was planned in Amer's home in Giza and given the code name Nasr [Victory]. Nasser contacted Shams Badran by phone and requested a list of all members of a secret security apparatus created around himself. Badran said that no such secret security apparatus existed inside the armed forces and that all soldiers were loyal to Amer and that no one could touch him. Badran threatened Nasser, saying that the armed forces would turn against him if he attempted to harm Amer.

This exchange aided Fawzi in getting Nasser to take drastic measures and move quickly against Amer. Soon after Nasser resolved to remove Amer—by force if necessary—he called on Fawzi to make the arrangements. It took Nasser from June 10 to August 24 to finally make this decision. In the meantime Fawzi worked with his cadre of officers to remove Amer loyalists from armed forces commands and formations.

Amer's Arrest

Fawzi recounts that at "1600 on August 25, Nasser charged me with the forcible entry into Amer's Giza home and the arrest of all officers and military personnel inside and around the property. Amer was scheduled to arrive at Nasser's home at 1900 that evening and remain there until I removed all vestiges of Amer loyalists from his home." Fawzi coordinated this task with Sharawi Gom'aa, Amin Howeidy, and Sami Sharaf, representing respectively the Interior Ministry and Civil Police, General Intelligence, and Communications. He writes, "Amer's home was cordoned off at 2100 hours, and I ordered that no one open fire except with my express permission. General Salah Mohsen, General Suleiman Muzhir, and Lieutenant Colonel Salah Saadani aided me with the plan."

When Fawzi approached Amer's front door, he found it locked with a chain. Shams Badran and two others, armed with assault rifles and grenades, stood guard. Fawzi began to talk with Badran when shots rang out from the rooftops; the shots were later determined to be celebratory and unrelated to the tense incident unfolding. Little did the revelers know that their shots could have started a bloodbath. Badran was burning incriminating documents, and the smell permeated the property. After Fawzi told him about his orders from Nasser and the futility of the situation, Badran surrendered his weapon and was taken into custody. Fawzi still had upward of three hundred Amer loyalists to deal with inside the villa, and using a bullhorn, he issued two orders. MP battalions formed to disarm Amer and his loyalists joined Fawzi, who issued the first order to those inside Amer's villa: "Military personnel inside, you are to surrender your weapons and proceed to a three-ton truck provided. After [battalion] MPs [loyal to Fawzi and Nasser] ensure that you are disarmed, you will be transported to the Cairo military prison." Second, he addressed the civilians: "All civilians are to execute the same sequence of events by surrendering their weapons, subjecting themselves to search, and then being transported to military prison for processing." Badran was taken to the Al-Qal'aa (Citadel) Prison.

Fawzi's forces entered the evacuated villa and seized enough weapons and ammunition to fill a three-ton truck. The search for weapons caches in the residence lasted all night. Fawzi arranged for Amer's property to be guarded by civilians and had a phone installed in a guard shack outside the villa for this civilian guard force. At 0500 on August 26, Fawzi informed Nasser that the mission was completed without any bloodshed or casualties. Amer was then escorted back to his Giza home by Vice President Zakariyah Moheiddine to reunite with his wife and children. He would remain under house arrest and was allowed access to his family only. However, Amer still tried to sway public opinion against Nasser using his telephone. Nasser had no choice but to place Amer in comfortable isolation, at a rest house near the Pyramids in Giza.

Amer's House Arrest and Suicide Attempts

Fawzi was in charge of moving Amer from his Giza home to the rest house. With him on this mission were General Abdel-Moneim Riad (see appendix 3 for a profile of Riad) and General Saad Abdel-Kareem (chief, Presidential Guard). Fawzi writes that Riad asked "Amer to come with him, and the field marshal hesitated reaching for a large stick. Riad was attempting to coax Amer when the field marshal placed something [a poison capsule] in his mouth." This was Amer's first suicide attempt. He was put in a waiting car and taken to Ma'adi Hospital, where his stomach was pumped and his life was saved. Unused capsules were located on his person and sent for analysis.[2] From the hospital, Amer was taken to the Maryutiyah Guest House, and General Muhammad Laithi was placed in charge of the field marshal's security and needs. Laithi was assisted by army medical personnel and a service staff from the Republican Guard. All the field marshal asked for were glasses of guava juice.

Amer spoke with Fawzi and General Riad about the military situation. He inquired about the massive arms shipment from the USSR and said that upon its off-loading the fighting could resume. According to Fawzi, Amer said, "The president must cease this [incarceration of me] within twenty-four hours, or he will be responsible for the outcome."

General Laithi found a two-villa complex in the Cairo district of al-Ma'adi, near the hospital, to accommodate Amer and his medical and security teams. While General Fawzi and General Laithi were inspecting the new quarters on September 14, they received word of Amer's second suicide attempt at 1900 hours with what was believed to have been a cyanide tablet. Upon arriving at the guest house, Fawzi found Anwar Sadat and Amer's older brother. Fawzi quotes the duty medical officer, Major Ibrahim Ali: "Amer was thought to be sleeping and then it was noted that he was unconscious at 1800. They attempted to revive the field marshal but pronounced him dead at 1840." On September 19 the newspaper *al-Ahram* reported that 149 men were detained in Amer's plot to seize control of the armed forces.[3]

Conclusion: Amer's Death as a Political Conspiracy

Amer's death was controversial, and Al Jazeera produced a splendid two-hour documentary on the event, including interviews with his children and other family members. The documentary explores all the conspiracy theories surrounding his suicide, from laced guava juice and slow-acting poisons to Nasser's ordering him to commit suicide.[4] In his memoir Fawzi mentions that he read the prosecutor's report that contained the autopsy, which said Amer ingested a poison on September 13 that was subtle and slow acting. The poison's effects did not appear until September 14. This may explain why the duty medical officer thought Amer was asleep before he realized he was unconscious.

Current generations of Egyptians, while generally aware of the struggle between Amer and Nasser, are familiar only with sound bites. As this generation of Egyptians struggle to form a more perfect government, it is imperative that they delve into the details of the Nasser-Amer relationship. Creating a government that accommodates the diversity of 82 million Egyptians demands wisdom, which can be derived only from understanding the past. Many SCAF generals were shaped by the events of 1967, but the war was not merely the battles fought and lost; it was a series of events and consequences that shaped the future of Egypt and the character of its people, politics, and society, from secular to Islamist.

As mentioned in previous chapters, struggles within the Egyptian government led the country to be gravely unprepared for the 1967 war. Specifically, the tumultuous relationship between Nasser and Amer took the focus away from battle strategies and efficient frontline communication, where it was desperately needed. Domestic politics drove the two leaders, especially Amer, to be more concerned with safeguarding their power than with a war victory. Ultimately, the power struggle between Nasser and Amer reached a disturbing level to include plotted coups, personal betrayals, and Amer's eventual suicide. Mohamed Heikal, the preeminent historian of Nasser and Sadat, referring to Fawzi's march on Amer's villa with an armed contingent, writes, "Processions such as this happen only in Greek tragedies and not in the real life of politicians."[5] This is why the Amer-Nasser relationship continues to fascinate Egyptians even to this day. For example, in 2012 Cambridge University's Hazem Kandil wrote an excellent revisionist history of Egypt from 1952 to 2012, focusing on the evolution and struggles of various military and security entities over political control in Egypt.[6]

Beyond having a lasting effect on the perception of the 1967 war, Nasser and Amer's relationship and Amer's suicide have affected current events. With Egypt's government—and its overall stability—presently uncertain, the country's past is as important as current tribulations, if not more so. Therefore, people must understand the intricacies of the 1967 war in order to handle future plights, especially those that may shape Egypt for decades to come. The next chapter will delve into Fawzi's thoughts as newly appointed Egyptian armed forces commander in chief, as he begins to lay the groundwork for his rebuilding of Egypt's shattered military. The general calls this section of his memoir "Starting from Zero."

Chapter Six

Starting from Zero

The Initial Plans and Strategy to Rebuild the Egyptian
Armed Forces after the Six-Day War

Happy is that city which in time of peace thinks of war.
—Inscription in the Armory of Venice—

Foreword by Barry Scott Zellen, editor in chief of the Naval Postgraduate School's
Culture and Conflict Review and author of State of Doom: Bernard Brodie,
the Bomb, and the Birth of the Bipolar World; the four-volume series
The Realist Tradition in International Relations: Foundations of Western Order;
and the forthcoming The Art of War in an Asymmetric World:
Strategy for the Post–Cold War Era

After the stunning defeat of the Egyptian armed forces by the Israelis in the 1967 Six-Day War, Egypt's leadership had to assess how best to reorganize and strengthen its armed forces. For the first time, the perspective of Egyptian military planners is made available to U.S. military readers through Commander Aboul-Enein's exposition of the memoir of War Minister General Mohamed Fawzi. The first order of business after the 1967 defeat was to designate someone as commander in chief of Egypt's armed forces. Egyptian leader Gamal Abdel Nasser appointed Fawzi to this post. In turn, Fawzi had to make necessary and vital decisions regarding the manner in which to rebuild the shattered forces. His memoir offers insight into how Fawzi and Nasser assigned other command positions within Egypt's military. Readers will understand how Nasser and Fawzi developed an ordered summation of political and military tasks. It was also necessary for the two men to organize other rankings of the armed forces and to name commanders of the various military units.

Ultimately, Fawzi and Nasser's rebuilding of the Egyptian armed forces, and the directives that went along with its rebuilding, set the stage for the War of Attrition, which lasted, as Fawzi recounts, from 1967 to 1970. While preparing for this next phase of the Arab-Israeli conflict, it was necessary for Nasser and Fawzi to gather up aid and assistance from Egypt's allies, particularly the Soviet Union. Commander Aboul-Enein, through his translation and analysis of Fawzi's memoir, illuminates the robust support that the Soviets provided Egypt after the Six-Day War. After securing military support in the form of essential military equipment, Fawzi's next task was to combine the posts of war minister and commander in chief into a single position. This combined post is a permanent fixture in Egypt's leadership to this day.

Having had the great privilege of serving as a journal editor at the Naval Postgraduate School and as author of numerous books on American national security and strategic thought, I understand the need to foster greater empathy and understanding and to thus better advise our leaders. Commander Aboul-Enein has written several important articles for our journal, *The Culture and Conflict Review*, and he has brought to those writings the same depth of insight that we find here, derived from his understanding of the region. Today, he shares his sources of information with a wider U.S. military audience in an attempt to educate future leaders within the U.S. armed forces. I applaud *Infantry Magazine* for providing Commander Aboul-Enein with this important forum for his multi-part series as the United States navigates the new and challenging strategic, diplomatic, and political environment in Egypt resulting from the 2011 Arab Spring. Many officers of the ruling SCAF in Egypt have lived through this history, and consequently, understanding this history is an important step toward understanding their mind-set.

Fawzi in Command

On the evening of June 9, 1967, and through the morning of June 10, General Fawzi sat at the Command Center at Nasr City. He writes that he "was the most senior officer in the building amid a military command structure in collapse." Fawzi calls this part of his memoir "Starting from Zero" and recounts the immediate steps he took when granted authority by Nasser to become Egypt's armed forces commander in chief. He saw his immediate tasks as securing the west side of the Suez Canal from further Israeli incursions and as getting the army into an orderly withdrawal and demobilization. The latter task included disarming the returning soldiers and having them report to their respective units. Fawzi assigned the first task to General Sadek Sharaf and the second task to the Military Police Command. Fawzi recounts, "The radio was used to issue orders to retreating troops arriving from the Sinai and to guide them to transport depots to take them back to their units." A third immediate task was "addressing the massive Soviet airlift arriving on June 9 and containing a much needed military resupply of hardware, equipment, and ordnance. This material needed to be off-loaded, stored, and distributed to field units along the western Suez Canal," which Fawzi considered to be the new defensive line. Airfields needed to be repaired to increase the level of Soviet military resupply and to receive forty MiG-17 jet fighters made available from Algeria.

Fawzi relied on many officers who chose to remain at their posts despite the chaos created by the decisive Israeli strike of the Six-Day War and the Israeli take-over of the Sinai. These men did not flee in the face of a disintegrating situation and were therefore available to help Fawzi organize the immediate tasks necessary to stabilize the Egyptian armed forces. Many of these officers were given orders to form a defensive line along the west side of the Suez Canal, using whatever military equipment necessary. Fawzi ordered the defensive line not just for national security reasons but, as his book reveals, also "for the purpose of reassuring the Egyptian public. It was also important to counter Israeli propaganda that made claims that Israeli units had crossed the canal and were headed toward Cairo." Fawzi describes how his thoughts, and thereby his assignment of tasks, became clearer with each passing hour. He realized he needed to build the defensive line along the entire length of the canal. By June 11, 1967, the Six-Day War had ended, and a sense of normalcy began to take hold in Egypt's major cities.

The Assignment of New Commanders in Chief and Military Directives

Fawzi's evenings and early mornings following the war were spent with President Nasser at his private home, where the two discussed the assignments for a new chain of command. Fawzi recommended Aswan governor and former air force pilot Madkoor Aboul-Eez as EAF commander in chief. He also recommended the Joint Arab Command commander in Jordan, Egyptian general Abdel-Moneim Riad, an air defense officer, as armed forces chief of staff. Nasser and Fawzi discussed the composition of the General Staff from flag officers to the ranks of major. In addition, Fawzi created a secretariat to allow him to issue formal orders to units in the field, after learning how Amer's verbal orders had caused confusion and created chaos on the battlefield. Nasser told the general, "This [responsibility of yours] is bitter and hard, and it will need an extra special effort under these circumstances." After Fawzi reassured Nasser that he was up to the challenge, they set about discussing the composition of a new General Staff. Fawzi, as armed forces commander, convinced Nasser that Abdel-Moneim Riad should be chief of the General Staff.

Fawzi is unique in Egyptian military history as the only flag officer to sit in private with his president in order to completely and conceptually redesign the shattered armed forces. He and Nasser outlined a series of political-military directives to be taken immediately. First was "the importance of stabilizing the armed forces and having them focused on a defensive line confronting the Israelis." Nasser and

Fawzi discussed Israeli broadcasts about Egyptian losses and about the nonexistent Egyptian conspirators who planned to rise up and topple Nasser. Israeli broadcasts picked up by Egyptians also alleged that the public was demanding a cease-fire with Israel and that Israeli defense minister Moshe Dayan was dictating terms to Nasser by telephone. Fawzi asserted that it was vital for Egypt to prevent Israel from gaining politically from its military successes. According to Fawzi's memoir, at this point Nasser made the momentous decision to take public responsibility for the crushing defeat and to offer to step down in a live televised broadcast. This decision had domestic and regional repercussions that will be discussed later.

Second, "Nasser wanted to bind the Egyptian public to the military and decided to exercise his position as president and leader of the Arab Socialist Union [his party] to direct military and civilian affairs. He expressed to me a desire to restructure the armed forces by entirely removing the condition of a state within a state that plagued many Arab armies." One can argue that this goal was never fully realized by Egypt, even to this day.

Third, "Nasser began to formulate a foreign policy that refused to negotiate with the Israelis until they returned lands taken in the 1967 war and recognized the rights of Palestinians. Nasser realized that he could not confront Israel militarily, but he also wanted to paint a narrative that Egypt did not seek war for its own sake but to take back its land that had been taken by force and aggression. Nasser resolved that the Sinai could be taken back only by force and not through negotiation." This perspective necessitated the rebuilding of the armed forces and, while doing so, the gradual resumption of hostilities along the Suez Canal. Nasser and Fawzi were laying the groundwork for what would be the War of Attrition (1967–1970). The Soviet Union's weapons, technical support, and diplomatic leverage were needed for the objective of gradual violence along the canal. Nasser announced an Arab policy whereby Egypt would not be the only frontline state to take on the Israelis; rather, Arab League members should also participate based on their capability. This was a gambit that would pay off for Nasser, because by binding all Arab states to Egyptian military policy, he would in effect influence the foreign policies of several Arab states, as well as extract economic contributions for Egypt.

Fawzi writes of Nasser's "deep strategic thinking, such as making the Soviets a partner in Egypt's failure by arguing that the prestige of Soviet weapons and technology were on the line." This argument allowed Egypt unimpeded access to modern arms, trainers, and Soviet technicians. Nasser ordered Fawzi "to prove to the Soviets that the new Egyptian soldier could quickly grasp the complexity of advanced Soviet weapons so that the Egyptians could justify to Moscow the requests for additional weapons."[1] In perhaps the most contentious discussion between Fawzi and Nasser, Nasser ordered Egyptian forces to be placed under the command of Soviet military trainers, and Fawzi ultimately relented. Fawzi wanted the placement of Egyptian forces under Soviet military trainers to be a concession and the quantities and nature of Soviet weapons to be different from those imported before 1967. These requests were meant to placate the ranks grumbling about being placed under Soviet training command.

The late Edgar O'Ballance, a noted scholar of the Arab-Israeli conflict, wrote, "Both General Fawzi, the Commander in Chief, and General Riad, his Chief of Staff, were capable and realistic officers, and in the reshuffling of command posts, they made some good choices."[2] This was written in 1974, less than a year after the 1973 Arab-Israeli War, but missing in O'Ballance's account are the mechanics of Fawzi's decision making, which, in fairness to O'Ballance, were not available to Arabic readers, much less an English audience, until a decade later, when Fawzi published his memoir in 1984.

Fawzi and Nasser's Strategic Formulation

Fawzi and Nasser discussed how to transform defeat into a war of liberation, a defensive war to restore Egyptian soil. They wanted to capitalize on the emotion of the Egyptian people after their defeat in the Six-Day War and to craft a national narrative in which the Sinai could be liberated only through force of arms, not through negotiation. Nasser indicated to Fawzi that "Israel understood only force, and the war should comprehensively deny Israel the means to absorb the Sinai into its new borders." The two realized that "for Israel to absorb its gains required massive amounts of money through grants and loans, which would be thwarted to the best of Egypt's abilities." Nasser was essentially proposing a diplomatic, legal, and economic campaign to make it difficult for Israel to develop and exploit the Sinai, the Golan, and the West Bank. He and Fawzi agreed that "the war for national liberation would occur between 1970 and 1971" and that they should "plan for a four-year timeline to restore the Egyptian armed forces so that they could take the offensive." Moreover, they agreed that "the Israelis would attempt to interfere with Egypt's effort to rebuild the armed forces through a variety of means, from undermining morale through propaganda, to economic warfare."

Fawzi's First Directive as Armed Forces Commander in Chief

Upon concluding his meetings with Nasser, Fawzi returned to headquarters and drafted his first directive as armed forces commander: Directive for the Functioning of the Armed Forces. This was an important document, according to Fawzi, as it began the process of shifting the main mission of the Egyptian armed forces from being guardians of the revolution to liberating occupied lands. This single directive aligned plans for force structure, weapons, and training, but what came after those plans were laid was extraordinary. For the first time, military plans would be subjected to discussion and refinement by a higher council of the armed forces; no longer would the whims of one leader constitute final military policy. In addition, Fawzi's first directive shifted the focus of the Egyptian armed forces from internal security to external security.

The implementation of Fawzi's directive is a unique case study of the complexities of addressing civil-military affairs. Balancing civil-military relations in Egypt would be a long process, and in fact the issue remains unresolved to this day. But between the wars in 1967 and 1973, Fawzi attempted to subordinate military authority to civil authority, and Nasser steered the military away from the cult of personality created by Field Marshal Amer.

Arab Military Aid and Discussions with Nasser

During the Six-Day War, on June 7, 1967, Algerian foreign minister Abdel-Aziz Bouteflika (currently Algeria's president) arrived in Cairo. Fawzi was impressed with Bouteflika arriving as hostilities were under way and conveyed the Algerian leader's offer of troops and MiG fighters to Nasser. Bouteflika left Cairo and took with him on his personal plane twenty Egyptian fighter pilots who were charged with flying the bulk of the Algerian MiGs back to Egypt as soon as practicable. The forty Algerian MiG-17Fs would be the first fighters used to defend Egypt after the complete loss of its air force in the 1967 war.

On June 18 Kuwait engineered an Arab summit to plan for the Arab states' condemning Israel with one voice at the UN General Assembly. During the summit the Arab leaders also discussed placing an embargo on petroleum products against the United States and withdrawing their ambassadors in America. Although the oil embargo option was not exercised in the aftermath of the 1967 war, it would be revived and executed in the 1973 Yom Kippur War. The 1973 oil embargo affected international markets dependent on petroleum products; the price of oil never was the same and steadily increased from a spot price of $3.56 per barrel before October 1973 to $95.80 per barrel four decades later.[3] Americans began to realize that they depended on oil to sustain economic growth.[4]

Jordan's King Hussein arrived in Egypt on July 11 to meet with Nasser. The two agreed to present a coordinated front by refusing defeat and affirming the Joint Defense Pact. They also agreed to develop a unified pan-Arab strategy. Nasser and King Hussein discussed increasing Egypt's ties with the Soviet bloc to counter the United States' binding ties with Israel and purposefully denying Israel a peace deal with Egypt, Jordan, and Syria. These maneuvers would result in the Israelis' ignoring the Palestinian question because they felt collectively isolated in the region and internationally isolated within the UN. Fawzi recounts, "Nasser intended to use the UN as a means of gaining time for Egyptian rearmament and tasked Hussein to speak at the UN General Assembly with one Arab voice. Jordan was also selected to be the interlocutor between the aggrieved Arab states of Egypt and Syria, and Washington."

Two days later Fawzi discussed the meeting between Nasser and King Hussein with Algeria's Houari Boumidienne, Syria's Nureddin al-Atasi, Iraq's Abdel-Rahman Arif, and Sudan's Ismail al-Azhari in Cairo. The leaders coordinated strategy and, more important, talking points for briefing Moscow on Egyptian and Syrian needs for restructuring their armed forces.[5]

Soviet Aid to Egypt

In his memoir Fawzi discusses the massive Soviet airlift and sealift of military hardware to Egypt in the aftermath of the 1967 Six-Day War:

> On June 9 the Soviets provided thirty-one MiG-21 fighters and ninety-three MiG-17 fighter jets via Yugoslavia. Antonov-22 cargo planes arrived hourly to Egyptian airfields, and during the month of June, ships disgorged military equipment replacements in the ports of both Alexandria in Egypt and Latakia in Syria. . . . Five hundred forty-four cargo sorties and 15 ships delivered 48,000 tons of equipment to the Egyptian military. The USSR did not request compensation for this installment. Warsaw Pact nations Poland, Yugoslavia, and East Germany provided MiG fighters, artillery, air defense systems, communications equipment, and transport trucks. On June 16 Soviet general Lashinkov arrived to supervise the off-load and distribution of equipment to Egyptian units.

Fawzi and Lashinkov created a defensive line west of the Suez Canal. Soviet premier Nikolai Podgorny arrived in Cairo on June 21 with Soviet marshal Matvei Zakharov (d. 1972), the deputy defense minister and former chief of the Soviet military staff. Fawzi writes, "The Soviet military delegation would be immersed in talks with Nasser, Egyptian Vice President Zakariyah Moheiddine, Ali Sabry, and Foreign Minister Mahmoud Riad, as well as myself. The meeting concluded with an agreement between Cairo and Moscow to erase all traces of the Israeli occupation of the Sinai. Egypt would be given priority in newly designed Soviet arms."

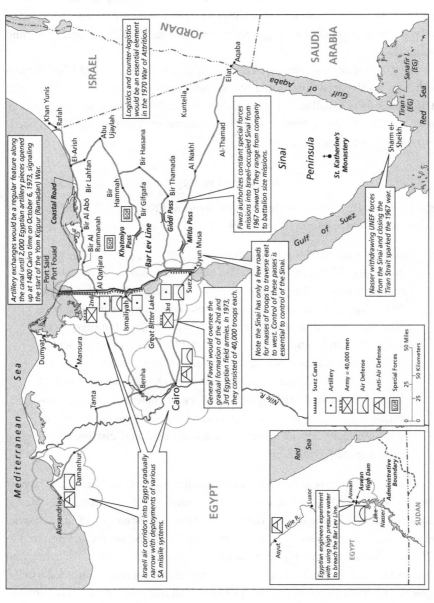

MAP 2. FAWZI'S VIEW: EVOLUTION OF EGYPTIAN TACTICS, 1967–1971

Map created by Christopher Robinson.

Artillery exchanges would be a regular feature along the canal until 2,000 Egyptian artillery pieces opened up at 1400 Cairo time on October 6, 1973, signaling the start of the Yom Kippur (Ramadan) War.

Logistics and counter-logistics would be an essential element in the 1970 War of Attrition.

Fawzi authorizes constant special forces missions into Israeli-occupied Sinai from 1967 onward. They range from company to battalion size missions.

Nasser withdrawing UNEF forces from the Sinai and closing the Tiran Strait sparked the 1967 war.

General Fawzi would oversee the gradual formation of the 2nd and 3rd Egyptian field armies. In 1973, they consisted of 40,000 troops each.

Note the Sinai has only a few roads for masses of troops to traverse east to west. Control of these passes is essential to control of the Sinai.

Israeli air corridors into Egypt gradually narrow with deployments of various SA missile systems.

Egyptian engineers experiment with using high pressure water to breach the Bar Lev Line.

Legend:
- Suez Canal
- · Artillery
- ⊠ Army = 40,000 men
- ◡ Air Defense
- ◠ Anti-Air Defense
- SOF Special Forces

0 25 50 Miles
0 25 50 Kilometers

Mediterranean Sea

ISRAEL

JORDAN

SAUDI ARABIA

EGYPT

Sinai Peninsula

St. Katherine's Monastery

Gulf of Suez

Gulf of Aqaba

Red Sea

Tiran I. (EG)
Sanafir I. (EG)

Alexandria
Damanhur
Tanta
Mansura
Dumyat
Benha
Cairo
Asyut
Luxor
Aswan
Lake Nasser
Aswan High Dam
Administrative Boundary
SUDAN
Nile R.

Port Said
Port Fouad
Al Qantara
Ismailiyah
Suez
Great Bitter Lake
2nd
3rd

Coastal Road
Khan Yunis
Rafah
El-Arish
Abu Ujaylah
Bir Lahfan
Bir Al Abd
Bir Al Rummanah
Bir Hassana
Bir Hammah
Bir Gitgafa
Khatmiya Pass
Bar Lev Line
Giddi Pass
Mitla Pass
Uyun Musa
Bir Thamada
Al Nakhl
Al-Thamad
Kunteila
Eilat
Aqaba
Sharm el-Sheikh

Zakharov-Fawzi Discussions on
Soviet Military Assistance to Egypt

Marshal Zakharov and Fawzi retreated with their staffs to discuss the mass distribution of Soviet military hardware, the absorption of these weapons into Egyptian combat formations, and the inculcation of Soviet military doctrine among Egyptian forces. Zakharov and Fawzi's delegations spent four hours discussing weapons systems, with the Egyptians asking probing questions in order to comprehend both Soviet systems developed but not exported and those under development. The discussions extracted a concession from the Soviets to treat Egypt like a Warsaw Pact nation in terms of weapons aid and sales.

The two senior delegations also discussed the Canal Zone and the deployment of forces. Talks then turned to agreements to deploy an initial contingent of twelve hundred Soviet military advisers, plus the treatment of these advisers and their authority over and relationship with Egyptian military personnel. Afterward, Nasser and Fawzi met privately to coordinate talking points about extracting Soviet economic aid. Premier Podgorny departed for Moscow on June 24, leaving Marshal Zakharov to continue advising the Egyptian General Staff.

Fawzi writes, "Marshal Zakharov concurred that the immediate need was to ensure Egypt's air defenses, with a focus on varying models of surface-to-air missiles, radar, and fighter interceptors." He also recounts strategic discussions between Nasser and Podgorny: "Nasser desired a tangible demonstration of the depth of Soviet support for Egypt. He proposed to the Soviet premier a visit by Soviet warships and the eventual basing of Soviet naval assets in Egypt as a challenge to the United States." In Nasser's mind Israeli forces considered the U.S. Sixth Fleet a strategic reserve. The Egyptian president also used his understanding of the limitations of Soviet jet fighters, as related to Israeli Mirage and Mysterie jets, to argue for Egypt's need to acquire the Soviet Union's newest deep-strike fighter-bombers.

Zakharov requested a meeting on June 29 with Nasser, informing him via Podgorny that the Politburo approved of all their discussion points. He also informed Nasser that Egypt would get the newly developed Sukhoi long-range bombers, then the state of the art in Soviet jet bombers. In addition, the Politburo agreed to provide the newly developed and evolving T-72 main battle tank, as well as additional MiG-21 jet fighters. The Politburo, through Premier Podgorny, affirmed its commitment to Egypt's defense.

Yugoslav leader Marshal Josip Broz Tito visited Damascus and Cairo, where he outlined Soviet diplomatic pressure being exerted on U.S. president Lyndon Johnson. The pressure centered on a fair and just resolution of the Arab-Israeli conflict in the United Nations. The Yugoslav leader reminded Nasser that Egypt was the frontline nation for Moscow's ability to airlift and send by rail cargo for sealift through Yugoslav ports.

When Egypt was at its most vulnerable, Fawzi recounts, "the efforts by Arab and Eastern bloc nations, in particular aid, saved the country from immediate catastrophe." Nasser and the Egyptian General Staff did not rest until November 1967, when they were assured that the defensive line along the canal was stable. From June to November 1967, Nasser worked sixteen to eighteen hours a day.

Conclusion

Aside from organizing Soviet military assistance to Egypt, Fawzi and Nasser also had to continue the restructuring of the Egyptian national security apparatus. Amin Howeidy (1921–2009) was appointed as war minister, in addition to his duties as director of EGIS. He would be the only person in Egypt's modern political history to serve as both war minister and EGIS director. On January 20, 1968, Fawzi assumed the war minister portfolio in order to allow Howeidy to focus on intelligence collection, analysis, indication, and warnings. The photo on page ii is General Fawzi formally accepting his assignment as war minister from Nasser. This meant that Fawzi worked as both war minister and commander in chief of the armed forces. The positions of war minister (occasionally referred to today as defense minister) and commander in chief of the armed forces remain combined to this day. Combining the two positions was Egypt's way of having cabinet oversight of military affairs. It is unclear if this will change in light of the 2011 revolution in Egypt.

Restructuring Egypt's armed forces, as well as the military leadership, was an important first step in the country's path toward restoring itself. Fawzi and Nasser's ability to collectively rebuild Egypt's military and gain assistance from the Soviets was an incredible feat. The two men were able to begin to remove the humiliating shadow of defeat that had been placed on Egypt during the partial leadership of the mentally unstable Amer. Fawzi and Nasser's accomplishments allowed them to focus on further preparing for the War of Attrition, which would begin in 1967.

Chapter Seven ★★

Plan Granite

Creating a Strategy Centered on the Suez Canal Zone
and the Sinai Peninsula

History is littered with wars which everybody knew
would never happen.

—ENOCH POWELL, BRITISH POLITICIAN AND SCHOLAR—

Foreword by Frederick Kempe,
president and chief executive officer of the Atlantic Council

The Atlantic Council's mission is to promote constructive U.S. leadership and engagement in international affairs on the basis of the central role of the Atlantic community in meeting the international challenges of the twenty-first century. Engagement in international affairs requires knowledge and understanding of the Middle East, and this is gained only through reading and studying the works of those nations. General Mohamed Fawzi's memoir is an example of one of such crucial Arabic works of military significance. Works like Fawzi's memoir expose America's military leaders to Egypt's historical military strategies, enabling the United States to use this historical knowledge to more efficiently partake in current international affairs and the formulation of U.S. national security policy. When I researched my best-selling book *Berlin 1961*,[1] I found that President John F. Kennedy and Soviet premier Nikita Khrushchev would have come to the abyss of nuclear confrontation were it not for advisers providing them a degree of empathy for one another. This tension played itself out again among Khrushchev, Kennedy, and Castro a year later in the Cuban Missile Crisis. Commander Aboul-Enein's series provides Americans with much-needed insight as we navigate the complexities of the Middle East. Fawzi reveals in vivid detail the ways in which Egypt capitalized on the Cold War to derive advantages against the Israelis in the aftermath of the 1967 Six-Day War. Fawzi also reveals the difficulty both Israel and Egypt have in confronting one another through conventional means. For Egypt this means vulnerable logistical tail through the Sinai, and for Israel this demonstrates the difficulty of keeping a civilian army mobilized to the detriment of the economy. Nasser and Fawzi discussed the vulnerability of the Israeli economy and closely followed the impact of their plans to gradually escalate tensions along the Suez Canal. As tensions escalated between the superpowers, the Suez Canal from 1967 to 1973, like Berlin in 1961, became the center of hostility, not just between Egypt and Israel, but by extension between the Soviet Union and the United States. I commend the U.S. Army *Infantry Magazine* for providing Commander Aboul-Enein a forum for this innovative series designed to educate our military leaders using direct Arabic sources. It is certain that the ruling generals in Egypt today have read this memoir, and this series gives us a glimpse into their military educations.

President Nasser and General Fawzi's War of Attrition

After Fawzi and Nasser had efficiently restructured Egypt's armed forces immediately following the 1967 Six-Day War, their focus turned toward preparing for the War of Attrition. Specifically, Egypt's goal was to liberate the Sinai and solve the problem of Palestine. Nasser and Fawzi began to strategize an eventual Egyptian offensive against Israel, taking into account the components necessary to defeat Israel. The two leaders decided that it was essential to create new committees under the General Staff in order to better organize military strategies and sectors. They also devised three plans over several years that would be used to counter Israel's military efforts: Plan 200, Plan Granite, and the Rogers Plan.

In the three years of the War of Attrition, Egypt constructed three operational phases that, according to Fawzi's memoir, would serve as strategies for defeating Israel. The phases included the *summud* (stabilization) phase, the *muwajahah* (confrontation) phase, and the *tahadee wa radeah* (challenge and response) phase. Along with the different phases, Egypt experimented with SAMs as a defensive tool against Israeli air strikes. However, one of the most important components of Egypt's efforts against Israel was support from other Arab nations in the form of aid and equipment. This support came even though the Arab League proved ineffective and had to be replaced by the Arab Revolutionary Liberation Front, a collection of Arab nations and nonstate actors Nasser cobbled together to support frontline Arab countries that were in a state of war with Israel and that bordered Egypt.

General Strategy

Fawzi describes Egypt's strategic objectives as removing all traces of aggression, liberating the Sinai, and pressuring Israel for a resolution to the Palestinian conflict. These objectives became the cornerstone of Egyptian grand strategy after the July 1967 Egyptian-Soviet summit. From this grand strategy, a three-year timetable was drawn to have Egypt take the offensive by 1970. While Fawzi worked with the General Staff and army commands, Nasser took this strategy to his cabinet ministers and then arrived for the August 1967 Arab summit in Khartoum with the plans in hand. Fawzi discusses the division of labor for the grand strategy: Nasser had final say on general strategy, while he and Foreign Minister Mahmoud Riad dealt with the formulation and implementation of military strategy (the trauma of the Six-Day War led to surprising levels of coordination between the War and Foreign Ministries). In his memoir Fawzi reveals, "It would take six months to bring the Egyptian air force into balance with the Israeli air force quantitatively, but two and a half years to plan, train, and rehearse the force." He reconfigured units, creating new formations, and considered the countering of Israeli psychological warfare as an important near-term objective.

General Abdel-Moneim Riad, the armed forces chief of staff, was placed in charge of laying plans for the Sinai's liberation. He was aided by generals in two new positions: chief of organization and administration and chief of military research. The two new chiefs researched the size and types of forces needed to fulfill Egypt's strategic objectives. A chief of training position was also created, and four new committees were formed under the General Staff: Armaments, Military Welfare and Morale, Military Medicine, and Transport and Logistics. By December 1967 the General Staff, having worked round the clock since June, had drafted Plan 200, which would be revised, updated, and implemented, with updates to the plan conducted every six months based on shortcomings and problems identified in the implementation of the plan.

In January 1968 Fawzi chaired a General Staff meeting to discuss how much time each service chief needed to plan and equip for Plan 200. He details this meeting, during which the staff collectively decided, for three reasons, to gradually escalate hostilities along the Canal Zone. First, escalation would allow the Egyptians to test and to probe Israeli defenses and the fielding of new weapons systems, either that the Egyptians acquired or the Israelis deployed. Second, it would provide opportunity to test the plans of the General Staff and to get Egyptian troops used to warlike conditions, which Fawzi writes "was necessary in order to cultivate their ability to hold their nerve under fire. The General Staff also wanted to probe for Israeli artillery fields of fire, kill boxes and kill zones along their side of the canal." The final reason for escalating hostilities came from discussions between the Egyptian generals and Fawzi about getting the Israelis used to a certain tempo of hostility and maintaining the initiative of escalation. The January 1968 General Staff discussions outlined hostility that would evolve into the War of Attrition, which, as previously mentioned, consisted of three operational phases: *summud*, *muwajahah*, and *tahadee wa radeah*.

Phases of the War of Attrition

The War of Attrition's *summud* (stabilization) phase (July 1967–March 1968), according to Fawzi, "focused on exerting political pressure and isolation on Israel." Although this phase (and, thus, the war itself) started in July 1967, it was not given a name or coherence until January 1968. Egypt's primary task during this phase was to restore the United States as a conduit for exerting pressure on Israel. Fawzi recollects this phase as "having the highest level of psychological warfare directed by the Israelis onto the Egyptian army and people. Three small skirmishes along the canal began the process of restoring confidence in a demoralized military."

During the *muwajahah* (confrontation) phase (March 1968–April 1969), according to Fawzi, "Egyptian forces were reconfigured and the Sinai front along the Gulf of Suez was designated a combat zone. It would be important to conduct a consistent level of constant harassment of Israeli units all along the canal and the Gulf of Suez. This constant level of readiness was seen to be taking a toll on Israeli GDP [gross domestic product], economic production, and productivity." By 1969, Fawzi notes, Egyptian pressure on Israel led the United States to provide its ally with fifty modern combat jets, a response to Soviet military aid to Egypt and Syria. In late 1969 Nasser met in closed session with the Majlis al-Umma (People's Assembly). He explained to the parliamentarians Israel's position vis-à-vis the United States and the concept of an attritional war mobilizing all Egypt's resources. Nasser openly said that "the United States would never allow an imbalance of power between Israel and the Arabs."

During the *tahadee wa radeah* (challenge and response) phase (April 1969–September 1970), according to Fawzi, Egyptian strategy shifted from canal harassment to operations conducted deep within the Sinai. Fawzi devoted a significant part of his book to this phase, boasting that "Egyptian conventional and special forces operations were conducted as far as Arish near Gaza." The structure of the Egyptian 2nd and 3rd Armies began to take shape between 1968 and 1969. EAF probes into the Sinai began to test Israeli reactions, and the Canal Zone settled into what historians later called the War of Attrition. Aside from dictating the tempo on the Israeli side, the *tahadee wa radeah* phase forced the Egyptian soldier to become used to confronting the IDF. Fawzi writes, "It was a physical effort to restore troop confidence and to break the mythology of Israeli invincibility."

The harassing Egyptian offensive was also an intelligence collection opportunity. Not only were the Egyptians able to gauge Israeli reaction times, but they could begin to understand the layered Israeli system from the canal eastward. This knowledge laid the groundwork for Egyptian strategy in the 1973 Yom Kippur War. Fawzi and Nasser saw in these gradually escalating military skirmishes the wider goal of putting economic pressure on Israel, as the Israelis now had to invest in additional troop and equipment presence to defend the Sinai. General Moshe Dayan commented, "Hardly a night passes without a battle," and the Israeli casualty rate between June 1967 and June 1969 was seven hundred killed.[2] That the Egyptian tactic of gradual escalation took a toll on Israeli domestic policy is interesting to ponder, as Fawzi and his generals had attempted to engineer just such a by-product.

Fawzi, Soviet Advisers, and SAMs

Fawzi believed that the economic pressure on Israel led the Israelis to respond to Egyptian harassment with a cost-efficient air strike deep into Egypt. The Egyptians thereafter began to conceive concentrated SAM defenses for their bases. In 1969 experimentation with SAM configurations commenced. This experimentation laid the conceptual foundation for the massive forest of SAMs deployed along the canal to counter the IAF in the Yom Kippur War. At this stage, however, Egyptians and their Soviet advisers began to see a decline in IAF strikes as a result of SAM deployments starting deep in Egypt along the Nile Delta and eventually leading along the canal. The Israelis, in response to the SAMs' effective erosion of their previous air dominance, became more defensive and switched to SF raids along the canal.

Fawzi considers 1969 a pivotal year, as the Egyptian General Staff began to understand and configure an air defense made up of a combination of SA-6, SA-3, and ZSU-23 AA guns and to assess the impact of these weapons on Israeli Skyhawk and Phantom jets. The Soviets were also eager to see how their equipment would stand up to American-manufactured close air fighters. Although Fawzi does not mention it in his memoir, it is assumed that the Egyptians provided Soviet technicians access to downed U.S. technology for reverse-engineering purposes. Fawzi and Nasser thought that the United States had resigned itself to the fact that the canal would be a hostile area, a problem then as it is strategically now for global shipping.

Wider Arab Battle Plans

Nasser wanted to find ways to collect and leverage all Arab capabilities in the conflict with Israel. He sought a wider effort against Israel, not one limited to the frontline states (Egypt, Syria, Jordan, and Lebanon). He discussed with Fawzi a means to operationalize the statements made by Arab leaders during the Arab summit in Khartoum in August 1967. After shoring up a steady and copious supply of Soviet arms, Nasser turned his attention to organizing economic aid to frontline states from the Arab League. Fawzi traveled to Algeria, Sudan, Morocco, Iraq, Jordan, and Kuwait to coordinate aid in the form of troops and capabilities. This resulted initially in the deployment of one division of Algerian troops, technical units, and logistical companies. The Algerians also supplied French-made 155-mm artillery. Sudan and Kuwait contributed one battalion each. Fawzi writes, "The next phase was to form agreements over unity of effort, primarily with Syria." This would be his next focus.

Fawzi describes the difficulties of forming the Unified Command Council under the Unified Arab Command. First, he had a conceptual discussion with Nasser, as the Egyptian president would have to enter into discussions with not only the Syrian president but also both countries' defense and foreign ministers. Resolving thorny issues such as assigning a single military commander within the unified chain of command and priority for air and air defense planning for both Syria and Egypt would be the first serious coordination of military effort between two Arab countries in modern Arab military history. The structure of the unity of effort agreement needed to ensure that any other agreements could not impinge on the efforts on the Syrian, Egyptian, and Jordanian fronts. After exhaustive discussions Fawzi was named commander in chief of the Unified Arab Command.

The May 1969 coup in Libya (led by Colonel Muammar al-Qadhafi) and September 1969 coup in Sudan (led by Colonel Jaafar al-Numeiri) aided Egypt by adding two Arab nationalist regimes that were avidly anti-Israeli to the mix. Egypt was delighted that the Libyan coup meant the U.S. loss of Wheelus Air Force Base (AFB) and the termination of the American military presence in Libya. Fawzi believed that "Wheelus offered an intelligence platform for the United States to collect on Egyptian deployments as well as order of battle, which would then be passed to the Israelis." Not everything was cordial between Nasser and Qadhafi, however (see the notes section for a transcript of a discussion between the Egyptian and Libyan leaders on June 10, 1970).[3]

Arab Revolutionary Liberation Front: Addressing the Ineffective Arab League

On September 1, 1969, Sudan's Numeiri called for a meeting in Khartoum with all frontline states. Egypt's President Nasser, Jordan's King Hussein, Syria's President Atasi, and Iraq's Vice President Mahdi Ammash attended the meeting, which was part of a mini-summit within the Arab League, separate from the wider Arab League. In Cairo, in November 1969, Lebanese army commander Emile Boustany and the PLO's Yasser Arafat signed a coordination protocol with Fawzi and Foreign Minister Mahmoud Riad in attendance. Fawzi writes, "During the same month the Arab chiefs of staff met to agree on a series of unified efforts and the steps to be taken against Israel. The armed forces chief of staff meeting in Cairo was to pave the way for the Arab League summit meeting in Rabat in December 1969."

Fawzi prepared a comprehensive report that consisted of the agreed upon contributions from the Arab states and their deployment along the Suez Canal Zone. As the Unified Arab Command commander, he joined Arab military chiefs of staff to discuss ways to undermine the U.S. military presence in the Middle East, as they viewed Washington as the main obstacle to undermining Israel. They agreed that military plans against Israel could not be undertaken without an understanding of what U.S. geostrategic power projection capabilities could be extended to Israel.[4]

Fawzi prepared documents that outlined the maximum extent of contributions for each Arab state and shared them at the Arab League summit in Rabat, Morocco, in late December 1969. When Nasser left the summit before an agreement giving structure, resources, and forces to a unified command could be reached, the bravado of 1967 and 1968 evaporated. Fawzi was deeply frustrated by "the unwillingness [by some Arab League members] to provide alternate landing options for the Egyptian air force, and the lack of ability to coordinate effort along a single front."

On December 23, 1969, members of the Khartoum mini-summit met in Tripoli. The summit brought Egypt together with the Arab revolutionary states of Libya and Sudan. The three states represented themselves as the Arab Revolutionary Liberation Front as a reaction to the inaction of the Arab League and failure of the Rabat summit.

Wheelus AFB Dismantled: Part of the Perception War

The perception war continued when Libya engineered the ceremonial dismantling of the U.S. Air Force's Wheelus AFB and renamed it Uqbah ibn Nafeeh Air Base in June 1970.[5] Under the guise of this event, Fawzi met with the military leaders of Libya, Syria, Jordan, Iraq, Sudan, and Algeria to lay the foundations of a strategic plan against Israel on two fronts, Egypt and Syria. Qadhafi proposed a union between Egypt, Syria, and Libya to revive the defunct UAR. Nasser agreed only to study the feasibility of a federal union. Fawzi writes, "Egypt's senior generals resigned themselves to the fact that Egypt would bear the brunt of responsibility for any military actions against Israel and that Syria would be viewed as a secondary front." This military thinking shaded the Egyptian General Staff through the 1973 Yom Kippur War.

By July 1970 Fawzi had secured a steady and reliable supply of Soviet arms, and he focused his attention on Plan 200 to liberate the Sinai in stages. Since its initial conception in 1968, Plan 200 had been revised every six months, taking into account not only intelligence collected but also new fully equipped Egyptian military units. Within Plan 200 was a subplan called Granite, which focused on crossing the canal with overwhelming force and sustaining several bridgeheads.

Nasser's Final Meetings, July and September 1970

Nasser visited Moscow in July 1970 for a summit with Soviet foreign minister Andrei Gromyko to discuss the Rogers Plan proposed by the United States. The plan involved cessation of aerial attacks for three months and of the construction of military bases; the Israelis could only renovate those bases already constructed. Nasser and Fawzi saw in the Rogers Plan a chance to amass more SAMs along the canal. The Egyptian leader accepted the plan's ninety-day moratorium on attacks, although Fawzi expressed concerns the Egyptian soldiers' training could be eroded as a result of the inactivity along the canal, which had been constant from 1967 until 1970.

The tactical problem of moving the SAMs within the ninety-day period required an elaborate deception and the constant transfer of SAM sites to and from the Canal Zone. The missiles were deployed at sunrise and dismantled at sundown; a few were always left behind while others were moved. The Israeli troops trying to keep up with the transfers experienced action at the tempo of an exercise or training. The Egyptian operation involved fourteen SAM battalions.

Conclusion

In September 1970 Fawzi joined Nasser on a train ride from Cairo to Mersa Matruh, along the Mediterranean Sea. During the trip Fawzi laid out fourteen maps that made up the latest iteration of Plan 200. The maps covered the following:

- Plan Granite (canal crossing)
- 2nd Field Army plan
- 3rd Field Army plan
- EAF plan
- Egyptian navy plan
- artillery plan
- communications plan
- logistical plan

The two also discussed what the Syrians had provided regarding their plans to liberate the Golan Heights. The fourteen classified maps had been endorsed by each commander and Fawzi.

Nasser ordered that practice runs of Plan Granite be conducted inside Egypt. This was Nasser's last order to Fawzi, for the Egyptian president died on September 28, 1970, the victim of a massive heart attack. Fawzi laments that the Egyptian leader "did not provide the armed forces with a [specific] time line to begin a new Arab-Israeli war." That decision was left to Nasser's untried, untested, and then inexperienced vice president, Anwar Sadat.

The next part of Fawzi's memoir highlights the extent of the Egyptians' tactical understanding of Israeli deployments in the Sinai and the three key altercations he used to create a sense of joint accomplishment among Egypt's army, navy, and air force. What Fawzi omits from his narrative are discussions he had with Anwar Sadat about Egypt's military readiness and options regarding extending the Rogers Plan. According to Mohamed Heikal, confidant to President Nasser and President Sadat, Sadat posed two questions to Fawzi in late 1970: "Would it be fair to give orders for a war to start only a few days after taking office? Would it be fair, distracted by grief, to plunge [the nation] into war?" After their discussion Sadat extended the cease-fire. Heikal recounts a side conversation during this meeting: Sadat asked, "Are you ready [for war] or do you need more time?" Fawzi replied, "If I am given an order in writing, I will do whatever is required of me by my political leadership." This response not only did not answer Sadat's question but also did not engender Heikal's confidence.[6]

Chapter Eight

Formulating a General Strategy
for the War of Attrition

---

*To those for whom war is necessary, it is just; and resort to arms
is righteous for those to whom no further hope remains.*

—Livy—

---

*Foreword by Brigadier General Peter B. Zwack, USA,
U.S. defense attaché designate to the Russian Federation*

This *Infantry* series provides an understanding of the Middle East region from the perspective and cultural vantage of those who actually live there, which is vital to the formulating of policy options strategically advantageous to the United States and its allies. I first met Commander Aboul-Enein in 2008, receiving important insights on Islam from him before my deployment to Afghanistan. Four years later, while I prepared to assume my duties as America's senior military representative to Moscow, he gave a presentation at the Joint Military Attaché School on the Arab Spring and terrorism that left me wanting to learn more. Since our meeting in the winter of 2012, I have relied on Commander Aboul-Enein for advice not only about the Middle East but also on the militant Islamist problem in Russia and neighboring countries, particularly in the Caucasus and Central Asia, including Afghanistan. He has been an ardent advocate of teaching America's military using direct Arabic sources, which is exactly what the U.S. armed forces need to best understand the complex nuances of Islam in this rapidly evolving twenty-first-century threat environment. In this part of the series, you will be immersed in a level of discussion never seen in the English language as Egyptian war minister General Mohamed Fawzi writes of the architecture for what would become the War of Attrition between Egypt and Israel (1967–1970). You will gain insights into the pivotal role the Soviet Union played in the reconstruction of the Egyptian armed forces in the aftermath of the 1967 Six-Day War, down to the actions of the Soviet military mission to Egypt, which oversaw the gradual deployment of arms shipments from Moscow along the Suez Canal front. Until the end of the 1973 Arab-Israeli war, the Suez Canal was a flashpoint in the Cold War between the superpowers. Readers will gain an appreciation of Egyptian tactical analysis, which is influenced by Soviet tactical doctrine, such as assessing a front not from the tip of the spear but from back to front, from the logistical tail to frontline combat units. I applaud the U.S. Army *Infantry Magazine* for providing Commander Aboul-Enein a forum in which to bring to life the blending of Egyptian and Soviet tactical thought. This is the first time Fawzi's memoir has been made available for an English-speaking audience, and it is my earnest hope that this series will be debated and discussed in America's war colleges and military and noncommissioned officer (NCO) academies as well as among our allies and partners.

Introduction: Egyptian Efforts to Gather Tactical Intelligence

This chapter provides readers a rare glimpse of what the Egyptians knew about Israeli military activities in the Sinai. It offers a picture of the intelligence pieced together by the Egyptians and allows the Western reader to rethink stereotypes about the lack of creativity of the Egyptians specifically, and Arabs generally, when conducting data collection on and analysis of an adversary. The worst thing that America's military planners can do is think that the Arab mind is somehow frozen in time and does not evolve in response to contingencies and pressures.

The large deployment of Israeli combat forces in the Sinai required a huge logistical sustainment effort. Fawzi writes that "water was assessed to be a constant battle for Israeli military logisticians," and the Egyptians took great care to note the elaborate water pipeline system gradually constructed by the Israelis. This was the beginning of the Egyptian General Staff's understanding of the Israeli army's supply chain in the Sinai and exploration of ways to exploit its vulnerabilities. The Egyptians' logic is interesting. If one is asked to start assessing an adversary's deployment, one may naturally begin with the tip of the spear and assess infantry, tanks, and artillery and then the supply chain. The Egyptians, however, likely with Soviet assistance, worked their way from the supply chain to infantry, artillery, and armored units. Fawzi writes, "The Israeli water pipeline network stretched from Arish along the Sinai Mediterranean coastal road and all along the Suez Canal until Ayoon Musa, very near to Egyptian-held Port Tawfik. In addition, ships outfitted as water tankers shipped water to the port of Eilat, which was distributed by truck to Israeli units deployed all along the southern Sinai and into a series of storage tanks. Allowances for the provision of fifty thousand Israeli troops deployed in the Sinai were assessed by the Egyptian General Staff, which then led them to collect on troop rotation within the Sinai."

According to the Egyptians, the Israelis rotated their frontline troops every three months. Over time it became clear that fewer regular forces were being deployed, and those that were deployed were substituted by reservists. Fawzi writes, "There was an increased number of Eastern European and Russian Jews, which led Egyptian intelligence to collect on the types of units being deployed to the Sinai." This observation, coupled with the deterioration of discipline in the units, led the Egyptians to assess if reserve units were being used and if regular forces were being deployed deep into Sinai or back in Israel.

Monitoring the supply chain also had significant operational repercussions. As Fawzi notes, "Maintaining large formations in the Sinai caused strain on the Israeli economy." Gradually, Egyptian leaders recognized the need to increase that strain, and plans for an attritional war began to take shape. The plans began with daily artillery bombardments and small skirmishes along the Canal Zone and escalated to Saaqa raids deep into the Sinai. Fawzi writes, "Soon after one of these raids I listened to criticism by Israeli general Moshe Dayan in the Israeli Knesset debate about the deployment of Israeli forces in the Sinai. The general stated the need to reposition forces along the Giddi and Mitla Passes and rely on them to be a rapid reaction force to reinforce the Canal Zone."

Fawzi writes of "the detection and monitoring of three Israeli airfields in the Sinai: Sharm el-Sheikh, Bir Tamada, and Mil'eez-South Naqib. Israeli naval patrols were also monitored, which were providing naval gunfire support to areas like Ras Nasrani." Over time the Egyptians developed a picture of the Israeli side of the Canal Zone. The evolving Bar-Lev line (named after its architect, General Chaim Bar-Lev) was a sand berm with guard towers at intervals of four to seven kilometers. Each tower contained a thirty-man unit, and there was a gap along the Great Bitter Lake. Egyptians took note of barbed wire, mines, and flamethrowers that could ignite areas of the canal waters. Fawzi writes that the Israelis deployed two infantry divisions, two tank battalions, and three artillery (reserve) battalions in the center of the Sinai. He continues, "The area of Umm Hasheeb contained a command and control center with one tank division in reserve, as well as a mechanized division. The Mediterranean Coastal Road from Rumana to Arish contained Israeli mustering locations, logistical bases, as well as rest and recreation centers for their troops." Fawzi was convinced that the Israelis reacted to Egyptian harassing artillery and raids by reinforcing the Bar-Lev line with concrete bunkers and by extending their area of operation along the Canal Zone from 170 to 450 kilometers of aerial, naval, and land surveillance. Egyptian military intelligence noted the locations of oil refineries and drills, settlement activity, and tourist resorts being developed in Rafah, Sharm el-Sheikh, and Sheikh Zuweid. The intelligence report noted that Egyptian Bedouins were being used as laborers for these projects.

Egyptian Tactical Reconnaissance Teams

Fawzi describes how Egyptian military intelligence sent two- and three-man reconnaissance teams into the Sinai for fifteen days. They were to collect information on Israeli military routines and locations, reserve unit routines, reinforcement routes, and logistical routes, as well as timetables for Israeli deliveries, terrain, and air landings. The EAF used reconnaissance MiG variants for aerial reconnaissance and intelligence collection on topography. General Mehraz Mustafa Abdel-Rahman was chief director of military intelligence (DMI) at this time, and it was his duty to use classified and nonclassified sources to provide Fawzi with an ever-improving picture of the Israeli order of battle inside the Sinai.

The Israelis also dispatched reconnaissance patrols and developed monitoring stations along the length of the Suez Canal to determine Egyptian intentions and activities. Fawzi mentions "Israeli psychological operations on their side of the canal designed to provoke a response from Egyptian soldiers. The tactics included Israelis fishing, playing Arabic songs, and Arabic jokes making fun of Egypt, Egyptians, and Egyptian arms." Some Egyptian troops opened fire, destroying loudspeakers, in response. Fawzi describes how gunfire escalated from light machine guns to heavy machine guns to mortars and artillery duels in sectors all along the canal. Egyptians and Israelis dug deeper, created concrete bunkers, and increased the height of their sand berms along the edge of the canal. When the Israelis erected electronic monitoring posts, the Egyptians targeted them, leading the Israelis to reconstruct them with reinforced steel and blast-proof protection.

Battle of Ras el-Aish

The June 1967 war ended with the Israeli occupation of the Sinai except for a small sliver south and east of Port Fouad, which was held by Egyptian infantry, SF, and an antitank unit. Fawzi writes,

> This small collection of Egyptian army units took initiative and reinforced their positions, laid antitank mines, and coordinated artillery strikes from Port Fouad against advancing Israeli armored and mechanized infantry units. The Israelis attempted to capture the eastern environs with a force of ten tanks reinforced with a mobile infantry battalion and engineers on July 1, 1967. This Israeli force was reinforced with close air support. Despite heavy concentrated air and ground fire, the Israelis met stiff resistance, leading to a loss of three Israeli tanks. The Israelis regrouped and attempted to take Ras el-Aish by flanking it from the coastal side, but tanks became stuck in the shallow tides. In

addition, Egyptian artillery, coupled with the antitank mines, allowed the Egyptians to maintain this toehold in the Sinai.

The Egyptian General Staff derived many lessons from fortifying defenses to mitigate the effectiveness of Israeli tanks and used AA artillery concentrations in and around Ras el-Aish to reduce the effectiveness of Israeli CAS. The lessons of Ras el-Aish were incorporated in the creation of a robust defense all along the Egyptian side of the Canal Zone and led to serious consideration of counterair measures.

Fawzi suggests that the Israelis were not idle either and also learned from Ras el-Aish; they were particularly concerned with the mass AA defenses they encountered in that engagement. The Egyptians had developed concentrated AA kill zones and were becoming more disciplined in their AA fire. This development led to Israeli reconnaissance overflights along the Canal Zone to assess AA defenses. The Egyptian General Staff responded to Israeli overflights by disguising ammo dumps, command centers, artillery positions, and eventually SAM sites as they were fielded. Air Marshal Madkoor Aboul-Eez, the EAF chief, took charge of denying Israelis the ability to capitalize on their overflight missions to gather intelligence.

Egyptian Naval and Air Force Engagement of the Israelis

The Egyptian Air Staff planned a demonstration of concentrated airpower on Israeli reconnaissance planes to show that the EAF was not out of the picture. Fawzi notes, "On July 14, 1967, in the southern part of the canal, ten MiG-17 jet fighters, supported by another ten MiG-17s, surprised Israeli reconnaissance planes by striking two and causing them to return to base. On July 15, 1967, two dogfights occurred and again Egyptian swarm tactics overwhelmed Israeli fighters, causing them to withdraw." Fawzi does not discuss EAF losses in this engagement.

Egyptians wanted to challenge the Israelis not only in the air and on land but also in the sea. The INS *Eilat*, Israel's largest warship at the time, sailed with impunity along the coast of Port Said. Fawzi had given standing orders for the *Eilat* to be challenged if it once again penetrated Egyptian national waters. On October 21, 1967, the Egyptians dispatched two Soviet-designed torpedo boats with KUMAR/ Styx antiship missiles from the naval base at Port Fouad. Fawzi calls the boats "TP-501 and TP-504. The TP-504, commanded by LtCol [Navy] Ahmed Shaker, scored the first hit on the *Eilat* with its missiles, causing the warship to list. TP-501, commanded by Lutfi Jadallah, fired two missiles, scoring a hit, and after two hours the INS *Eilat* slipped beneath the waves eleven miles northeast of Port Said. Naval Headquarters at Port Said tracked the *Eilat* on radar until she disappeared from the screen at 1900 hours with 250 on board." It was the first time a warship had been sunk by antiship missiles. Fawzi oversaw the awarding of medals of valor to the commanding officers and their crews, and October 21 became Egypt's Navy Day. Nasser was personally informed by Fawzi of the INS *Eilat*'s sinking, but their jubilation was short lived.

Fawzi notes, "On October 24, the Israelis began a fierce artillery barrage that targeted petroleum depots and refineries, causing damage to 60 percent of Egypt's petroleum stockpile." The Egyptians decided to move these facilities deeper along the Nile Delta toward the Libyan side of Egypt. A complete military fuel plan was drawn, creating smaller depots closer to the front and larger ones deep inside Egypt.

Fawzi tied together the Egyptian army engagement at Ras el-Aish in early July, the EAF engagements in mid-July, and the Egyptian navy's sinking of INS *Eilat* in October to create a sense of joint accomplishment among Egypt's three services. He accomplished this by holding joint award ceremonies, talking to all ranks about the relationships between these operations, and emphasizing that success in modern warfare could be accomplished only through interservice cooperation. Fawzi also took the added steps of implementing interservice training and command and control exercises.

Civilian Evacuation of the Suez Canal Zone

Fawzi writes of "the evacuation of over 1.5 million Egyptian civilians from the Canal Zone, including from the cities of Port Said, Ismailiyah, and Suez. . . . It was a Herculean effort and the first time Egypt's military and civilian leaders worked together to arrange for the moving, feeding, and housing of these people. Militarily, it sent a clear message to the Israelis that Egypt was laying the groundwork for a resumption of hostilities." Fawzi thought that Israeli protests against this mass civilian evacuation were not due to humanitarian concerns but instead stemmed from their concern that they would be deprived of an opportunity to apply pressure to Egypt to accept the status quo. Fawzi's memoir indicates that this mass evacuation was used as a pretext to begin the mobilization of the entire nation for war.

Establishment of the First Line of Defense

Fawzi recounts frantically that

> my first order of business when Nasser made me war minister in the
> midst of the Six-Day War was to restructure small retreating battalion
> side units. I equipped them with small arms and ammunition and sent
> them back to guard the western side of the Suez Canal. General Ahmed
> Ismail, Canal Zone commander, took the initiative and organized

retreating Egyptian soldiers into new battalions, assigning officers who remained in the field of battle to command these units. Throughout the next few days, these newly organized frontline units were provided with small arms and heavy machine guns, then mortars, and finally artillery all along the canal.

Fawzi pushed troops and matériel from the Nile Delta to the Suez Canal Zone, and General Ismail assigned the general of air defense, Abdel-Moneim Riad, to travel along the canal and tend to shortages and gaps in the defensive line. Within a month these three generals—Fawzi, Ismail, and Riad—had concentrated five infantry divisions, two armored divisions, five SF battalions, and one Algerian infantry division along a 170-kilometer line from Port Said to Adabiyah Port. Fawzi was assisted by Soviet general Lashinkov, who was now designated chief of the Soviet military mission in Egypt.[1] The Soviet arms shipments created two Egyptian armored divisions in addition to those already deployed along the canal. These extra two divisions would serve as a reserve force.

Early Tactical Problems: Artillery, Communications, and Constant Supply

Fawzi's next step was to work on an artillery fire plan, while working through such tactical issues as artillery resupply, communications, and the concentration of forces in a battle space 170 kilometers in length and on average 60 kilometers in depth. The efforts of the Egyptian generals and the Soviet military mission evolved into the Egyptian 2nd and 3rd Field Armies, which had eighty thousand soldiers total. It was only in November 1967 that Fawzi and the Egyptian generals thought they had stabilized the front line against any Israeli attempts to penetrate the west side of the canal into Egypt proper.

The Nag Hammadi Operation in October 1968 struck Egyptian refineries and petroleum depots deep in Egypt and near Aswan. In addition, Israelis raided portions of the Aswan High Dam at midnight on November 1, 1968, with two Israeli helicopters laden with Israeli SF. The attack caused minor disruptions to Cairo's electrical grids, and Egyptian engineers worked round the clock to restore power. The attacks led Fawzi to link an early defense warning system from the Aswan High Dam to the border with Sudan. As a result of the Israeli raids during the last months of 1967, Fawzi had overseen the creation of a civilian defense force for the Nile Valley. He finally organized the 141st Palestinian Fedayeen (Sacrificers) Battalion for the purpose of harassing Israeli sites from a base in Amman, Jordan.

Conclusion

This segment of Fawzi's memoir contains the Egyptian military perspective on many complex facets of the Arab-Israeli conflict. The action and reaction of each side, both on defense and offense, were key factors in the ongoing conflict. In addition, it is important to note that Egyptian arms gradually became proficient. While the Egyptians at this point did not have the expertise needed to pull off the initial surprise attack in 1973, the intellectual seeds had been planted owing to the physical and mental restructuring of the Egyptian armed forces.

The next chapter will feature Fawzi's thoughts on asymmetric warfare as a means of supplementing conventional warfare. It will also focus on efforts to reduce inefficiencies in the Egyptian armed forces and to transfer some military assignments to other ministries in order to allow the Defense Ministry to focus on war. Finally, it will examine Fawzi's thoughts on attaining unity of command while solving additional tactical problems in the field.

★★ **Chapter Nine** ★★

Redesigning the Egyptian Armed Forces

The Russians can give you arms,
but only the United States can give you a selection.
—ANWAR SADAT—

Foreword by Paul J. Murphy, director, Russia-Eurasia Terror Watch,
former assistant national intelligence officer for counterterrorism,
congressional adviser, and author of Allah's Angels:
Chechen Women in War, The Soviet Air Forces, *and other books on Soviet*
and Russian political and military matters

I am delighted to write this foreword for Commander Aboul-Enein. We share a common passion for analyzing authoritative original-language materials and educating America's future military leaders. My own experience goes back to the mid-1970s, when, as a young intelligence analyst, I translated and wrote about Soviet military strategy and tactics as part of the U.S. Air Force's Soviet awareness program. I commend Commander Aboul-Enein for carrying on that tradition by making available for the first time the memoir of Egyptian war minister General Mohamed Fawzi. Thanks also go to the U.S. Army *Infantry Magazine* for dedicating space in several issues for this work.

This essay sheds light on how Egyptian strategic thought evolved after 1967 and how it was shaped by the experience of the Six-Day War and the massive influx of Soviet advisers and sophisticated military equipment that followed. The latter is of particular interest to me because Fawzi confirms many conclusions drawn in my 1984 book, *The Soviet Air Forces*.[1] While relations between Egypt and the Soviet Union began as early as 1955, the years after 1967 saw a significant increase in the quantity and quality of Soviet military equipment going to Cairo. Soviet air power played a particular role. Egypt became the paramount recipient of Soviet combat aircraft. The MiG-21 Fishbed fighter appeared there a year after it became operational. Chief Marshal of Aviation and Commander in Chief of Soviet Air Forces Pavel Kutakhov, along with Defense Minister Marshal Andrei Grechko, visited Cairo in February 1972. By mid-1972 Egypt had some six hundred Soviet combat aircraft, almost two hundred helicopters and about a hundred transports in its air inventory.

In his analysis of Fawzi's memoir, Commander Aboul-Enein writes, "The Kremlin's goal was to draw Egypt into the Soviet sphere of influence. The Kremlin ultimately failed in Egypt under Sadat, but Soviet doctrinal pronouncements at the time made very explicit the view that modern Soviet military power was created not only to win wars, but to obtain global political objectives through military power projection." Fawzi's perspective does not take into account the wider view of Soviet foreign policy after the death of Stalin in 1953 and the sidelining of his generation of apparatchiks, like Vyacheslav Molotov and Lavrentiy Beria. Stalin's death brought to the fore a new generation of Soviet leaders who would realign the communist view of capitalist encirclement to the more inclusive socialist encirclement and evolution of Khruschev's "rolling crisis" theory of creating tension in Lebanon, then Formosa, then Berlin.[2] Whereas Stalin focused on immediate neighbors, the new post-Stalin generation of Kremlin leaders shifted to global reach.[3] Egypt would be among several areas Moscow would use to create a rolling crisis for the United States in Cold War global brinksmanship. The Soviets viewed Egypt as an example of a noncapitalist path toward development, as opposed to the typical communist model. Pragmatic Soviet policy makers saw no problems with engaging the bourgeois leaders of India and revolutionary democrats in Egypt. V. Rumiantsev, a Soviet policy intellectual of the period, captures this post-Stalinist pragmatic approach toward Egypt in an exquisite way:

> Significant transformations have taken place during the last several years in the views held, first of all, by the leaders of the Egyptian revolution. In the initial stage these leaders paid homage to petty bourgeois illusions, forced "peace class" and tried to reach compromises with reactionaries. But beginning with the sixties, President Nasser and his comrades in arms started to carry out important socio-economic transformations in their country which were directed against the great and part of the middle bourgeois and corresponded to the working people's interests. Thus the Egyptian revolution entered a new stage characterized by the intensification of its domestic and social character.[4]

Added to Egypt were Algeria, Iraq, Syria, Sudan, and Libya, which provided Moscow the ability to assert itself in the Mediterranean to challenge the United States. From Moscow's view, undermining the chain of alliances such as the North Atlantic Treaty Organization (NATO), Central Treaty Organization (CENTO), and Southeast Asia Treaty Organization (SEATO) was a priority, and this dovetailed nicely with Nasser's plans to undermine the Baghdad Pact created in 1955 and renamed CENTO in 1959, when Iraq withdrew from the alliance. Nasser saw this organization as a mechanism for bolstering Arab monarchies at the expense of Arab progressive republics. In the final analysis, nuanced changes in leadership between, for example, Nasser and Sadat, Kennedy and Johnson, and Khruschev and Brezhnev, as well as Israeli prime ministers Levi Eshkol, Yigal Allon, and Golda Meir, all changed the calculus of regional relations, bringing subtle changes in policies that had an escalating or de-escalating effect. Personalities matter: for instance, in 1971, Sadat not only refused to recognize a pro-communist coup in Sudan but sent military advisers to restore the deposed Sudanese strongman Jaafar al-Numeiri to power within five days of his being removed in a communist-backed coup.[5]

In reading and rereading Fawzi's memoir, one is struck by the complete absence of appreciation for recent global events that brought superpowers to the brink, such as the Cuban Missile Crisis, which had happened only five years before Fawzi began his tenure as war minister in 1967. The Suez Canal developed as a fault line for Moscow and Washington, and Egypt's war minister does not mention this in his memoir. Nor does he address how Cold War tension resulted in nuclear threats during the 1973 Yom Kippur War.

Introduction: Asymmetric Warfare in Egypt's General War Plans

Chapter 8 saw General Fawzi immersed in solving tactical problems with the Egyptian armed forces. He worked with several generals "on the restructuring of Egyptian military units to solidify a defensive line along the Suez Canal that was 170 kilometers long and 60 kilometers in depth." Among the tactics he considered was

> the leveraging of asymmetric warfare in the form of Palestinian guerrillas launched from Jordan to harass and raid Israeli targets. In December 1967 Palestinian Liberation Organization guerrillas attacked the settlement of Bitah Tikvah on the outskirts of Tel Aviv and damaged an oil pipeline linking Jerusalem and Tel Aviv. In addition, they attacked a train between Tel Aviv and Bir Saba. In March 1968 Fatah launched what would be called the Battle of Karameh, which led to twenty-nine deaths and seventy casualties. . . . In August 1968 military bases and industrial areas were harassed inside the West Bank during the Battle of Sullah. While known in the Middle East as battles, [these actions] are aptly described as guerrilla raids.[6]

General Fawzi exploited the raids as an additional means of applying pressure to the Israelis: "In 1969 elements of the Egyptian special forces and frogmen, coupled with Palestinian guerrillas, assaulted the Israeli port of Eilat from the sea, damaging fuel depots."

Unity of Command and Effort: Fawzi's Constant Obsession

One of Fawzi's focal points in the late 1960s was unity of command. He spends several pages in his memoir discussing such concepts as the military operational art and the unity of effort. After the Six-Day War, Fawzi unified the offices of the war minister and the chief of staff, and then he convinced the chief of staff to become the deputy chief of staff. He abolished the Office of High Command and the Office of the Chief of Staff, which he viewed as unnecessary layers of bureaucracy separating himself from the chief of staff. These offices were reduced and merged with the war minister and chief of staff posts to create the High Military Council.

Fawzi discusses the trial and error involved in organizing the military command structure before he found an efficient format. The High Military Council consisted of Fawzi (that is, the war minister), the chief of staff (now a separate position), functional and service chiefs, and corps commanders. This council became the single entity from which orders emanated. Gone were the days of Field Marshal Amer issuing verbal orders with no authentication. General Ahmed Zaki Abdel-Hamid served as Fawzi's liaison and helped him to craft clear chains of command. Fawzi understood how the conflicting orders that Field Marshal Amer issued as the Six-Day War unfolded had caused confusion and how the haphazard way the order to retreat from the Sinai was issued had led to not only confusion but chaos and a rout.

Designing a Post-1967 Egyptian Armed Forces

The plan developed in 1967 called for the liberation of the Sinai by 1970. This three-year timetable dictated the size of the armed forces. Fawzi took into his calculations census data, demographics, and the Israelis' ability to sustain field units for certain lengths of time. A second consideration in determining the size of the armed forces was the theater of operations at air, land, and sea. Other considerations included the speed of Soviet shipments, the types of weapons, and the training necessary to use the equipment, as well as the education of technical units to maintain the equipment. These considerations became acute issues for the EAF and the Egyptian Air Defense Forces (EADF). Fawzi writes of the careful balance among the numbers, training, time, and acquisition of proficiency in advanced weapons systems.

The core ground forces, according to Fawzi, should include the following:

- five infantry corps
- three mechanized corps
- two armored corps
- three field artillery divisions
- one reconnaissance division
- two paratroop divisions
- forty-four Saaqa battalions
- two air assault divisions

Given this core force, Fawzi and his generals determined sustainment, self-sufficiency, and the number of days the ground troops could operate independently before needing resupply. This force would gradually become the infamous 2nd and 3rd Field Armies that crossed the canal in October 1973. What Fawzi's memoir offers is the initial conception and rationale for the balance of forces in the aftermath of the Six-Day War.

The core air force consisted of six hundred fighters and eight hundred pilots. Each air division was assigned two airstrips or one major air base. The divisions included the following:

- 2 light fighter divisions
- 2 heavy bomber divisions
- 5 helicopter divisions
- 2 transport divisions
- 120 trainers, both jet and propeller aircraft

The EADF, Fawzi writes, consisted of

> eight air defense groups, each organized around three or five divisions of combined antiair guns, and various surface-to-air missile variants. Eight radar battalions also aided this force, and each of the eight air defense groups had an operations center, with a ninth as the overall air operations center linked to all eight operation centers. This setup had the effect of combining antiair defense with vectoring jet fighters to target and ensured minimal friendly fire. This design was the reason that the Air Defense Forces, a separate service from the air force, was created on the advice of the Soviets in 1968.

The EADF was given an overall mission that overlapped with the EAF's mission of providing air support and denying the enemy air space.

The technical and logistical units were "the most complex to train and to prepare for deployment," according to Fawzi. The war minister's priority was "to provide logistical support, maintenance, and resupply units to fighting units along the Suez Canal first and then to develop a support and lines of communication system extending back into the Nile Delta."

For the Egyptian navy, Fawzi concentrated "on maritime reconnaissance, the development of amphibious landing capabilities, frogmen, fast attack boats, and maintenance facilities in the Mediterranean and Red Seas to sustain [the] force. It was deemed by the Egyptian General Staff that these assets would aid in the mission of the Sinai theater of operation."

For Fawzi, control units were not an afterthought. He considered it important to field competently trained military police units, not just to maintain good order and discipline in this massive force, but to control the flow of traffic. In addition, a stand-alone education formation balanced the basic training at intake. It provided training for complex weapons systems and advancement training and development. It was important for this cadre to visit the Canal Zone frequently and apply the lessons of an active combat zone in both basic and advanced training.

Working with Soviet Advisers to Develop the Force

General Ahmed Zaki Abdel-Hamid, Fawzi's liaison to the Soviet military mission in Egypt, was designated commander of the Coordination Council. Abdel-Hamid worked closely with Soviet advisers to train Egyptian units on the military hardware being air- and sea-lifted from the Soviet Union and Eastern bloc nations. To illustrate the magnitude of Abdel-Hamid's task, Fawzi writes, "40,000 drivers had to be trained per year on various military vehicles, from jeeps and trucks to armored personnel carriers [APCs] and tanks. Driving schools had to be established and managed throughout the country."

Egyptians worked closely with hundreds of Soviet military advisers to create a fully equipped infantry division with accompanying support units. The Egyptians, with the help of Soviet officers, would field self-propelled artillery units for the first time and revamp reconnaissance as well as radar units. The Soviets aided the Egyptians in establishing monitoring and early warning posts from Port Said to Mersa Matruh.

Fawzi complains of "Nasser's meddling in the size of the armed forces and the attempts by the Egyptian leader to politicize the process. This would have a chain reaction and interfere with the timetable of starting offensive operations with Israel in 1970." Fawzi and the General Staff debated the mobility of Egyptian units, down to the amounts each soldier could carry before becoming encumbered. The General Staff also took coastal artillery duties from the army and gave them to the navy. In the realm of education, technical schools for the armed forces were created. In addition, an air force high school was created to help students matriculate into the Air Force Academy, and an air defense college was established.

Fawzi comments, "During the massive Soviet arms shipments, Egypt was provided the latest weaponry even before many of the Warsaw Pact nations were provided them. This included the latest T-55 variant with night-vision capabilities and the MiG-21. The massive amounts of Soviet hardware were calibrated through three or four Soviet-Egyptian Military Coordination Council meetings per year from 1968 to 1971. Moscow and Cairo negotiated a financial agreement in which the first payment would not be due until ten years later, and the debt for military hardware would be settled over forty years at 2.5 percent interest." Fawzi is among the few Egyptian generals who discuss the nuts and bolts of financing agreements for military hardware in their memoirs. He writes that "a MiG-21 would be priced at 750,000 Egyptian pounds, the Mirage at 1 million Egyptian pounds, derived from Libyan purchases of the French Mirage fighter, while the U.S. F-5 Phantom export variant would be priced at between $6 million and $8 million; the United States did not accept local currency," but the Soviets did. The Soviets clearly subsidized their equipment, not to make a financial profit but to penetrate and influence Egypt's centers of power and gain basing rights. The Kremlin's goal was to draw Egypt into the Soviet sphere of influence. The Kremlin ultimately failed in Egypt under Sadat, but Soviet doctrinal pronouncements at the time made explicit the view that modern Soviet military power was created not only to win wars but to obtain global political objectives through military power projection.

Maintaining primacy over the United States in the Mediterranean Sea and achieving influence in key global lines of communication were Moscow's chief concerns. On a naval tactical level, the Soviets needed bases to enhance their anti-submarine warfare (ASW) capabilities so that they could counter U.S. Polaris-equipped submarines. Soviet naval access at Alexandria and Sollum, coupled with airfield access, allowed Moscow options for reconnoitering U.S. Sixth Fleet assets.[7]

Teaching Soldiers to Respect Themselves and Their Weapons

Fawzi was interested in the ways that his subordinates were reorienting Egyptian soldiers to respect both themselves and their weapons. This reorientation was accomplished through drills, military parades, inspections, and weekly weapon cleaning and inspection. These rituals were meant to fuse soldiers to their weapons and officers to their soldiers.

Egyptian armed forces research facilities conducted tests and then proposed improvements to Soviet equipment, identifying shortcomings caused by usage, endurance, terrain, and weather. Fawzi personally sent reports about Soviet weapon performance to the Soviet defense minister. The reports included "specifications and engineering notes to improve Soviet weapons systems. These technical improvements in use and engineering were shared with other Warsaw Pact nations. An example was the use of concertina wire around tanks to counter antitank missiles. It is comparable to a bird caught in netting, flying in and around the wires until it exploded, leaving tanks undamaged. Concertina wire was deployed along the defensive front line with extra bundled wire around deployed equipment. Constant experimentation was conducted using floating modules, crossing bridges, looking at speed of construction, ease of deployment, durability, and tonnage." Egyptians also shared information with the Soviets on the payload, distance, endurance, and altitude envelope of the new MiG-21 jet fighter.

Fawzi notes, "The Soviets had no half-track vehicles for Egypt to purchase, and the Egyptians supplemented their Soviet equipment with open-market purchases of military hardware from the United Kingdom, Belgium, and West Germany. The Egyptians used front companies and third-party purchasing agents in order to conceal these purchases. Egyptian freighters brought this equipment in as early as late 1967."

Conclusion

Through Fawzi's memoir Egypt's growth as a nation, from a defeated and humiliated country after the 1967 Six-Day War to a successful and strong sovereign state, can be tracked and deciphered. Leading up to, throughout, and after the 1967 war with Israel, it was apparent that Egypt was not equipped, trained, or prepared for combat or defense against aggressors. From its humiliating and swift defeat came the realization that critical improvements were necessary for Egypt's survival as a sovereign state and advancement toward becoming a powerful nation. Improvements came in the form of restructuring leadership, completely redesigning the armed forces, and seizing military advancements in weaponry.

After the Six-Day War, it was clear that changes in Egypt's leadership were imperative. Field Marshal Amer's compulsion for power led to chaos and confusion throughout the war and Egypt's eventual retreat. His mental instability kept the country's leadership from effectively commanding its troops and strategizing throughout and after the war. After Amer's suicide Egypt's leadership was reorganized, with Fawzi at the helm of the restructuring. Nasser and Fawzi ensured that new individuals—not Amer's old cronies—were assigned positions as war ministers and chiefs of staff, and a new, more solid leadership began to take shape.

Egypt's armed forces also required improvement, as they would be tested in the War of Attrition. Fawzi understood that the armed forces needed to comprise various, separate components with different responsibilities. Advancements in air, land, and sea reserves and supplies ultimately allowed Egypt's armed forces to become organized and resilient. From the Soviets Egypt was able to procure advanced weapons systems and necessary training. Fawzi ensured the establishment of training schools and facilities to further strengthen Egypt's armed forces. The ultimate goal was to eliminate any possibility that the humiliation and disaster of the 1967 Six-Day War could be repeated. Fawzi's memoir traces Egypt's military leadership, faults, mistakes, triumphs, and most important, transfiguration, illustrating how small details can make for tremendous advancements. His writing provides not only insight into Egypt's history and current situation but also an overall understanding of how one nation can affect another.

Chapter Ten

Overhauling the Egyptian Armed Forces

Strategy, Unity of Command, Civil-Military Authority, Drill, and the Need for Statutory Legislation

There is only one decisive victory: the last.
—Carl von Clausewitz—

*Foreword by Colonel Norvell "Tex" DeAtkine, USA (Ret.),
former U.S. defense attaché to the Arab Republic of Egypt and
eighteen-year instructor at the JFK Special Warfare School*

Having written the foreword to the updated edition of Raphael Patai's *The Arab Mind*,[1] as well as a controversial 1999 article, "Why Arabs Lose Wars," in the *Middle East Quarterly*,[2] and having spent eight years on active duty in the Middle East, I have pondered the Arab way of war for decades. Commander Aboul-Enein and the U.S. Army *Infantry Magazine* are helping current and future generations of America's military planners understand with precision and clarity the rationale behind Egyptian operations and national strategic thought. In 1981, as U.S. defense military attaché, I was in the reviewing stand with Anwar Sadat. In a matter of seconds, I witnessed the proud celebration of a rare conventional achievement—the crossing of the Suez Canal (known to Egyptians as *al-ubur*, or simply, the Crossing)—destroyed by the asymmetric warfare of militant Islamists' gunning the Egyptian leader down before live television cameras. General Mohamed Fawzi's memoir offers an understanding of the architecture of the 1973 Yom Kippur War and, now available in English through this series, should be studied in our war colleges and military academies to instill a sense of empathy for the creativity and planning that took place in the lead-up to the fifth and final conflict between Egypt and Israel. With the changes of the Arab Spring, never has it been more important for Americans to explore Arabic works of military significance. Many of the generals who currently rule Egypt are officers I interacted with as an attaché, and Fawzi's memoir provides not only an understanding of his own thoughts but a frame of reference for understanding Egypt's top military leaders today. It is my privilege to introduce the tenth essay in this series, and I look forward to the debate and discussion it will generate.

Introduction: The Overhaul of Egyptian Military Formations

Fawzi writes of how he pressed "Nasser to draw up and pass a series of republican orders disestablishing units and transferring others from Defense to other ministries. This was to allow the Defense Ministry to focus on warfare." The Counterdrug Unit, Customs, and the Border Guards, for example, were transferred to the Interior Ministry, and the Border Guards and Customs administrations were merged. Fishery, avian, and food inspectors were transferred from Defense to the Ministry of Supply and Food. The war minister writes, "Three divisions of 50,000 soldiers total were used for agricultural projects such as raising crops on tens of thousands of acres. All these responsibilities were transferred by orders of the republic submitted by Nasser and endorsed by Parliament to restructure and utilize every soldier for actual war-fighting efforts or in support of the canal front. In the past soldiers were organized into engineering units and assigned to maintain housing complexes in downtown Cairo. This practice was discontinued, and a budget was passed and provided to the Housing Ministry to address housing projects."

Within the Defense Ministry, Fawzi moved scientists for missile and plane development into the Research and Development Section of Armed Forces Industries. He created oversight centers to get maximum performance from the massive quantities of advanced weapons from the Soviet bloc. The General Staff deemed it unsustainable to devote resources to the development of stand-alone jet engines and indigenous jet fighters and missiles at a time of war when Egypt was receiving the latest Soviet equipment. Thus, Fawzi wanted scientists to maximize, alter, and get the most engineering-wise from the Soviet planes, missiles, armor, and EW equipment.

The Constant Quest for Unity of Command

One of the main failures of the Six-Day War was in designating a clear line of authority from President Nasser—the supreme commander of the armed forces—to the troops themselves. In addition, there was confusion over the responsibilities of the armed forces commander in chief, the armed forces chief of staff, and the deputy armed forces commander in chief. War Minister Field Marshal Abdel-Hakim Amer had created senior positions without thinking about how they fit in the Egyptian command structure and how they would affect the chain of command, which heightened the lack of command unity and functional responsibility.

Fawzi laments that the military leadership did not learn from the parade army's dismal performance in the 1948 Arab-Israeli War, except that the armed forces were strong enough to overthrow the Egyptian monarchy in 1952. Neither were important lessons taken from the 1956 Suez Crisis, a military defeat for Egypt that was overshadowed by Operation Musketeer, the American and Soviet intervention to rein in the British, French, and Israeli forces in the Sinai and the Canal Zone. The Egyptian armed forces had neglected their primary mission—preparing officers and troops for war—and prioritized secondary missions, such as making money and creating a sphere of power separate from civil authority. This negligence led to the crushing defeat of 1967.

Fawzi reflected on the 1967 debacle and thought of ways to create strategic armed forces commanded and controlled efficiently and with civilian oversight. He thought about the relations between the state and its armed forces. In developing and implementing his ideas, Fawzi relied on General Abdel-Moneim Riad, General Mustafa al-Jamel, and General Ahmed Zaki Abdel-Hamid. These generals led the Center for Military Research, a brain trust created for and by the General Staff in the aftermath of the Six-Day War. The Center for Military Research was equivalent to the Office of Net Assessment in the U.S. Office of the Secretary of Defense. Fawzi writes that he and other generals derived lessons from Eastern and Western strategists, but sadly, he does not tell the reader which strategists they discussed.[3] These unnamed strategists, however, influenced several important strategic objectives guiding the Egyptians' thinking in the aftermath of the 1967 war, including assigning responsibilities for the overall strategic goal of placing the nation on a war footing, understanding how the Egyptian armed forces fit in with the state, and defining the role of the president as commander in chief.

Fawzi's focus on unity and efficiency of military effort was also influenced by these strategists. He writes of "the constant task of exerting command and control from the Ministry of War, understanding ways to prevent the duplication of effort unless tactically necessary and to avoid the encroachment of the armed forces in areas best handled by civilian ministries." The Egyptian military is perhaps one of the most efficient institutions in the country, and it has been a constant struggle to balance military efficiency with running and controlling the economy.[4]

Lessons learned from the Eastern and Western strategists also convinced Fawzi to develop ways to deal with major decisions involving questions of national defense as a collective so that no one person dominated the formulation of military options. Fawzi thus established war committees for various aspects of Egyptian defense policy. In fact, he undertook the effort to furnish the tools needed to accomplish all of Egypt's strategic objectives and to equip the armed forces from the battalion commander upward.

In reflecting on the 1967 war, Fawzi realized that during hostilities political leaders without fail lose some or all control of events. In Egypt this loss of control is doubly perplexing. Many Middle Eastern leaders have unleashed their armed forces only to become victims of a military coup. In other cases these leaders have been sidelined as the military took control of one or more organs of the state. This was in fact the case for Nasser and Field Marshal Amer in the lead-up to the Six-Day War.

Bridging the Political and Military Gap: Insights into Civil-Military Affairs

Fawzi discusses how he and the General Staff considered bridging the *siyasi-askari* (political-military) and the *strategi-askari* (military strategy–tactics/operations) gaps. Fawzi engineered the political-military system so that Nasser, as president of the republic and head of the National Defense Council, would be its apex. The president would have the final say on matters pertaining to national defense. Among the items with which Fawzi would need Nasser's assistance was preparing the Egyptian economy for war. He aligned industry, agriculture, transportation, and communications at the national level for the needs of war. Nasser needed to sign off on the construction of bases, logistical depots, command and control centers, and roads and the conversion of aspects of civilian industry to military needs. Fawzi used the Egyptian leader to prepare the people for war and instill a sense of national morale and civil support for military objectives. He also needed Nasser to give the final say on national strategic objectives and balance of power so that the war minister could assess the armed forces in times of peace and war. Fawzi also interlocked the relationships among the president, the military leaders of the National Defense Council, and the civilian leaders of the cabinet.

Civil-military affairs had never been so integrated before the crushing defeat in 1967. Before that year there had been a fatal disconnection and decoupling among the institutions charged with national defense and civilian authority. In addition, the War Ministry became disconnected from the main mission of national defense planning and war planning and more concerned with promotions, retirements, benefits, and appointments of officers.

The General Staff was responsible for training and operational planning; the War Ministry took over personnel matters and the provision of resources for operational units. A chain of command began to form going from the president to the National Defense Council to the War Ministry and the General Staff. Fawzi sought to remove duplication of effort by different offices. In his memoir he provides fascinating insight into the relationship between authority and responsibility: "You cannot have responsibility without authority. . . . [The year] 1967 taught Egyptians that general strategy needs to be outlined, and the command should be left to accomplish those outlines with authority and resources. The General Staff should not meddle in command but hold field commanders responsible for delivering results, but only if both authority and resources are provided."

Legislating a New Egyptian Armed Forces

From the failure of 1967 came Law 4 of 1968 restricting the armed forces, which was presented to Nasser in draft. Fawzi and Nasser made sure that the law took into account modern strategic principles and defined authorities and responsibilities from the president down to the brigade level for the first time in modern Egyptian military history. Law 4 of 1968 defined Egyptian civilian-military affairs and clearly enshrined civil control over the military in legislation. In theory, the law eliminated the armed forces as a competitor for civilian political power and integrated civil and military leaders into one body with the same national strategic objectives.

After working on drafts of Law 4 of 1968, Fawzi turned his attention to reforming Egypt's military justice system. He noted that Law 25 of 1966, which codified Egypt's military law, contained within it "regulations unchanged and lifted directly from Egyptian military codes issued in 1894." Fawzi offers as an example "shirking duties," an offense so vague that anyone could be charged with it without what Westerners would call "due process." Hence, Fawzi argues, the military codes were not aligned with Egypt's constitution. The wrestling among members of the Egyptian armed forces over retaining the ability to adjudicate their own is jealously guarded and remains a red line as Egyptian political and judicial leaders attempt to reform and revise the unpopular December 2012 Islamist-influenced constitution, after ousting President Morsi in July 2013. It is expected that any future constitutions will preserve many of the prerogatives of the military.

Raising the Offensive Capabilities of the Armed Forces

According to Fawzi, "Killing is the profession of all members of the armed forces. Therefore, preparing the soldier and his officer in times of peace [to practice] arts of war that are known, conceptualized, and theorized as well as to learn from various battles is the business of the military commander." He continued, "Proficiency has to begin with the individual soldier and from basic tactical training with other units trained in other military specialties (armor, artillery, and infantry). From there service combinations (army, air force, air defense, and navy) are applied to hone their fighting skills and to get them to operate as one, toward one goal, and at one time."

Egypt would benefit from an abundance of infantry, and thus Fawzi began a rudimentary inquiry into ways to protect and enhance infantry strength in order to negate, if not counter, Israeli proficiency in air and armored capabilities. Since the incoming sophisticated Soviet equipment demanded educated soldiers, Egyptian generals now had to concern themselves with draftees' and volunteers' levels of education. Rates of acceptance and rates of rejection preoccupied Fawzi, and he constantly adjusted standards to acquire the right balance of physical and intellectual capabilities among recruits, as well as those seeking officer commissions. Fawzi writes, "Intellect is the core of what makes a good fighting force, and training begins individually and culminates into ever complex levels of collective and integrated fighting. The chief of staff was assigned responsibility for training standards and goals. Field army commanders down to the unit commander were responsible for execution and improvement of training on the basis of field experiences. Top-down training is more efficient than bottom-up; however, training is the responsibility of the entire chain of command."

According to Fawzi, "Commanders must be present and oversee all aspects of unit training, and officers cannot be excused from leaving the training field." To emphasize that last point, he ordered that "an officer cannot depart the exercise area of operation even if summoned by me, the War Minister!" This standing order was a direct result of Egyptian officers abandoning their posts and their men in the Six-Day War, leading to a chaotic retreat from the Sinai. Fawzi observed the chaos firsthand and was determined never to see it happen again. He wanted exercises to cultivate confidence between commanders and troops.

Fawzi writes, "Stand-downs to derive of lessons learned from field exercises were to be conducted by the entire unit before dismissal, and the process integrated Soviet military advisers. Live-fire exercises were conducted on a regular basis to simulate real combat conditions." Fawzi, as war minister, reviewed reports and compared progress in weapons proficiency, deployment of forces, and maneuver of formations. He wanted to integrate infantry, armor, and artillery within the army before introducing it to elements from other services, such as the air force and navy.

Egyptian generals saw the Canal Zone not only as a combat zone but as an exercise field for preparing troops psychologically for combat. Israelis grew used to observing the Egyptians' constant activity along the canal and gained a sense of security, thinking that every action was either a training exercise or at worst an attempt at intimidation short of actual war.

Ammo, Fuel, and Training:
Exercise, Exercise, Drill, and More Drill

Fawzi discusses the fuel and armament needs to conduct his program of instill-ing confidence through training exercises. He writes, "Fuel consumption increased twenty-fold owing not only to ground forces but also to the fact that pilots were provided with three times as much air time than [they had been] pre-1967 and Egyptian naval units began spending longer deployment time at sea in the Medi-terranean and Red Seas. Between 1968 and 1971 Egyptians lost eighty-three planes owing to constant exercises. . . . The Egyptian Air Force in the actual 1973 war would lose twenty-three planes."

Overseeing Fawzi's vision for Egypt's new, intense military training program was General Salah Mohsen. The two found the most difficult aspect of training to be the cultivation of proficient fighter pilots. Fawzi did the math and decided that "for Egypt to have 1.5 pilots per plane in three years, they would need to train eight hundred pilots. In 1967 only fifty fighter pilots were on the active list; others were retired or transferred to serve in civil aviation or air freight pilots. Before 1967 only two pilots were added to the personnel inventory per year." Fawzi changed this statistic, envisioning a program in which between three hundred and four hundred pilots would graduate from flight school per year. This was accomplished by rotat-ing an entire Egyptian air wing, including the pilots and technicians, to advanced training in the Soviet Union. In early 1970 the Egyptians had reached 75 percent of their goal of eight hundred pilots; the remaining 25 percent gap would be made up by Soviet pilots and technicians serving in a defensive capacity. The Soviet air force personnel were integrated into Egypt's defense plans and arrived in March 1970. They partook in offensive strikes in the Sinai and deep into Israel.

Fawzi also discusses the second-most challenging aspect of training: develop-ing competent and proficient SAM crews. He notes,

> Fielding the SA-3 missile system required increasing the SAM training centers from two to four and required a new level of soldier who had proficiency in electronics. A complete division of air defense person-nel was sent to the Soviet Union in the hopes that they would return and train other units inside Egypt. The massive influx of Soviet advis-ers meant an increased need for Russian–Arabic translators; Egyptian SAM crews trained in Russia were broken up. Those who acquired a proficiency in Russian were kept busy shifting from command to com-mand and served as assistants and liaisons to Soviet advisers on the ground in Egypt. Every three months, three hundred were sent to learn

the deployment, operation, basic maintenance, and basic theory of the SAM systems. The goal of training Egyptian SAM crews was not met, and gaps had to be filled with Soviet crews.

Training Ground Replicas of the Suez Canal

Within the General Staff, the Operations Bureau cooperated with the Training Bureau to bring together field army commanders, military district commanders, and commanders of other services for true interservice exercises. Through constant trial and error during these mass military exercises, artillery, air defense, and ground forces became more and more integrated. With each exercise, Plan 200 was updated. Large swaths of Cairo West, which contained Nile tributaries, had terrain like the Suez Canal and were designated military zones for training. They included West Banha, Tel-el-Kibir, East Dumyat, El-Burjat, and areas of the Western Desert. In these areas the 2nd and 3rd Field Armies perfected their plans for crossing the canal.

Logjams were addressed with the establishment of beachheads in exercises Fawzi called Tabur al-Ubur (Crossing Queues). Fawzi attended a crossing exercise along a Nile tributary, and he writes that it "was estimated to take three days for each field army [80,000 troops] to cross a similar area along the canal and under fire." These exercises were the beginning of Egyptian experimentation with the bridges and breaches needed to quicken the pace of the crossings. Nasser also attended a crossing exercise, at Qarun Lake in the Fayyum area of Egypt; this exercise featured Soviet advisers as exercise judges.

A system was developed whereby a battalion of fifteen hundred soldiers would rotate from the front lines along the Canal Zone to train deep within Egypt on canal-crossing operations at least twice a year. Fawzi noted, "This would take a battalion off-line for ten to fifteen days. A complete armored and mechanized infantry division was assigned the role of playing the dug-in Israelis to simulate combat conditions in the exercise."

Air and Naval Exercises

Air forces and ground units involved in striking simulated targets based on the guidance of ground forces and reconnaissance exercises were a prominent feature of air and ground force integration. The navy was exercised in providing coastal support to ground forces to prevent the flanking of ground forces along the Sinai's coastal road. Egypt dispatched its aging fleet to India and Pakistan for retrofit upgrades, and the navy also practiced naval gunfire support to ground units and coastal denial of Israeli ground and maritime forces through the deployment of Egyptian missile boats, torpedo boats, and mining. Fawzi signed agreements with Moscow to conduct massive joint maritime exercises with the Soviet Mediterranean Fleet.[5]

IL-28 reconnaissance planes were used in maritime reconnaissance, evasion, and tracking exercises in the Mediterranean Sea. Along the Egyptian-Libyan coast, joint amphibious landing exercises were conducted and Soviet naval assets were given basing rights in Port Said. On September 29, 1969, a four-day maritime exercise included warships from Egypt, the Soviet Union, and Syria, with a Soviet command and control ship writing the exercise scenario and housing judges from all country participants. During this exercise Fawzi learned of the potential of EW and the necessity of advanced radar. The Soviets trained Egyptian submarine crews to loiter outside Israeli ports. These submarine missions lasted eleven to fourteen days, and Soviet advisers embarked with each submarine to help the crews get closer to Israeli ports to collect intelligence, particularly on Israeli maritime defensive routines. The objective of the mission was to remain undetected a certain distance off Israeli ports for two days. All of the air and naval exercises proved effective and necessary to ready Egypt's armed forces divisions for future combat.

Conclusion

Through his restructuring of the Egyptian armed forces, Fawzi proved himself to be an incredibly adept war minister. He successfully applied lessons from the immense failure of the 1967 war to future military endeavors. By better organizing the armed forces into effective specialty units, Fawzi was able to implement new military training strategies that would be useful in future wars. These new training strategies were based on real-life combat experiences, allowing troops to grow accustomed to combat conditions. The war minister also based training and reorganizing efforts on the successful military models of other nations, which was an extremely intelligent move. Integrating divisions of the armed forces allowed Fawzi to make sure that each unit knew how to work with the others effectively in combat situations. Fawzi's implementation of updated, specific training and organizing models in Egypt's armed forces was necessary after the embarrassing loss of 1967, and his changes are still effective today. U.S. military personnel can learn from Fawzi's bold advancements in military strategy and apply his concepts to improving troop training and division organization.

Psychological Recovery, Artillery, Special Forces, and Respect for the Adversary

---

Who dares, wins.

—Motto of the British Special Air Service Regiment—

Foreword by David Suiter, director of the Pentagon Library

It is a privilege to contribute to this series introducing for the first time the memoir of Egyptian war minister General Mohamed Fawzi to English readers. I have known Commander Aboul-Enein as a frequent patron of the Pentagon Library for six years. Providing support for his important work is one more demonstration of the way the Defense Department's library contributes to the department's mission. Over the years the Pentagon librarians have provided Commander Aboul-Enein Arabic-language works through interlibrary loan, as well as detailed maps and even research that enabled him to refine and craft speeches as he supported various subcabinet-level officials in the Office of the Secretary of Defense for Policy. I have sat and listened to him outline this series, and he clearly realizes the importance of this effort in educating our military decision makers. In this section of his memoir, Fawzi delves deep into the psychological trauma of the 1967 Six-Day War and outlines his thoughts on how to address the problem of binding closely the officer corps to the Egyptian soldier. He also discusses the evolving nature of the Suez Canal front, from sniper and artillery duels to the constant erosion of the IAF's air dominance. I would like to offer my high praise to the U.S. Army magazine, *Infantry*, for publishing this series. Finally, it is my hope that members of the U.S. armed forces fully utilize the Defense Department's libraries, whether they are stationed overseas or in the Pentagon, for their own education or so that they can teach others, as Commander Aboul-Enein does through his books, lectures, and courses at both the National Defense University and National Intelligence University. I speak on behalf of all federal librarians when I say, "How can we help you succeed?"

Introduction: The Psychological Aspects of War

The psychological shock resulting from the 1967 Six-Day War led to the radicalization of Egyptian politics from the Left and the Right and gave an added boost to the emerging Islamist trend, which took advantage of those seeking refuge in religion. This trauma, according to Fawzi, also affected the armed forces, and the war minister intervened to help the upper echelon of Egypt's flag officers get to know the greater army officer corps. Fawzi needed these flag officers to both counsel and foster the corps' military professionalism and to help restore morale for the wider ground forces and SF. Fawzi writes, "The distance between officers and enlisted within the Egyptian armed forces was detrimental to the psychological recovery of the military. This was not lost to the Israelis, who waged a creative information operations [IO] campaign directed at Egyptian soldiers and planted the idea that Egyptian officers cared little for them or their welfare." Egyptian officers who abandoned their units in the Sinai during the 1967 war reinforced this Israeli IO campaign.

Fawzi initiated interviews with Egyptian prisoners of war (POWs) from the 1956 and 1967 conflicts in order to understand the Israeli military ethos. He wrote, "Unlike the Egyptian military, the Israelis spent much time conversing with their troops on warfare, the mission, and previous battles both within the Middle East and globally." Egyptian officers behaved in a nearly opposite manner, as was reinforced by the pre-1967 Egyptian soldiers, who were uneducated but stubborn in their defense of ground. Fawzi pondered the contrasting mottos in infantry tactics: "the Israeli 'Follow Me!' versus the Egyptian, 'Advance!'" He was envious of the high casualty rates of Israeli officers—22 percent.

Fawzi dissects what he considers the Israeli way of war: the use of overwhelming, concentrated firepower and maneuver tactics. He determined that Israel's size and inability to sustain a long attritional conflict made it resort to "lightening," combined-arms warfare. He made connections between the Six-Day War and the Israeli plan of attack in the 1956 Suez War, and he deduced that the necessity of removing Arab air assets was a lesson Israeli generals had learned from the 1956 campaign. His exploration into Israeli tactical command methods led him to incorporate elements of them into the reconstruction of the Egyptian military, the restoration of morale, confidence building in the military generally, and new standards for leadership among Egypt's officers. The War of Attrition would be the baptism of fire that would allow Fawzi to mold and restore Egyptian military self-confidence.

Caring for the Troops

Fawzi actively and visibly listened to commanders' and units' complaints. When a new Soviet AA battery was switched on, he held an event to restore courage and address the Egyptian fear of Israeli fighter jets. Fawzi ordered administrative and support personnel to train as soldiers first, and for the first time many of them underwent extensive weapons training on par with the infantry to enable them to defend their posts and restore mutual confidence between combat troops and logistical military units. He took an interest in the quality of field rations, the cleanliness of the field kitchens, and water quality, and he urged his officers to show the same concern. Over time the Egyptian officers followed Fawzi's example. In the U.S. military, when we are deployed in the field, we take the understanding and bonds between officers and troops for granted; we instinctively line up for chow from junior to senior. This basic care for the soldier, which is part of the American and Israeli military ethos, was only rediscovered in Egyptian arms after 1967.

In March 1968 Fawzi orchestrated a field visit by Nasser. Among the war minister's ulterior motives was to "get the Egyptian leader to help solve some of the larger social problems of the armed forces, such as pay, disability benefits, death gratuities, and health care for the soldiers and their families." Nasser held an important meeting that year on Egypt's new warfare doctrine. He said that there could be no retreat after what occurred in 1967 and that Egypt could restore national dignity and the lost Sinai Peninsula only through warfare. Nasser then reinforced Fawzi's efforts, ending the meeting by urging field commanders to take a personal interest in the care, feeding, and social welfare of the personnel under their charge. Nasser said that centralization was a danger that had caused the Egyptian military many problems. Officers had to address this issue despite their traditions. Soldiers had to be allowed to speak honestly, and officers had to take into consideration their soldiers' complaints.

Nasser formed, for the first time in Egyptian military history, a committee to study psychological warfare and ways to counter it. According to Fawzi, "It is an enemy [Israeli] goal to turn the entire country against us and against the armed forces in order to create conditions favorable for . . . the preservation of the status quo. . . . The Americans will not furnish an acceptable solution, and America only accepts [that is, advocates Egypt's] surrender." Nasser and his generals understood that no progress could be made with the Israelis until they achieved a battlefield victory, even if only a partial victory.

Fawzi pondered how "to fuse three-quarters of a million men under arms who came from every region of the Egyptian Republic into a machine that achieved unity of goal while gradually raising military morale." The Egyptian war minister made field commanders responsible for morale and used the media, both civilian and military, to report on the accomplishment of units and individual soldiers in the Canal Zone or in field exercises. Fawzi made sure that every unit had an office that focused on morale. He writes, "The Egyptian military began to seriously take into consideration the psychological factors of the individual soldier and thereby the unit."

Starting in 1969, Egyptian SAMs downed Israeli Phantoms and Skyhawks. These successes were used to increase troop morale, and soldiers began to see the extent to which the national leadership acquired and deployed technology designed to protect them. This increased the troops' confidence and focus on training. Fawzi walked around commands, visited units, and whenever possible attended award ceremonies; occasionally he would personally award battlefield commendations. Through his example, Fawzi encouraged officers to see and to be seen among the troops. He writes, "The lifting of morale and self-confidence to reinstill a fighting spirit is the most important aspect of the War of Attrition."

Among Fawzi's first orders of business as war minister was the collection of retreating units and their reorganization into fighting units. He did not know if the Israeli advance would go beyond the Sinai and into Egypt proper, so it was vital to reinforce the Canal Zone with every soldier capable of fielding a weapon. Fawzi writes that standing between the Israeli armored advance and cities on the west side of the canal—and therefore on the road to Cairo—were the canal itself and a demoralized force equipped with small arms. The war minister broke into stockpiles and scraped together artillery, mortars, and heavy guns, closing the window of vulnerability with each passing hour. As the Israelis paused along the canal's east bank, Fawzi organized the chaos of the Egyptian retreat into standing formations and a defensive line extending 170 kilometers and built around two infantry divisions. Within weeks of the conclusion of the Six-Day War, Fawzi had signed orders allowing for fifteen-day reconnaissance missions into the Sinai. These missions continued throughout the War of Attrition and even up to the Yom Kippur War. Fawzi wanted to have the latest intelligence on Israeli deployments, routines, rounds, patrols, and perimeters.

The Artillery War

In November 1967 Fawzi turned his attention to the artillery shelling of Israeli positions on the canal and then coupled this shelling with SF harassment of Israeli armored convoys, static logistical depots, and convoys two to five kilometers east of the canal. The Egyptian artillery developed a response to Israeli counterartillery strikes. The response consisted of three minutes of concentrated fire, dismantling of the weapons, and then movement to another firing position. This movement gave the impression that the Egyptians had more artillery than actually deployed in 1967 and 1968 and saved Egyptian heavy guns from Israeli countershelling. Fawzi calculates, "An Egyptian artillery division had thirty-six howitzers. If trained well, they could fire ten rounds in three minutes. Each round had a minimum of five kilograms of high explosives [HE]; this meant a concentrated fire of five tons in three minutes per artillery division." By the end of 1969, Fawzi had two thousand artillery pieces concentrated along the Suez Canal. This number includes reserve artillery units concentrated no more than fifty kilometers behind the canal's west bank. The Egyptians also fielded 130- and 150-mm multiple-launch rocket systems (MLRSs). Fawzi thought the construction of the Bar-Lev line was a response to this artillery concentration. He estimates, "In 1968 the Israelis suffered twelve hundred casualties along the canal."

However, the war minister faced another problem: Egyptian forces consumed tons of ordnance per month that had to be not only replaced but also brought forward to the front. This problem was taken on by General Abdel-Moneim Riad, who was killed in an active artillery duel while inspecting artillery positions along the Canal Zone on March 9, 1969. An Israeli round scored a direct hit inside his foxhole.

The War of Attrition allowed for adjustments in the way artillery shells were stored and distributed by Egyptian combat forces. Fawzi established a system of one artillery depot per artillery division along the canal. The Israelis did not remain static in response to Egyptian fire but lobbed shells onto the cities of Suez and Port Tawfik, causing military and civilian casualties. Israelis also deployed their air force deep inside Egypt. Fawzi obsessed about these Israeli countermeasures, and it became his mission to knock down this wall of fear. Egyptian SF reconnoitered locations of Israeli artillery shelling Egyptian cities along the canal, and over time these reconnaissance teams became larger and incorporated infantry, artillery, and engineers who assessed Israeli positions three to five kilometers east of the canal. Egyptian artillery destroyed an Israeli convoy of nine tanks, two jeeps, and an MLRS and caused three hundred casualties as a direct result of Egyptian reconnaissance that called accurate strikes onto Israeli positions. Fawzi used Egyptian artillery successes coupled with SF successes to slowly shatter the myth of Israeli invincibility established in 1948 and reaffirmed with spectacular success in 1967.

The Sniper Wars

The General Staff planned, trained, and deployed snipers along the Canal Zone and inserted them deep in the Sinai. The snipers' mission was to instill fear in Israeli bases, trenches, and lines of communications. The Egyptians were gratified when signs in Hebrew warning of snipers appeared along the canal and took this to be a measure of tactical success. Whether using artillery, ground rockets, or snipers, the objective was to make movement along the Canal Zone and the Sinai dangerous for Israeli combat units. Although Fawzi never mentions the famous World War II Soviet sniper Vasily Zaytsev (1915–1991), who scored 242 kills, he does write that he "used the exploits of Egyptian snipers to raise morale," and he likely discussed Zaytsev's impact in the Battle of Stalingrad with his Soviet advisers.

Assessing the Big Picture

Among the priorities of training was crossing the canal en masse. Fawzi writes, "The obsession with this single tactical problem began as early as 1968, and I viewed the mere exercises in crossing the canal as psychologically important for Egyptian ground forces. It also demonstrated the seriousness of placing the nation on a war footing, when Egypt's civilian leaders came to view these exercises. On March 10, 1968, Nasser visited the front to raise morale, and his itinerary included a visit to the Algerian infantry contingent deployed along the canal."

Fawzi writes of "an overall evolving combat canal zone, in which howitzers, rockets, and snipers continued harassing fire while combat engineers simultaneously prepared the combat area. The gradual increase in SAM systems was not only part of an elaborate program to deny Israeli overflight of the Canal Zone, but an integral part of morale building and knocking down the wall of fear using a wall of AA systems from guns to missiles reaching low, middle, and high altitude." The war minister developed the active defensive line gradually, adding artillery operations, reconnaissance missions, reconnaissance in force, special operations raids, sniper operations, crossing and infantry raiding force, and night raids. These additions not only increased Egyptian capabilities and necessitated coordination but also tested Israeli defenses and responses. Egyptian reconnaissance teams gradually came to understand Israeli fire plans and kill zones and were sent to Egypt's military training centers to share their experiences and help develop countermeasures to Israel's order of battle in the Sinai.

Israel's strong defenses at Deversoir at the northern end of the Great Bitter Lake became the template on which Fawzi based the perfect reconnaissance. By authorizing several reconnaissance missions starting in October 1968, he began over time to gain a picture of Israel's logistics, watch routine, and perimeter security for that segment of the Bar-Lev line. Fawzi took a personal interest in Egyptian raid missions on Israeli positions. He cites a raid on Tel Salom for which he reviewed ingress and egress plans, cover fire from heavy machine guns, mortars, and artillery, pushing the artillery, infantry, and SF to integrate their plans for the raid. Egyptians created mock-ups of the Israeli defensive position along brackish tributaries of the canal near Ismailiyah to rehearse offensive raids. The Israelis responded to successful Egyptian raids with mass sweeps of artillery fire and overlapping defensive trenches to reinforce the areas that were raided.

Plan 200 was Fawzi's obsession during this period. He consulted it daily, looking for ways to update it according to reconnaissance on Israeli capabilities and the increasing Egyptian capabilities provided by personnel training and Soviet technology. Fawzi integrated aspects of Plan 200 into military exercises drawn up for the 2nd and 3rd Field Armies and their supporting units.

Fawzi's memoir shows his obsession with Israeli killed and captured. He considered June 1969 in particular a good month for Israeli losses. The war minister issued directives ordering that Israeli troops from the Sinai be captured or, if capture was not an option, killed. He used this directive to integrate Egypt's SF and military intelligence for penetration deep behind Israeli lines. In October 1969 Egyptians captured their first Israeli officer, and this officer had in his possession military documents. The 117th Egyptian Reconnaissance Division's five-man team captured an Israeli soldier whose jeep struck an antipersonnel mine, and an Egyptian unit behind Israeli lines captured another injured soldier wandering the Sinai. These prisoners were smuggled out of the Sinai to Egypt, and they became the first Israeli POWs held by Egypt since the 1948 Arab-Israeli conflict. Fawzi read their debriefings with great care in his effort to cultivate empathy, not sympathy, for Israeli military methods.

Hebrew University professor Raphael Israeli refers to Fawzi as the "Father of Plan 200" and highlights the controversy among Fawzi, General Mohammed Sadeq (who would eventually replace Fawzi as war minister in 1971), and Sadat over the sections of the Egyptian defenses that were six feet high and offered no protection against Israeli defenses that were fifty feet in height. Fawzi had specified that the Egyptians should have two feet for every foot of Israeli defenses to give them fire dominance and superior points of observation.[1] Sadat disparaged Fawzi as perpetuating the Soviet plan and, in turn, Egyptian dependence on Soviet arms and spare parts. He wanted the war minister instead to focus on cultivating Egypt's manufacturing potential.[2] This accusation is unfair, as Fawzi had not only to absorb Soviet hardware but to educate his soldiers and officers in its use, all while developing offensive tactics against the Israelis. Developing Egypt's arms manufacturing took a backseat given the flood of Soviet hardware pouring into Egypt in the aftermath of the Six-Day War. What Fawzi could not appreciate was President Sadat's strategy to gradually decouple Egypt from the Soviet Union, while still gaining Soviet arms and military advice.

Battle of Lissan Port Tawfik

Lissan, or "lip of," Port Tawfik became a prized piece of combat real estate for the Egyptian General Staff, according to Fawzi. From that point Israeli artillery shelled refineries south of the city of Suez and Adabiyah Port. Fawzi tasked the 3rd Field Army with neutralizing Israeli artillery in this sector and retaking Lissan Port Tawfik. The 3rd Army designated the 43rd Saaqa Battalion for the mission, and a plan was designed to take the area in a surprise assault laying heavy suppressive fire. On the night of June 9–10, 1969, the entire battalion (thirteen hundred men) crossed into Lissan Port Tawfik without being detected and established a beachhead. The Israelis had a mixture of troops in the narrow strip of land that numbered no more than two hundred men. Fawzi does not provide any tactical details, except to say that the Israelis were overwhelmed and had to yield the ground.

Battle of Jazeera al-Khadra (Green Isle)

In July 1969 the Israelis responded to the Battle of Lissan Port Tawfik, according to Fawzi, by attempting to dislodge an Egyptian AA company on Jazeera al-Khadra, south of Lissan Port Tawfik. The Israeli company-size force was repulsed by heavy artillery fire, and the Egyptian commander on Jazeera al-Khadra was commended for calling in the concentrated and close artillery fire that was the decisive factor in denying the Israelis this ground.

From July 20 to 28, 1969, Israeli jet fighters pounded Egyptian positions along the Suez Canal; this had a slight effect on morale among Egyptian troops.

Operation Zafaraniyah

A company of Israeli troops reinforced with amphibious assault vehicles took the Zafaraniyah sector, an area one hundred kilometers south of Suez overlooking the Gulf of Suez on the Egyptian side in September 1969. The area had been guarded by a handful of Egyptian border guards. The Israeli takeover posed a tactical problem as it threatened the road from the city of Ghardaga and Suez. Fawzi writes, "Regrettably, the area was not a priority for Egyptian ground forces, and reinforcements had to be sent from Cairo to retake the area." An infantry division reinforced with a mechanized company and MiG-17s was placed on alert.

In dealing with the Zafaraniyah situation, Fawzi had an argument with his chief of operations, General Ahmed Ismail. Nasser had ordered Ismail through Fawzi to head toward Zafaraniyah and make plans for retaking the area. A few hours after delivering Nasser's order, Fawzi found Ismail in his office in Cairo directing operations. The operations chief had dispatched the Soviet adviser to Zafaraniyah to assess the situation. Fawzi tersely told Ismail, "The Soviet adviser executes my orders, and the chief of operations prefers to remain in his office. I shall await the Soviet adviser with you!" Fawzi, upon receiving the update from the Soviet officer, updated Nasser and relieved Ahmed Ismail of duty.

In his memoir Fawzi does not discuss how the Egyptians removed the Israeli company from Zafaraniyah or how they closed the gap in Egyptian defenses in that sector. However, this operation seems to have been significant for both Fawzi and Nasser, as described in his memoir, as it represented the loss of additional Egyptian territory after the 1967 Six-Day War. Fawzi writes with a tone of frustration that can be captured only by reading the original Arabic.

Radar Operations along the Gulf of Suez

The night of December 23–24, 1969, the Israelis conducted a commando raid in Ras Gharib, destroying a P-12 radar that was providing warning coverage in the Gulf of Suez. The Israeli raiders carried away some of the electronics, and the Egyptian officers, having left their post unguarded, were held responsible for the damage and lost equipment. Fawzi notes, "The P-12 was an old radar, and the Soviets did not lose out in the expropriation of the technology by the commandos." The P-12 "Yenisei," known by NATO as "Spoon Rest," was a two-dimensional very high frequency (VHF) radar.

The raid, known by the Israelis as Operation Rooster-53, was a combined operation using the Nahal Brigade's 50th Battalion, the special reconnaissance paratroop unit Sayeret Tzanchanim, and the IAF. The Israelis, concerned about their eroding aerial superiority, attempted to acquire radar units intact in order to reverse engineer them and develop countermeasures. Two CH-53 heavy lift helicopters made away with radar, caravans, and antennae, weighing several tons.[3]

According to the Israeli account, provided in Stacey Perman's *Spies, Inc.*, the raid was conducted at 2:00 a.m. on December 27, not the night of December 23–24, as reported by Fawzi. Fawzi may have been recalling dates from memory. Also, his comment that the P-12 was old technology may have been a means of saving face. However, the radar was fielded by the Soviets in 1956 and was used not only in Egypt but in the Vietnam conflict. Understanding the engineering of the P-12 would have been useful to American air forces serving in Vietnam.

Operation South Balah Island

The 2nd Field Army Command, along with the 2nd Infantry Group, planned a company-level raid of approximately two hundred men along the Israeli-controlled reinforced trenches at South Balah Island, east of Qantarah and north of Suez, off the coast of Suez. In the closing weeks of 1969, a company was sent to challenge Israeli forces in this sector. Fawzi writes,

> Egyptian commanders began to understand for the first time the utility of task-organized units, creating a reinforced company combining mechanized infantry with armor and leaving behind robust occupying forces as the mobile-reinforced company continued to push the Israelis off South Balah Island. . . . The taking of this sector represented the first time the Egyptian flag was raised in occupied Sinai since the 1967 war. The Israelis attempted to retake the area but were met with a larger Egyptian force now quickly reinforced with artillery, and saturation fire degraded their ability to gain a foothold on South Balah Island.[4]

Another important aspect of this operation, according to Fawzi, was that this was the first time Egyptian forces crossed the canal in force under hostile fire. Revisiting this operation time and again was the function of Egyptian military planners in the lead-up to the 1973 war.

Fawzi's Opponent

In April 1970 the Israelis appointed General Ariel Sharon (d. 2014) commander of Israeli forces on the Sinai front. Fawzi keenly studied Sharon, reading everything he could about his opponent. He writes of "reading about Sharon's development as a commander, his patterns of taking risks, his special forces as well as commando experience." Fawzi told the Egyptian General Staff to brace for increases in Israeli commando raids and air strikes behind Egyptian defensive lines. Sharon led Egyptian military planners to reexamine the map; they sensed that Sharon would conduct air strikes on the city of Suez as a diversion to infiltrate Israeli commandos in other defended areas, like Qantarah, Port Said, or the Port Said to Dumyat Road. Fawzi ordered the 2nd Field Army commander, General Abdel-Moneim Khalil, and the 3rd Field Army commander, General Mohammed Fahaiq Bourini, to discuss countermeasures, offensive operations, and increases in the tempo of canal crossings by Egyptian combat forces in light of Sharon's appointment. The generals discussed the likelihood that Sharon would attempt to erode Egypt's SAM and AA sites and decided that overlapping AA sites would be built to provide coverage for Egyptian forces extending eight kilometers behind the Israeli side of the canal. Egyptians stepped up reconnaissance, trying to detect changes in routine, maneuver, response methods, staging areas, logistics, and concentrations of Israeli forces after the appointment of Sharon.

Fawzi writes, "This reassessment based on the appointment of General Sharon led Egypt to understand the utility of gradual but constant escalation of hostile action along the canal." The war minister had noticed that the Israelis were settling into a routine as the Egyptians began to escalate from company- to battalion-level raids. This escalation was coupled with platoon raids along the canal to keep Israelis guessing as to the point of concentration of battalion-level forces. In 1970 Fawzi monitored the integration of air defense systems with battalion-size crossings to negate Israel's air superiority. That year Fawzi and his military planners conceived of the massive air defense system that in 1973 provided cover for 80,000 Egyptian troops swarming the Bar-Lev line in the opening gambit of the Yom Kippur War.

Conclusion

One of Nasser's last meetings with his generals before his death in September 1970 was a series of three discussions from January 6 to 10 with the General Staff. The next chapter will detail the January 1970 conference Nasser held with his generals, reassessing Egyptian military capabilities vis-à-vis the Israelis. The discussion was the most candid Egyptian generals had had with their leader about what could and could not be done at that juncture and what would be needed to solve operational and tactical problems. Fawzi's recollection of the discussions offers insight into sophisticated Arab military thinking that is crucial for twenty-first-century war planning.

Chapter Twelve

Nasser's Conferences with His General Staff

I have given instructions that I be informed every time one of our
soldiers is killed, even if it is the middle of the night.
When President Nasser leaves instructions
that he is to be awakened in the middle of the night if an
Egyptian soldier is killed, there will be peace.
—GOLDA MEIR—

Foreword by Joseph J. Collins, professor of national security strategy,
National War College, and former deputy assistant secretary of defense
for stability operations

It gives me great pleasure to be among those who are introducing Commander Aboul-Enein's effort to make the memoir of General Mohamed Fawzi accessible to English-speaking readers. During my tenure as deputy assistant secretary of defense from 2001 to 2004, my staff and I had to concern ourselves with the stabilization of countries using the assets and capabilities of the Department of Defense; this could range from keeping warlords from breaking agreements to considering overall structural stability options for Afghanistan. There is nothing more vital in the business of national security than cultivating a deep understanding of the region and the culture of an area of strategic interest to the United States. I applaud Commander Aboul-Enein for his long-term effort to introduce America's military planners to Arabic works of military significance. Nothing beats understanding a country from the point of view of its people. War Minister General Fawzi offers not only a fresh way to look at the Arab-Israeli conflict but also insights into the architecture of what would evolve into the 1973 Yom Kippur War. We often make judgments about world leaders based on sound bites or stereotypes; this is not adequate for defending America's interests, for that requires nuance and an understanding of mind-set to enable the prediction of changes in behavior or approaches that could disturb regional stability. The U.S. Army *Infantry Magazine* has done a great service by publishing this series, which is an additional tool that can be used to teach empathy with the region.

Introduction

Nasser conducted three sets of meetings with his General Staff in January 1970. These were candid discussions between the Egyptian leader and his generals. Fawzi's memoir details these discussions, which have never been made available in English. The first meeting opened with this question to Nasser: "We have decided to undertake the War of Attrition for two years now. Are we to continue on this course, or is this [conflict] a double-edged sword?" The question exposes the generals' concern about when the best time to initiate hostilities was and whether the conflict would simply become a cross-canal war of attrition. Nasser replied,

> You must know the importance of issuing and executing joint directives. The enemy's success is built upon a foundation of integrating planning, reconnaissance, and training and their execution of operations on that basis. I now wish to hear your views candidly. The enemy has achieved the goal of delaying the deployment of SAM batteries, and losses owing to Israeli Air Force raids have been high. We must integrate air with ground operations more efficiently. Operations conducted in December 1969 [by Egyptian forces] did not involve the air forces. We must have competent fighter pilots to challenge Israeli air dominance!

According to Nasser, the Israelis were convinced that offensive operations along the canal would begin in the summer of 1970. He said, "They [the Israelis] will prevent our crossing with their air dominance, and we must negate this with air defense missiles and jet fighters. We must strike Israeli air bases in the Sinai first. Israel's first strike will be [Egyptian] air defense systems, and [their] second strike will be air bases." It seems Nasser and his generals reduced the opening phase of hostilities in the Sinai to who would wield the element of surprise and strike first with overwhelming force.

A 1969 report of Israeli sorties targeting Egyptian AA systems, according to Fawzi, said that 3,500 Israeli sorties hit forces involved with Egyptian AA defenses destroying 2 37-mm AA batteries, 10 howitzers, and 19 AA guns. The sorties killed 16 Egyptian officers and 150 soldiers and wounded 19 officers and 299 soldiers. The Egyptians claimed to have downed 5 propeller planes, 2 Mirage jets, 3 F-4 Phantoms, and 1 Mysterie jet, some of which were retrieved from wreckage in Egyptian-controlled territory. Fawzi writes, "In 1969 the Egyptian air force conducted 2,900 sorties, which translated to 170 ground strikes and 70 reconnaissance missions. There were 22 aerial engagements resulting in 23 Egyptian planes lost to 14 Israeli planes. These data were among the many statistics used as a basis of discussions with Nasser."

During Nasser's closing session with his generals, they discussed the president's upcoming visit to Moscow on January 22, 1970. The Egyptian leader intended to press the Soviets to assist in closing the gaps in Egypt's AA missile defenses and shortages of trained pilots.

The Battle of Shadwan Island

Shadwan Island is located in the entrance to the Gulf of Suez and is the largest island off the coast of the port of Ghardaga. In 1970 an Egyptian infantry company reinforced with AA and heavy machine guns was stationed on the island. The company possessed two torpedo boats. On the night of January 22–23, 1970, the Israelis conducted an assault on the southern part of the island using helicopters, fast-attack boats, and a wing of jet fighters. Although the Israelis were unable to dislodge the Egyptian infantry on the island, they succeeded in sinking two Egyptian fast-attack boats. Egyptians in Ghardaga opened up with long-range artillery along the west bank of the Gulf of Suez, and under mass artillery fire, a sizable mechanized infantry force was brought up from Cairo and deployed on the island. The Israelis, monitoring the buildup of forces, withdrew. Fawzi received the casualty report: sixty-two Egyptians killed. The Battle of Shadwan Island led the Egyptian General Staff to plan for retaliatory strikes against the Israeli port of Eilat using a combination of fedayeen, Saaqa, and *dafadaa* (frogmen).

Escalation of Hostilities

In the first months of 1970, Fawzi wanted Egyptian combat forces to operate at a reinforced battalion level along the canal. Until this time operations had been conducted at the company level. The war minister advocated for two simultaneous battalion-size assaults, and he discussed with his field commanders the right mix of armor, rocket-propelled grenade (RPG) tank-killing teams made up of SF, and engineers as part of this task-oriented battalion. The first successful operation (Shaheer) on February 15, 1970, was conducted, according to Fawzi, against Israeli defensive positions on Balah Island, five kilometers from Qantarah. The objective was to capture Israeli soldiers, but the battalion-size force overwhelmed the Israelis. The defensive area they had constructed north of Balah Island was destroyed, along with ammo stores, and the Egyptians captured their weapons, including an Israeli 81-mm howitzer. The Israelis withdrew their ground forces and responded with air strikes. Fawzi writes that the Egyptian military leaders thought "that the Israelis would counterstrike with air assets, and while good, initial offensive operations could not hold ground owing to disadvantage in numbers." The General Staff and field armies began to realize their proficiency in combined ground operations and integrated combat arms, according to Fawzi.

May Day Operations

On May 1, 1970 (May Day), Egyptians celebrated International Labor Day. Nasser planned to send a message to President Richard Nixon that day through the airwaves. Just as he had done in 1956, with a radio address that triggered the nationalization of the Suez Canal, Nasser planned to commence military operations during his May Day speech and coordinated these plans with Fawzi. The 2nd Field Army pushed one reinforced battalion to swarm an Israeli position north of Qantarah. Three SF teams were dispatched to lay mines and conduct ambushes five kilometers past the Israeli side of the canal. Their mission was to delay an Israeli response team. The Egyptian battalion remained north of the Qantarah sector the entire day (May 1–2) before withdrawing and taking two Israeli POWs with them.

May 30, 1970

What is interesting is Fawzi's obsession with taking Israeli POWs. He writes that Egyptian forces initially met with little success at capturing Israeli troops, but after collecting reconnaissance along the entire front, small teams were sent to lay ambushes for Israeli patrols. Throughout 1970 Egyptians monitored Israeli activities and troop concentrations, searching for lightly reinforced areas. Fawzi noted "a pattern of Israeli convoys being protected by two Mirage fighters to deter Egyptian [ground] swarming attacks."

On May 30 two ambushes were conducted. The first ambush was on Kilometer 30 (KM-30) North of the Qantarah–Port Said Road and used an eight-man SF team from the 83rd Saaqa Battalion. The second ambush was planned for Kilometer 8 (KM-8) South of Ras el-Aish Road and conducted by a twenty-one-man team from the 135th Infantry Division based in Port Said. The Israeli convoy on KM-30 was composed of four tanks and four half-ton trucks. They were ambushed on Kilometer 14 toward Port Said, with one prisoner taken and a few men wounded or killed. The prisoner was taken across the canal to Port Said, and within twenty-four hours he was in Cairo. Fawzi does not mention the results of the second ambush, so it must be concluded that the infantry division failed to take prisoners or was repulsed by the Israelis.

Fawzi deems these ambushes an important milestone in that they confirmed for him that the Egyptian soldier, when trained, cared for, and led, is capable. The Israelis responded to the ambushes with ferocious aerial strikes on June 17, 1970, using 1,000-pound bombs and napalm from Port Said to Qantarah. Egyptian 100-mm AA guns received a concentrated pounding with 80 bombs of between 1,000 and 500 pounds. The result was 1 killed Egyptian. South Balah Island received 4 hours of Israeli aerial pounding with the loss of 1 wounded Egyptian soldier. Twelve IAF fighters were damaged or downed. The Egyptian government newspaper, *al-Ahram*, ran photos of the area to stir up local and Arab outrage.

Fawzi writes of

> how through trial and error with every Israeli air strike, a defensive combination of antiair guns and missiles were deployed and moved by engineers and troops. The army and Air Defense Forces learned to cooperate, as they slowly acquired proficiency to lay concentrated antiair fire in ground combat areas the Israelis were likely to strike. . . . The American-produced [Douglas] Skyhawk F-4 Phantom II posed the most serious challenge to Egyptian air defenses. They would be countered using antiair guns and SAMs placed along predicted approaches to the narrow Suez Canal. The Egyptians produced kill zones for Israeli war planes.

Fawzi visited an Egyptian AA gun crew burned in place, a statue of ash, while manning their weapons. He describes them as beautiful martyrs.

Among the combinations that showed promise was the 100-mm and 37-mm AA guns coupled with the SA-2 to counter Israeli CAS, and in 1970, in response Israeli air strikes deep inside Egypt, the Soviets provided the more sophisticated SA-3. Egyptian air defense planners tracked Israeli reactions to locks from SA missile guidance systems and found that as soon as the Egyptians got a lock, the IAF pilot reacted by pulling upward for more altitude. This led the Egyptians to experiment with deploying AA defenses in a way that would ensure the highest probability of successful strikes and preferably give the Israeli pilot no choice but to crash on the Egyptian side of the canal.

The EAF Offensive

Two squadrons of MiG-17s were deployed against Umm Hasheeb (also called Khaseeb), an Israeli forward command center in the Sinai, and against a concentration of armor around the Bar-Lev line. Fawzi considers this operation "the start of the development of Egyptian aerial tactics." The MiG-17s would be protected by a squadron of the more advanced MiG-21s, with the MiG-17s being the strike force and the MiG-21 the shielding force against Israeli interceptors. From July 1969 to the conclusion of the War of Attrition in August 1970, Fawzi monitored the increasing tenacity of Egyptian aerial strikes, conducted ever deeper in Israeli-occupied Sinai. The Egyptian squadron commanders and their pilots were eager to conduct deeper strikes against Israeli positions in the Sinai, but Fawzi needed to conserve the EAF strike capability and had them contain their excitement. The war minister writes that the EAF strike capacity had not reached its full potential for a full-scale breach of Israel's canal defenses and the occupation of the Canal Zone and portions of the Sinai. Fawzi and the General Staff wanted Egyptian air strikes not only to demonstrate air capabilities but also to combine with mass AA systems to neutralize Israel's air strike qualitative edge.

On September 9, 1969, a hundred jet fighters organized into offensive strike MiG-17s, with MiG-21s as a shielding force, attacked Rumana, Mitla, and Heytan. This was the first time the EAF and EADF had coordinated that many planes in an assault, and the strike demonstrated increasing capabilities to the Israelis. Captured Israeli POWs provided information of an impending attack on October 23, 1969, allowing a wing of MiG-21s to prevent the IAF strike force from attacking an Egyptian command center in Deversoir. What pleased Fawzi, as war minister, was the coordination between the EAF, EADF, and military intelligence. Unfortunately, Egyptian NCOs and officer teams that coordinated and vectored air strikes had little understanding of Egyptian and Israeli jet fighter capabilities. Fawzi planted pilots who were not approved to fly for various administrative reasons on these ground teams. Pilot-to-pilot communications between air and ground produced a dramatic improvement in CAS.

Fawzi took great interest in Israeli radar and air defense systems that provided early warning of mass Egyptian MiG formations. He discussed with the EAF and EADF chiefs how to achieve aerial surprise and how long Egyptian fighters could loiter before an Israeli response. They discussed sending four Egyptian MiG-21s as bait to entice the Israelis to send up their fighters. The Israelis would then be led to a swarm of MiGs or directly into AA kill zones along the canal. Fawzi preferred ground-to-air vectoring to target over aerial vectoring. He does not say why. Fawzi does highlight that Soviet advisers provided detailed lessons to Egyptian pilots on refining aerial tactics. Dogfights were frequently used as a training tool, and Fawzi specifically mentions one that occurred on February 26, 1970, involving sixteen Egyptian MiG-21s.

Aerial duels would also have geopolitical repercussions, and Nasser as well as Fawzi crafted a narrative to undermine the pride Israel had in its air force. Domestically, Nasser used aerial duels to raise popular morale and to demonstrate to the Soviets that Egypt was worthy of its most advanced military hardware. Whenever an Israeli aircraft was downed, both Nasser and Fawzi worked on press announcements, and Fawzi insisted that no announcement be made unless either an Israeli pilot was shown or wreckage was produced. Gone were the wild exaggerations of the 1967 Six-Day War. They were replaced with aerial footage of Israeli casualties. Fawzi writes that Israeli casualties were actually higher than what was reported and that international and Israeli media were monitored to deduce as accurately as possible the results of Egyptian military engagements.

The northern coast of the Sinai contained concentrations of Israeli military units for training, logistics, communications, and even recreation. Throughout October 1969 Fawzi authorized a series of air strikes in this sector. Egyptian MiG-17s took only minutes to approach targets along the northern Sinai (also known as the coastal road), strike, and withdraw. Israeli sorties that gave chase were lured into designated AA kill zones south of Port Said. Reading reports of the Six-Day War, Fawzi found that some Egyptian aircraft were destroyed by friendly fire, and he set about exploring identification friend or foe (IFF) systems and training on those systems with Soviet advisers.

October 1969 saw the introduction of the Ilyushin-28 (IL-28) bomber. Two IL-28s, escorted by four MiG-21s, were sent to target areas east of Rumana. Within thirty minutes, four MiG-17s were sent to bomb the same area again, impeding Israeli rescue efforts. Throughout the War of Attrition, the EAF would strike with a small contingent of MiGs protected by a larger contingent of MiGs. On October 26, 1969, Egypt began to conduct varying attacks on Israeli Hawk AA missile sites, probing the capabilities of the U.S.-made system. In one attack Egyptian jet fighters destroyed two Hawk sites, and a second sortie returned to lay down fire on the surviving crew. This operation cost one Egyptian plane, brought down by Israeli AA gunfire.

Fawzi writes, "One experienced squadron leader was paired with three proficient pilots on most missions, so they could acquire actual combat experience in the air." By 1970 the EAF was conducting deeper strikes in the Sinai and planned a strike a hundred kilometers east of the Canal Zone with MiG-21 formations. The Israelis responded with deep strikes of their own, created an aerial map of Egyptian radar coverage and AA systems, and found gaps that enabled their jet fighters ingress and egress to Egyptian air space. Egyptians began assessing these aerial gaps and found, for instance, a large one south of the city of Suez for Israeli fighters flying at low altitude. Israelis used two-plane surgical hit teams, in stark contrast to Egypt's swarm aerial tactics. Israel conducted several high-profile attacks on Egypt, and Fawzi lists them as follows:

January 1970
> Tel el Kibir
> Inchass-Cairo Air Base
> Dahshour
> Maʾadi-Cairo

February 1970
> Abu Zabal Factory (over seventy workers killed)
> Cairo East Air Base

April 1970
> Bahr al-Baqar School (thirty-one students killed)

The introduction of SA-3 missiles in quantity began to close gaps in Egypt's aerial defenses. However, Israeli strikes on April 14 and 15 delivered a thousand tons per day of ordnance on Egyptian targets. Fawzi writes, "The introduction of the U.S. F-4 Phantom in the Israeli inventory was noted in September 1969 when it was noticed that [Egypt's] AA systems and radars experienced jamming." The war minister discussed the plans for an Egyptian retaliation against Israel's deep air strikes. Between April 18 and 28, 1970, the Egyptian Air Staff planned and conducted six air strikes targeting logistical and communications lines, troop and armor concentrations, radars, Hawk sites, and command centers. MiG-21s acted as shields, providing protective cover, and engaged Israeli interceptors. Fawzi issued an order to his Air Staff that "the Umm Hasheeb forward command center be targeted multiple times and be given priority" because this command center monitored Egyptian air and defense activity on the Egyptian side of the canal. Antennae, electronic surveillance, and signals intelligence collection conducted by the Israelis at Umm Hasheeb concerned Fawzi. He writes that the command center "provided Israelis sophisticated early electronic intelligence [ELINT] of Egyptian radars and gathered communication intelligence [COMINT]." The Egyptian-controlled heights overlooking Umm Hasheeb provided electronic coverage on a good section of the Canal Zone, and the Egyptians connected the EW capabilities of these heights with a command center as well as three Egyptian airstrips to scramble MiG fighters. The War of Attrition was entering the EW phase, during which the rudiments of what would become information dominance would evolve.

Conclusion

The next chapter will continue to discuss Fawzi's insights into the evolution of the EAF and transitions to the section of his memoir on the development of the Egyptian navy. As Fawzi continued to explore modernization, his discussions with the Soviets intensified.

Chapter Thirteen

Egypt's Air Defense Problem and
Egyptian Naval Capabilities

In the future, war will be waged essentially against the unarmed
populations of the cities and great industrial centers.
—GENERAL GIULIO DOUHET, FATHER OF AIR POWER THEORY—

Foreword by S. Diane Lamb, president of the Association of the
Industrial College of the Armed Forces

Having served as manager for the Egypt program in the U.S. State Department's Office of Political-Military Affairs, I know firsthand how technology provides policy options for nations. In addition, the acquisition of weapons systems can alter the strategic balance of the region. As Commander Aboul-Enein reveals, General Mohamed Fawzi and his military staff, in the quest to provide Nasser with strategic options in the aftermath of the 1967 Six-Day War, acquired massive quantities of sophisticated Soviet equipment. This would enable Nasser to order an escalation of tensions along the Suez Canal and necessitate a response from Israel and the United States to address this escalation of weapons systems. This series is unique, for it offers insights that have to date been made unavailable to English-speaking readers, such as the levels of involvement of Soviet field marshal Andrei Grechko (d. 1976) and the Commander of Soviet Air Defenses Pavel Batitsky (d. 1984), as well as the decision by the Soviets to send their forces to Egypt and undertake the largest deployment of Soviet personnel outside the Warsaw Pact since World War II. Commander Aboul-Enein is a colleague whose advice and counsel I valued as we served together from 2004 to 2005. He was director for Egypt and North Africa at the Office of the Secretary of Defense for Policy and I at the Department of State in the Political-Military Bureau. My first encounter with him was in the Pentagon, as we tried to work through and understand steps to be taken in the effort to plan for the modernization requests of the Egyptian armed forces. I found in Commander Aboul-Enein a consummate student steeped in the mind-set of the region, always curious to understand the complexities of the countries for which he was responsible to the secretary of defense. I must confess our discussions, even at a social level, digressed into a debate about such books as Alistair

Horne's classic on the Algerian War of Independence, *A Savage War of Peace*,[1] and the classic 1972 biography of Egyptian president Nasser by Anthony Nutting.[2] Our nation demands a more nuanced understanding of the Middle East, its political history, and its military narrative if we are to derive strategic advantages for the United States in the twenty-first century. As president of the Association of the Industrial College of the Armed Forces, I am privileged to find ways to provide our graduates a continuing education through speakers, seminars, and meetings. If history and progression of the times are important to the growth of an individual, then they are equally important to the development of institutions composed of personnel who need to better understand the global climate to preserve U.S. national interests. Commander Aboul-Enein has graciously supported our programs by giving us insights into the Arab Spring, counterterrorism, and the ever-evolving events in the Middle East. I give the U.S. Army *Infantry Magazine* high praise for making space available for Commander Aboul-Enein's series on Egyptian war minister Fawzi and look forward to the debate this series will produce. I agree with Commander Aboul-Enein that Arabic works of military significance must be a staple in the education of our nation's armed forces and its future leaders.

Introduction

In the last chapter we left General Mohamed Fawzi pondering the closing of aerial defense gaps exploited by Israeli fighter-bombers. The Egyptian armed forces increased and layered their AA defenses, and an electronic surveillance war between Egypt and Israel ensued in and around Umm Hasheeb. The Egyptians would target Umm Hasheeb as part of a massive Egyptian aerial strike on Israeli targets in the Sinai in April 1970. On April 18, 1970, deep strikes inside Egypt by the IAF began to decline. Fawzi credits the degrading of Israeli air-strike capabilities along with blinding the enemy's surveillance capacity to EW efforts at Umm Hasheeb. MiG-21 squadrons were manned inside Egypt by Soviet pilots and acted in a defensive capacity; this also gradually challenged Israel's aerial capabilities inside Egypt. Fawzi discussed with Soviet military advisers the need for advanced electronic jamming equipment. He wanted to place jamming and surveillance stations in areas such as atop Ahtaq Mount, southwest of Suez, and link them with a command and control center. After April 1970 the wall of Egypt's AA defenses became a duel not between planes but between air defense systems. In a 1970 graduation for pilots that included aerial exercises, Fawzi discussed the gradually improving state of Egypt's air force; he was joined by Chief of Air Operations General Ali al-Baghdadi and a young and newly minted chief of staff for the EAF, General Hosni Mubarak.

Upgrading the MiG-21

Fawzi also details discussions with his Air Staff about improving the performance envelope for the MiG-21 when the newly built Y-511 jet engine was installed. He noted with pride, "Egypt was the first country in the Soviet sphere to get this new jet engine, and Moscow armed the Egyptians at this phase to demonstrate the advanced nature of its weapons in combat." Improving Egyptian equipment was a form of deterrence directed not only against the United States but also against NATO; it was also a signal to Washington that no peaceful solution was forthcoming with America's ally Israel. Egypt fielded three MiG-21 wings, complete with pilots and technicians, along with their Soviet technicians and trainers, to provide defense in depth against Israeli air strikes. These forces, representing between sixty and sixty-five jet fighters and twenty-five hundred personnel per wing, came online in March 1970 and were placed under the command and control of the EAF and EADF commanders jointly. Fawzi regrettably does not discuss how this aided or hampered unity of command.

In July 1970 the first equipment for EW arrived from the USSR. This enhanced Egyptian reconnaissance, jamming, and electronic interference. Egypt was now in the game of counterjamming and emitting false signals to mislead Israeli collection efforts. Fawzi takes great pride in being able to close the gap between Egypt's and Israel's EW capabilities. Heavy bombers were stationed in Aswan, as well as in Wadi Sidna in Sudan, along with Soviet technicians and advisers. These two bases also housed the battlefield-range ballistic missiles with a maximum range of 200 kilometers. While Fawzi refers to the missiles as Zina, he likely means the 9M21 or the 9K52 Luna-M missile, the NATO-designated Frog series of missiles.

Balance of Air Power

In July 1970 the Soviets stationed ten heavy bombers equipped with long-range missiles in Egypt. Fawzi writes that these were Soviet assets placed under Egypt's disposal as a second-strike weapon in case of an Israeli first strike. The bombers offered Egypt a retaliatory capability, but only at Moscow's direction. Special bases were designated for these strategic forces and to accommodate follow-on Soviet strategic forces in case of all-out war with Israel and the deployment of American forces to counter Soviet deployments. Fawzi reveals, "Egyptian crews were trained to receive Soviet bombers within six hours of first alert." He does not mention the types of bombers the Soviets sent, but the Egyptians had already fielded the Tu-16 "Badger," so they were likely Tu-95 "Bears," which were available only to Soviet air forces and were not exported at that time to any country, even Warsaw Pact nations.

The Soviets based four MiG-25 reconnaissance jets, which were crewed by Soviets and not part of military sales or grants to Egypt, in Mersa Matruh. Strategically, this merely meant that Fawzi was able to present an offensive air plan to Nasser as part of the overall planning for the liberation of the Sinai. In discussions, Fawzi indicated to Nasser that Egypt had reached parity in air defense vis-à-vis the Israelis. The approximate numerical figures Fawzi discusses are as follows:

	EGYPT	ISRAEL
Jet fighters	740, of which 300 were MiG-21s	500, of which 300 were F-4 Phantoms and A-4 Skyhawks
Heavy bombers	45 Tu-16	0
Helicopters	124	73

EADF Operations

After 1967 the air defense arm was created as the fourth and newest service in the Egyptian armed forces. Jordan was invaluable in supplementing Egypt with Western AA defense equipment that possessed capabilities beyond what the USSR was willing to provide. In addition, Amman provided Cairo with access to a myriad of Western weapons to field and for which to develop countermeasures. Stitched together through trial and error was a combination of the following weapons to close the air defense gaps the Israelis were using. The weapons included in Fawzi's recollection were as follows:

◆ 37-mm line-of-sight AA guns

◆ 57-mm radar-guided AA guns

◆ 100-mm radar-guided AA guns

◆ SA-7 low-altitude AA missiles

◆ Western 40-mm AA guns

◆ SA-1 and SA-2 missile batteries for strategic locations

◆ Man-portable Strela AA missiles for ground formations

Radar Coverage over Egypt

Radar grids were developed gradually from Port Said and Ras Banas to the Nile Valley toward Cairo, Alexandria, and Fayyum. The last major centers to receive radar and early warning coverage were the city of Aswan and its environs, although the Aswan High Dam was a priority owing to fears of sabotage by Israeli commando teams. Fawzi's memoir shows the urgency of creating an overlapping radar grid that would make it more challenging for the Israelis to bomb strategic, operational, and tactical targets in Egypt. In early 1969 the Egyptians experimented with a combination of 37-mm, 57-mm, and 100-mm AA guns along with SA-3 mobile missiles. Fawzi wanted this air defense combination linked to the MiG-21 assets of the EAF. He constantly thought of ways to increase integration between the detection and interception of Israeli jets over Egyptian air space.

The year 1969 was rough for the EAF, as many pilots were lost in Israeli dogfights owing to inadequate training and inexperience. A July 20, 1969, raid by the Israelis along the canal revealed insufficiencies in the EAF's preparedness. These were remedied initially with mobile SA-3 batteries linked to a squadron of MiG-21s that scrambled and swarmed Israeli jet fighters. On September 19, 1969, the IAF targeted two radar sites west of the Suez. The SA battery commander moved his missiles to another location but left behind a skeleton crew and obsolete AA equipment and lit fires to give the feel of an active site. This was the first of what would be many instances of the Russian art of *Maskirovka* (military deception) practiced by the Egyptians. It is disappointing that Fawzi does not mention this technique by name in his memoir, but there is no doubt that its implementation was a result of the mass infusion of Soviet military advisers and consequently their intellectual influence among Egyptian officers. The actions of the battalion commander saved his missiles, and likely a good portion of his troops, from certain destruction.

Another Egyptian tactic was to have two 57-mm AA guns throw up flak on Israeli jets, enticing them to bomb a location. The guns were bait designed to lure the pilots into an SA kill zone. Using this technique, three Israeli jet fighters were downed, and among those hit was the wing commander. Egyptians shared their military tactics with Jordan, and on November 23, 1969, when the Israelis attempted to bomb the Jordanian radar site at Ajloun, it cost them two planes and only minimal damage to the radar site.

In mid-1969 Egypt's air defense system was integrated, overlapped, and brought online with an elaborate web of radars, AA missiles, and AA guns. Now the EADF would have to improve through trial by fire, as the Israelis probed for gaps in Egypt's aerial defenses.

Nasser's Escalation of Tensions along the Canal

In late 1969 the political situation demanded an escalation of military operations against Israel. Nasser conducted a series of meetings, as previously discussed, in

January 1970 with his General Staff. The main focus of the discussions was the Egyptians' ability to escalate tensions along the canal and conduct assaults inside the Sinai. After their three-day meeting, Nasser, Fawzi, and the General Staff decided to undertake small operations using the capabilities of the 2nd and 3rd Field Armies and the SF battalion. There would be a gradual escalation from using only a battalion to combining the infantry battalion with SF units. With each escalation Egyptians took note of Israeli response and reactions. The first months of 1970 saw Israeli raids inside Egypt against economic and military sites. January saw Israeli strikes at Tel el Kibir, Inchass, and Dahshour. In February Helwan and Abu Zabal were struck. At Abu Zabal a strike killed seventy factory workers and demoralized the Egyptian populace. IAF low-altitude strikes were not detected by Egypt's early warning systems. This led the General Staff to scramble to close the gaps and led to the idea of combining SA-3 missile batteries and MiG-21s in a response system. Cairo put pressure on Moscow to fill aerial defense gaps with Soviet personnel. The Egyptians argued that Israeli raids were shaking the people's confidence in their leaders, and this unstable situation was only reinforced by Egypt's inability to strike beyond the Sinai and in Israel proper.

Soviet Field Marshal Pavel Batitsky

In 1969 the Soviets dispatched their commander in chief of air defense, Field Marshal Pavel Batitsky (d. 1984), to discuss with Nasser and Fawzi ways to eliminate inefficiencies in Egypt's air force. Batitsky had been chosen in 1953 to personally execute Stalin's hatchet man and feared People's Commissariat for Internal Affairs (NKVD) chief Lavrentiy Beria after a sentence of death passed by the Supreme Court of the USSR.[3] He was accompanied by a delegation to assess Egyptian air defenses and to come up with plans to counter Israeli air strikes inside Egypt. Nasser charged Batitsky with laying out a comprehensive air defense plan for Egypt, and the two discussed low-altitude penetration by Israeli jet fighters. Batitsky personally visited and inspected Egyptian air defense units.

Batitsky's report was presented to War Minister Fawzi via General Muhammad Ali Fahmy, commander of the EADF. The Soviet marshal agreed that low-altitude gaps needed to be closed. He recommended four B-15 radar units. Fawzi writes of "being aware of the Soviet B-15 radar in September 1969 during my tour of a Soviet destroyer during the combined fleet exercises with Egypt and Syria that year." Batitsky also told Nasser personally that Egypt did not have the right balance of SA-2 and SA-3 AA missiles. Fawzi was tasked with following up with Moscow to obtain additional SA missiles and MiG-21s, along with shipments of the B-15 radars, which would further restrict Israel's ability to penetrate Egyptian air space.

Nasser found the additional matériel to be inadequate and wanted retaliatory strike capabilities against Israel.

Nasser's Secret Visit to Moscow

Despite it being only a month since Anwar Sadat's publicized December 1969 visit to Moscow with a delegation that included War Minister Fawzi and Foreign Minister Mahmoud Riad, Nasser told his inner circle he was traveling to Moscow for secret talks from January 23 to 25, 1970. Fawzi calls the talks "the most important with the Soviet General Staff since the massive Soviet arms lift in the aftermath of the 1967 Six-Day War." Fawzi does not mention that during the three-day talks conducted in December the Egyptians had added the MiG-21J to their wish list to match the capabilities of the F-4D and E Phantom II variants in the Israeli inventory.[4]

Fawzi was shocked when, in discussions with the Politburo, Nasser declared that he would leave the presidency to a successor better suited to dealing with the United States. Fawzi recounts,

> He [Nasser] felt that the Egyptian people were in an impossible predicament of either acceding to Israeli demands or of going to war without adequate air cover. Nasser demanded the deployment of Soviet-manned SA-3 missile units, as well as entire squadrons of Soviet-piloted MiG-21s with two Russian pilots per deployed plane. Finally, he demanded early warning radar systems manned by Soviet military personnel. Nasser said that time was not on Egypt's side and that it would take years to train Egyptians on the new Soviet weapons. He felt that there was nothing to immediately address the superiority of the Israeli Skyhawk and Phantom jet fighters, which attacked inside Egypt with impunity.

Nasser essentially wanted a Soviet defense of Egypt in order to free Egyptian forces to go on the offensive without worrying about deep retaliatory Israeli strikes. In addition, a direct Soviet commitment of forces would be a massive deterrent to Israel and its U.S. sponsors. These were high stakes that could draw the superpowers toward conflict over Egypt and Israel.

Soviet leader Leonid Brezhnev conferred with the Politburo and summoned Nasser and his delegation to the Kremlin on January 25, 1970. Fawzi recalls, "The Soviet leader agreed to most of Nasser's demands. Brezhnev reminded the Egyptians that this would be the largest deployment of Soviet forces outside the Soviet Union since World War II." There is no discussion in Fawzi's memoir of what lessons could be taken away from the last major deployment of Soviet strategic forces in Cuba, less than a decade earlier. Brezhnev then proceeded to read the following points, as recounted by Fawzi:

1. An entire Soviet air defense division would be deployed from the USSR to arrive in Egypt in one month. The division would be under Egyptian command for the explicit defense of Egypt only. The deployment would include Soviet technicians to support this division.

2. Three Soviet air divisions of ninety-five MiG-21s equipped with the latest high-performance turbojet along with technicians, radars, and operators would be sent to Egypt. This air division would also be reinforced by fifty Sukhoi-9 fighters, as well as the upgrade of fifty MiG-21s in Egypt's inventory.

3. Three Soviet B-14 radar groups would be deployed.

4. Egypt would be responsible for preparing for the arrival of these forces and their billeting.

Brezhnev ended by saying that this would be a temporary deployment until sufficient Egyptians were trained.

Nasser returned to Egypt and convened a cabinet meeting to announce the concession he had garnered from the Soviets. He authorized 110 million Egyptian pounds for the defensive and technical upgrades needed to receive the influx of Soviet military personnel. Fawzi coordinated the details with Soviet defense minister Andrei Grechko, including specifics such as timetables for training three Egyptian divisions to man SA-3 missiles. Fawzi and Grechko outlined the rotation schedule of these Egyptian trainees, MiG-21 pilots, and technicians for the support of this newly acquired Soviet war matériel.

Preparing for the Arrival of Division-Size Soviet Formations in Egypt

Fawzi writes of "the urgent need to prepare for the deployment of the Soviets and their equipment. Thirty-two locations for the SA-3 missiles alone needed to be prepared in forty days. General [Engineer] Gamal Muhammad Ali was placed in charge of this massive effort," and Fawzi met with him for daily progress reports and conducted weekly inspections. On the thirty-ninth day, a day ahead of schedule, all barracks, grounds, and infrastructure were in place for the arrival of the Soviets. Moscow issued public warnings to the United States that it would aid Arab countries if raids by Israel continued.

Fawzi notes, "This mass deployment of Soviet forces in Egypt upset the strategic balance for both Israel and the United States. Israeli raids into Egypt declined precipitously in mid-April 1970. An Israeli attempt to attack southwest of the Suez saw its squadron commander wave off his formation after detecting MiG-21 interceptors communicating in Russian." Although Fawzi takes satisfaction in this development, he does not discuss the wider problem of a possible dogfight between Russian and Israeli pilots over Egypt in what would be a tactical altercation that could ignite a war.

Fawzi recalls that the Soviet deployment and equipment arrived under escort by Soviet warships at Alexandria on February 25, 1970. Personnel off-loaded and deployed to Cairo, Alexandria, Janaklis, and Mahala. Concentrations of Soviet troops linked to air defense were taken to Cairo, Kom Awshem, and Bani Suef. MiG-21s began to land at designated airfields at Janaklis, Kom Awshem, and Bani Suef. The Soviets deployed SA-3 batteries and ZSU-23 AA guns from Cairo, working their way eastward toward the Canal Zone. Air defense areas were overlapped by a second and third and so on. Fawzi writes that twenty-three Soviet SA-3 battalions formed the core that was protected by ZSU-23 and portable SA-7 missiles as well as 37- and 100-mm AA guns. He continues,

> Between the Soviet and Egyptian air defense, assets deployed in the Canal Zone alone had eight divisions of troops, with one division dedicated to Port Said alone. All of the divisions would be linked by radar communications, as well as command and control centers. Each SA missile site with two missiles required six hardened shelters for personnel and equipment. Each air defense division had twenty-five missile battalions, which required 150 shelters or bunkers, spread over a distance of a hundred kilometers along the canal. Each battalion covered an aerial space of between thirty and forty kilometers in diameter and had to be overlapped.

Israel's Strike to Undermine Egypt's Closing of Aerial Gaps

The Israelis did not sit idle but instead harassed efforts to deploy these SA-3s by, for instance, using 1,000-pound bombs to destroy an area just completed. The Soviets and the Egyptians used these Israeli probes to test and readjust SA deployments and acquire tactical information from MiG-21s sent up to intercept the Israeli formations. By the spring of 1970, the war had digressed into an Egyptian SA versus Israeli jet fighter duel. What Fawzi's memoir lacks are discussions about the Soviets' sharing the effectiveness of the MiG-21 against the F-4 Phantom in the skies over

Vietnam with the Egyptians and whether even the Egyptians stopped to consider studying aerial tactics and countermeasures based on the ongoing conflict in Southeast Asia, which used the same warplanes that would be engaged in the skies over Sinai. Here are items Fawzi does highlight regarding the air defense picture:

> On May 30, 1970, an Egyptian SA destroyed an Israeli reconnaissance plane with twelve on board. What remained of the plane clearly showed it was imported from the United States. The United States provided Israel with surveillance equipment to probe Soviet advanced equipment being deployed in Egypt, collecting on Soviet reaction times, and the gathering of electronic intelligence. . . .
>
> On May 14–15, 1970, the Israelis conducted a ferocious aerial raid, dropping ten thousand tons of explosives per day, concentrating on areas near Port Said. . . .
>
> During April 18–24, 1970, the Israelis engaged in heavy aerial raids. Eleven were conducted around Suez and Port Tawfik. Nasser visited bombed out cities to raise morale and grieve with families.

While the Israelis continued their raids, Fawzi approved plans to move SA sites by night to create kill zones closer to the canal and also to confuse Israeli reconnaissance of missile sites. In July 1970 the Egyptians, using this tactic, were able to down Phantoms and Skyhawks in an aerial missile ambush. Fawzi writes, "July was the high-water mark for the battle for air supremacy. On July 2 two Israeli jets were downed, on July 3 three Israeli jets were struck, and on July 30 eight Israeli jets were downed and five pilots taken prisoner." In June and July, Fawzi estimates, the Israelis flew five hundred sorties.

Maritime and Naval Operations

While the EAF worked closely with the Soviets to close aerial gaps, Fawzi also had to focus on building up the Egyptian navy. Fawzi states, "Operations along the Mediterranean were more active than those along the Red Sea." The reason for this discrepancy, from his perspective, was "the lack of port facilities along the Red Sea coast," when Fawzi assumed charge as Egypt's war minister. The main ports and maritime repair facilities were Alexandria, Port Said, Abu Qir, and Mersa Matruh, all along the Mediterranean coast. A few destroyers were deployed to the Red Sea area of operation, but they could dock only in the port of Suez, which brought them within range of Israeli artillery fire. Suez was the last port facility to be brought into Egypt's air defense system. Fawzi and his Naval Staff contracted agreements for port facility usage in Pakistani and Indian harbors. The Red Sea Fleet was supported by repairs conducted along the Indian subcontinent. This required the development of the Egyptian ports of Safaga, Ghardaga, and Bianees into areas where warships could be made suitable for transit to India and Pakistan for extensive repair and upgrades. In 1969 the Libyan Revolution provided Egypt with strategic maritime depth when Libya's port of Tobruk was made available for Egyptian warships; that same year a pro-Nasserist coup in Sudan made Port Sudan along the Red Sea available for Egyptian warships and naval planners.

The Egyptian navy did not suffer damage in the Six-Day War owing to the nature of the conflict. However, the navy had not been integrated fully into the General Staff before 1967, which Fawzi considered a serious flaw. For the first time, in late 1967, Egyptian naval officers were designated billets in the General Staff and in the administrative sections of logistical and field commands. Fawzi saw this as part of a wider effort to integrate air, land, sea, and air defense commands to attain maximum unity of effort and ease of communications among the services. Perhaps this is one of the enduring legacies he bequeathed to the Egyptian armed forces.

After securing the navy billets in the General Staff, he made some hard decisions, including the following:

- Taking coastal artillery units from the army's artillery corps and giving them to the navy
- Instituting maritime reconnaissance as a navy mission and furnishing antiair missiles to the navy
- Changing the terms of tens of millions of dollars of Soviet naval vessels and requesting instead that the entire amount, estimated at $65 million [50 million Egyptian pounds], be in the form of reconnaissance equipment and technological upgrades to current warships

Fawzi questioned why Egypt had large destroyers and frigates, as well as antiquated Eastern bloc submarines. He saw smaller fast-attack missile boats, minelayers, maritime artillery, and amphibious capabilities to be more in line with Egypt's naval requirements post-1967. He argued that the time needed to train a full complement of sailors on new classes of heavy warships would be too much given the timetable for offensive action to liberate the Sinai. Fawzi ordered that the focus be on training sailors and officers on board units they were familiar with, which would be technologically upgraded. The Soviets constructed a new dry dock in Alexandria to help with the upgrades and repairs of existing Egyptian warships.

Another post-1967 development was the expansion of frogmen and the cultivation of a maritime SF capability. A naval infantry division was fielded to allow the navy a role in the liberation of the Sinai. Fawzi established the first integrated naval command center that provided real-time monitoring of ships in the Red and Mediterranean Seas. The two major engagements Fawzi writes of are the sinking of the Israeli warship INS *Eilat* on October 21, 1967, and a naval operation in which two Egyptian destroyers shelled Israeli camps for thirty minutes before withdrawing to Port Said. The navy worked with regular Saaqa to harass logistical lines leading to Arish along the coastal road. The sea raids were conducted against Port Nasrani and Abu Rudeis and targeted petroleum refineries. Attempts were made to harass, and possibly cut off, patrolling Israeli ground units along the Sinai coast.

In the overall plan to liberate the Sinai (Plan 200), the navy was given the task of covering the Egyptian 2nd Field Army's northern-most flanks as it crossed the Suez Canal. In addition, plans were made, in conjunction with the army and air force, to land a naval infantry force near Arish to harass Israeli logistical lines. Submarines were used for surveillance and to harass Israeli shipping with a focus on the port of Ashdod. The Egyptian navy rehearsed and drilled for plans to harass navigation in the Gulf of Aqaba to prevent or slow traffic bound for the port of Eilat.

Since the Mediterranean covered a large maritime area, Egypt integrated efforts with the Soviet and Syrian fleets and, in September 1969, attended fleet exercises consisting of naval units from all three countries. Fawzi relied on Admiral Mahmoud Abdel-Rahman to cultivate Egypt's maritime offensive capabilities.

Nasser's Final Visit to Moscow

Nasser traveled with Fawzi, Arab Socialist Union leader Ali Sabry, and Foreign Minister Mahmoud Riad to Moscow on July 29, 1970. Within two months Nasser would die of a heart attack. In this final meeting at the Kremlin, the Egyptian president pressed the Soviets for sophisticated jamming technology, more advanced communications, and the latest EW capability to link the air force to the deployed air defense units along the canal and in strategic bases throughout Egypt. Fawzi writes that after the talks "was the first time a real EW capability was introduced into the Egyptian armed forces."

The Egyptians and the Soviets also discussed areas in which Soviet forces were deployed throughout Egypt, including with SA-6 missiles around the Aswan High Dam. The SA-6 was experimental in 1970, and its chief designer, Ardalion Rastov (d. 2012), used Egypt as a testing ground to improve his designs for the AA missile and its connectivity with guidance and radar systems.[5]

Conclusion: The Rogers Cease-Fire Plan

As the Rogers Plan, imposing a cease-fire on August 8, 1970, was set to be implemented, Fawzi "used every hour to deploy and move forces before the agreement took effect." He adds, "Time itself became a weapon of war." The war minister details his priorities during this period as "moving fourteen SA battalions to the edge of the canal and also laying additional aerial kill zones. The movement of Egyptian forces was completed minutes before the 0100 cease-fire time." The Israelis protested and threatened to strike thirteen of the AA missile battalions if they were not moved fifty kilometers west of the canal. The Egyptians countered that they had been moved before 0100 on August 8 and would not be moved again. Fawzi writes, "The United States provided replacements for the eighteen Israeli Phantoms lost and fifty that were damaged in the summer of 1970 to placate Israel into accepting the Egyptian fait accompli." The SA batteries allowed Egyptian SF to operate with impunity and provided an option for conventional forces to operate on the Israeli side of the canal, should a deployment be necessary. According to Fawzi, the Rogers Plan was good for only three months, after which a state of no war, no peace resumed. The next part of this series will discuss Fawzi's insights on SF operations, as well as preparations of the area of operations for war on the strategic, operational, and tactical levels.

Chapter Fourteen

Egyptian Special Forces Operations

He who knows others is wise. He who knows himself is
enlightened. He who conquers others has physical strength.
He who conquers himself is strong.

—Tao-te Ching—

Foreword by Vance Skarstedt, dean of the College of Strategic Intelligence,
National Intelligence University (2007–2013)

Studying the strategic thinking of military leaders is a critical dimension of intelligence analysis and, if done thoroughly, provides an advantage in policy formulation and planning. General Mohamed Fawzi (1915–2000) served as the Egyptian defense minister and led the rebuilding of the defeated Egyptian army after the Six-Day War of 1967. Until now his memoir has never been made available in the English language, and his perspectives on the challenges of reconstituting the Egyptian armed forces provide deep insights into not only his thinking but the reasoning of the Egyptian General Staff, President Gamal Abdel Nasser, and their Soviet advisers. For example, Fawzi discusses the evolution of the Egyptian special forces and highlights the criticality of military logistics in operational planning. Like the French Revolutionary war leader Lazare Carnot (d. 1823), Fawzi argues that Egyptian military victory required the national mobilization of the Egyptian economy. After a revolution that mobilized the populace in a similar fashion to the revolution that produced Carnot, Egypt now transitions to a new experiment in government and possibly new directions in strategy. The new Egyptian ruling class will no doubt review thinkers like Fawzi and no doubt adopt some of their tenets. Commander Youssef Aboul-Enein, U.S. Navy, a lecturer at the National Intelligence University, has provided an invaluable insight to Arab military thinking. The changes in the Middle East demand a deeper understanding of the region and its intellectual influences, military and otherwise. Efforts such as this by Commander Aboul-Enein will help make that understanding possible.

Introduction

I n this chapter we backtrack a bit to focus on the evolution of Egyptian SF units under President Nasser. We will also discuss the detailed planning required for a nation to prepare for war and specifically Fawzi's and other Egyptian leaders' preparations for the 1973 Yom Kippur War. Saaqa and paratroopers were pre-1967 formations in Egypt's order of battle. After the Six-Day War, airborne assault troops, navy frogmen, and ranger reconnaissance units were added and would be developed to battalion size. War Minister General Mohamed Fawzi cultivated forty-four SF battalions and two paratroop divisions and oversaw the merger and training of Y-8 helicopter squadrons with newly created airborne assault troops. After the 1967 war, Egyptian generals reexamined every aspect of their SF capabilities, looking into types of weapons carried, carrying capacity, days of self-sufficiency, and realistic length for independent operations. Fawzi writes, "Not only should the training of special forces be unique and demanding by conventional army standards, but their morale and psychological outlook must be higher." He felt that SF units needed to have a high level of military readiness; be able to conduct operations on land, at sea, and in the air; and be able to conduct precise and synchronized operations.

Fawzi immediately deployed Egyptian SF units behind Israeli lines inside the Sinai. Initially, these were composed of three- or four-man teams. Over time a doctrine of ten days' self-sufficiency for SF before relief by conventional forces or withdrawal from the target area was developed. These three- or four-man SF reconnaissance teams were deployed throughout the War of Attrition. From 1967 to 1969, Egyptians gradually escalated the size of reconnaissance units and set a target of converting surveillance missions into offensive operations. These operations would begin at the platoon level and over time increase to battalion-size skirmishes. Egyptians began these missions humbly, opening small skirmishes all along the canal. These skirmishes were used as diversions to insert reconnaissance teams deep within the Sinai. Fawzi coordinated with PLO guerrillas in Jordan and Gaza, integrating them into the general Egyptian war plans for the liberation of the Sinai. On the Jordanian front, these plans with the PLO were amended after Arafat's failed takeover of the kingdom and the events of the "Black September" of 1970.

The Egyptian General Staff focused on targeting the Israeli ports of Eilat and Ashdod, with plans to attack petroleum infrastructure, such as pipelines, refineries, and fuel storage. SF-designated targets included lanes of shipping from Ras Muhammad around the Sinai to Eilat and petroleum pipelines in Wadi Araba leading to the port of Ashdod. "Egyptian frogmen attached mines to ships in these ports and left mines inside the port of Ashdod," according to Fawzi. He lists five successful operations in his memoir:

- Petroleum storage, Eilat
- Petroleum tankers, entrance of Eilat
- Port pier and troop transport ship, Eilat
- Pipelines north of Eilat (disrupting fuel supplies for one month)
- Two pipelines at Wadi Araba (synchronized and simultaneous explosions)

The Egyptian navy worked with army SF in sabotage operations at Ulma, Abu Zaneema, and Tur. Egyptians experimented with SF and helicopter insertions and gradually improved this capability in real-time operations. Fawzi recounts an operation on March 8, 1970, "involving the War Ministry and Egypt's General Intelligence Service. The operation involved destroying an offshore drilling platform being constructed by the Israelis that they planned to utilize off the Sinai coast with a Canadian firm. Nasser himself was briefed on the operation. The platform, at the time, was docked off the coast of Abidjan in the Ivory Coast. Using Egyptian SF teams an 'accidental' explosion was arranged." Egypt neither confirmed nor denied the event until the publication of Fawzi's memoir in 1984.

Preparing the Egyptian Nation for War on a Strategic, Operational, and Tactical Level

Fawzi spends a portion of his book stressing the importance of mobilizing what he calls "national capability" in the pursuit of modern war. Fawzi and Nasser instilled the principles of total war after the 1967 Six-Day War, first in Egypt's generals, then officers, then the entire armed forces, and finally the Egyptian people.

As discussed in chapter 10, one of the crucial pieces of legislation Fawzi undertook to restructure the demoralized Egyptian armed forces was Law 4 of 1968 for national defense. This law, for the first time in modern Egyptian political history, linked the political to the military in Egypt and the wider Arab world. Many defensive plans were drawn up by a committee under the leadership of General Abdel-Fatah Abdullah, deputy war minister, and approved by the Council of Ministers. Abdullah oversaw the process whereby generals and field commanders made regular briefings to the cabinet, which then withdrew to decide on budgetary allocations. Fawzi saw his role as developing plans with his officers and then working with the Council of Ministers and Nasser to get those plans approved and funded. He instituted linkages between the military and the civil authority that, after the 1973 Yom Kippur War, would erode; as a result, the Egyptian military regressed into an economy under Hosni Mubarak.

Fawzi also attempted to define the role of the Egyptian war minister, seeing it as educating the nation on what would be needed in terms of effort and sacrifice to liberate the Sinai. He became one of the few war ministers to meet with Egyptian provincial leaders, city mayors, and village chiefs. He even made a major address to the ruling Arab Socialist Union during its 1968 annual party conference. He appealed to party leaders as representatives of the people and searched for ways to bind the people to the project of liberating Israeli-occupied Egyptian territory. Fawzi got "Nasser to agree to the creation and appointment of a deputy defense minister responsible for defense and industrial security to calibrate every ministry to the war effort." He would read daily reports from various military and civilian sectors for the progress of assigned tasks. The prime minister organized monthly meetings to have Fawzi, the civilian ministers, and the generals report on the progress of the war effort.[1]

Nasser coordinated with his prime minister and cabinet on prioritizing strategic programs and working on complex issues to resolve competing demands on the national budget. They searched for ways to provide the Egyptian military with funding without impinging on annual economic growth. Fawzi highlights the dual civilian and military benefits of upgrading Egypt's communication system and establishing roads as a strategic priority. Strategic projects included the construction of new ports in Mersa Matruh, Abu Qir, and Ras Banas. Safaga was constructed as a merchant port to relieve pressure on the port of Suez, and Alexandria's port facilities were upgraded. Fawzi introduced the ministers to General Gamal Muhammad Ali to discuss the costs of military engineering and construction projects. They also discussed the importance of stabilizing the defenses of the canal, as the Egyptian armed forces undertook the offensive phase of liberating the Sinai. These procedures may sound self-evident given America's long tradition of military subordination to civilian authority, but in Egypt Fawzi's effort was extraordinary, particularly in light of his operating in Nasser's single-party system. Nasser's shaken charisma after 1967, coupled with his hold on Egypt's polity and pan-Arab appeal, meant Fawzi had to both link his military to civil authority and garner effort and support from Egypt's population.

The 1967 destruction of petroleum facilities in the Suez by Israeli shelling and air assaults deeply affected Egyptian military planners and caused a wider discussion of securing various military supply chains. Fawzi discusses civil-military plans to disperse Egypt's energy infrastructure. He wanted to ensure food and energy supplies for the armed forces and Egyptian citizens at large. Storage facilities were located far from main rail links and duplicated. Civil defense was organized at the village level and developed gradually as a first response to Israeli commando raids. Fawzi writes, "This required the psychological preparation of the civilian population to never hesitate to kill Israeli troops caught conducting raids inside Egypt."

From Nasser to Mubarak, Egypt has been the victim of single-person and single-party rule. In Nasser's time it was the Arab Socialist Union (ASU), and under Mubarak it was the National Democratic Party (NDP), originally formed by Anwar Sadat. With the collapse of Egypt's First Republic (1952–2011) and the establishment of the Second Republic (2011–present), the relationship between civilian and military authority still dominates the political landscape.[2] As of this writing, civilian and military relations have entered a critical phase with more fundamentalist Salafi groups challenging the armed forces, leading to hundreds of casualties in May 2012.

Preparing the Area of Operation

Fawzi reveals,

> Military engineers cooperated with their civilian counterparts in both the private and public sectors to constructs bases, ports, piers, airfields, bunkers, buildings, and fortifications. Egypt's military lacked the engineering capacity for such a massive undertaking, and for the first time military, public, and private sectors were fused and directed toward a national project of total war. This lofty construction project was placed under the direction of military engineers. Egyptians designed shelters for MiGs and Sukhoi jet fighters that could withstand the impact of 500-pound bombs and direct hits from 8-mm missiles. Vents were created to hot start jet engines inside shelters and provided with enough ordnance and spare parts to get jets airborne. Among the creative ideas put in place was the use of coiled barbed wire to act as netting to catch missiles and antitank projectiles.

Fawzi and his chief of staff, General Abdel-Moneim Riad, attended tests at proving grounds at Bilbais Airfield. Fawzi estimates that "fifteen shelters were needed per airstrip and thirty per air base. This meant that five hundred shelters would be constructed—a massive undertaking." He adds that reinforced shelters were constructed for two diesel generators per airstrip, radars, air operations centers, pilots, ordnance and missiles, and jet fuel. According to Fawzi,

> All of these were mostly constructed underground in support of jets. A minimum of two runways per airfield were constructed, and each was 3.5 kilometers long and 15 meters wide. These would be repaired annually, and twenty airfields would be added to the ten already in existence

before the 1967 [Six-Day] War. Each air division was assigned three airports at which to land, and they were designated as a headquarters field and two alternates. This designation had the added benefit of fusing together different squadrons operationally, since they now had to support one another in case of emergency landings or refueling.

Fawzi made it a priority to make these air bases self-sufficient in terms of water, food, and communications and to integrate them in the national early warning system. Sections of the Cairo-to-Alexandria highway were designated as emergency landing runways.

One of the last major air force construction projects conducted while Fawzi was war minister was a massive underground command center for 60 people. This command center was Egypt's first air operations center designed to monitor and track the air activity of the entire nation. The center would complement a reinforced operations center for the General Staff, built to accommodate 150, and the designated Operations Center 10 on the outskirts of Cairo at Wadi al-Qamar. The navy was allocated resources for its own command center in Alexandria, which was completed in 1971. A situation room was constructed underneath Cairo's Tahira Palace for Nasser.

Logistics, Construction, and Supply Chains for War

Preparing for the arrival of Soviet forces, equipment, and additional aid required the mobilization of the entire nation. Fawzi writes, "The massive construction effort can be compared to that conducted by the Pharaohs in ancient Egyptian history." Upon the conclusion of the secret talks between Leonid Brezhnev and Nasser on January 25, 1970, the Egyptians had to prepare for the arrival of division-level Soviet formations. On Fawzi's return with Nasser from Moscow, the war minister had to tap into emergency funds to help finance the massive crash construction effort needed, and even with the money, he had to elicit the assistance of private civil engineering firms to help with the effort. Fawzi recounts, "It took eight hour shifts of engineers and laborers, twenty-four hours a day for thirty days to prepare the groundwork for Soviet forces arriving in Egypt. Exhausted in the acquisition of domestic supplies of cement, several tons of cement were imported from India, Pakistan, and Somalia. Despite the threat of Israeli air raids, construction of several hundred hardened shelters continued." This is the unglamorous side of warfare: the preparation and logistics of war. Fawzi devotes several pages of his memoir to logistics, the sinews of war, and Port Said's transformation into a center of supply activity for Egyptian forces along the canal. Overlapping systems of supply were constructed, extending back toward the Nile Delta.

One of the main challenges was pushing potable water to troops along the Red Sea, Port Said, and the Canal Zone. Fawzi worked with civilian governors and mayors to come up with solutions to this problem. Among the solutions undertaken was a 70-kilometer network of pipelines extending from Qantarah to Port Said and another pipeline extending from Cairo to Port Said. This system was backed up by water trucks. In addition, temporary storage tanks from Cairo to Attaqa and from Port Said to Ismailiyah were constructed, along with 120 kilometers of pipeline designed to support the 3rd Field Army. Eleven water reservoirs west of the Nile Delta were allocated for the 2nd and 3rd Field Armies as sources from which these forces could get their water through underground pipes. Underground water tanks were also constructed closer to the Suez Canal front.

Side canals all along the city of Ismailiyah were utilized to practice bridging and to get Egyptian engineers used to coordinating with armor and mechanized infantry formations. Farmers had to be displaced and offered compensation as acres of land were designated military zones. Fawzi engineered an agreement by which the farmers would receive rent for their land and, at the end of the military's use, would be left with paved roads from their fields to the main highway, linking them and their produce to the major markets of the cities.

The memoir contains elaborate descriptions of the logistical preparations from the creation of telephone lines and switchboards to multichannel communications and overlapping lines of communication developed from the 2nd Field Army to Suez and the 3rd Field Army to Port Said. Both Suez and Port Said would relay communications to Abu Suweir Air Base and Cairo. Navy communications were channeled to Port Said and Alexandria. Since ground formations increased sevenfold after 1967, about eighty crossing units to bridge the canal and cross up to division-size formations needed to be developed. Along the Nile bridging training centers were established at Helwan, Amiriyah, Burqash, and Tel el Kibir. Maintenance of Soviet bridging equipment and the construction of Egyptian models took place in workshops concentrated in Bulaq (a district of Cairo) and Helwan. Engineers from the Suez Canal Company, now out of work owing to the closure of the canal, were drafted for this effort. Bridge sections were moved from Cairo to the Canal Zone at night and camouflaged.

Aswan High Dam engineers, led by Chief Engineer Sidqi Suleiman, solved the problem of breaching the Bar-Lev line, which was mainly constructed of massive sand barriers using high-pressure water cannon. Fawzi worried about Israeli forces using flammables to ignite the surface of the canal to complicate Egyptian breaching efforts. Egyptian frogmen were deployed to examine the pipes that spewed out flammables on the Israeli side and render them inoperable.

Fawzi writes of how the Israelis settled into a routine two years into the occupation of the Sinai (1967–1969). Despite changes and rotations every three months, the combat efficiency on the Israeli side gradually declined. In addition, the morale of Israeli forces in the Sinai began to deteriorate in 1969 with losses in troops and matériel caused by pressure exerted by the Egyptian 2nd and 3rd Field Armies. Egypt attempted to exploit this complacency in order to amplify the Israelis' sense of invincibility and to lull their leaders into a false sense of security. Fawzi writes, "1969 was also a year that Israeli air force strikes saw a gradual reduction in their ability to harass Egyptian troop concentrations. However, it would take the infusion of Soviet forces to close the aerial gaps exploited by the IAF in the spring of 1970." The revolutions in Sudan and Libya in 1969 changed the strategic balance in favor of Egypt, and Fawzi sought to capitalize on the strategic depth offered by these two revolutionary regimes. Nasser used Libya and Sudan to exert additional pressure in the United Nations on Israel and the United States.

Nixon's Dismissal of Brezhnev's Middle East Proposals

Arab states admired Egyptian steadfastness in the face of Israeli air assaults. This admiration translated to political, economic, and military support for Egypt. According to Fawzi, "President Richard Nixon's rejection of a Soviet proposal to resolve the Arab-Israeli crisis only increased Brezhnev's resolve to provide military aid." This was also, according to Fawzi, "part of the calculus in [the Kremlin] acceding to Nasser's demands to deploy Soviet forces in Egypt."[3] With the presence of Soviet troops, Nasser wanted Fawzi to escalate attacks on Israeli forces along the canal and in the Sinai. Fawzi approved plans to move sensitive commands to Libya and Sudan, including the following:

- Supply depots
- Maintenance facilities
- Egypt's military academy (from Cairo to the Sudanese capital of Khartoum to allow cadets a peaceful environment to hone their skills)[4]
- Egypt's naval academy (from Alexandria to the Libyan port of Tobruk)
- Egyptian naval units (to Port Sudan on the Red Sea coast and Libya's ports of Benghazi and Sirte on the Mediterranean coast)
- Egyptian fighter and bomber squadrons (to Uzma Air Base in Sudan and Wheelus Air Base in Libya)
- Fuel farms (along the Libyan-Egyptian border close to the coast)

Egypt's civil defense force, organized in 1968, aided in the movement of Egyptian military assets, and local police participated in the guarding of military property for movement to Sudan and Libya.

Conclusion

The next chapter will include Fawzi's recollection of superpower brinksmanship over Egypt and of Nasser's capitalization on the Cold War. Fawzi provides the tonnage and number of sorties of the initial Soviet airlift during the Six-Day War and explains how the airlift enabled him to stabilize the canal front. He highlights and discusses his observations in five Egyptian-Soviet summits from 1968 to 1970 and the strategic options each summit provided Egypt.

★★ Chapter Fifteen ★★

Translating Soviet Military Aid into Egyptian Strategic Options

The general who wins the battle makes many calculations in his temple before the battle is fought. The general who loses makes but few calculations beforehand.

—Sun Tzu—

Foreword by A. Denis Clift, vice president, planning and operations, U.S. Naval Institute, and president emeritus, National Intelligence University

The late President Harry S. Truman has been quoted as saying, "The only thing new in the world is the history you haven't read." Those lasting words apply to Commander Youssef Aboul-Enein's abridged and analyzed translation of Egyptian war minister Mohamed Fawzi's writings on the architecture of Soviet military aid to Egypt during the interwar period between the 1967 Six-Day War and the 1973 Yom Kippur War. This is important history, and there are lessons to be learned and applied now and in the future.

A sterling silver cigarette box engraved "Anwar El Sadat" in Arabic has a place of honor in my office. I had the pleasure of meeting with Sadat in 1975 and 1978. I was impressed by what I learned from him about Egyptian history and culture. On the first occasion, I was a senior member of the National Security Council staff traveling with President Gerald R. Ford. The setting was Salzburg, Austria. Before the president's talks with Sadat, Chancellor Bruno Kreisky hosted a dinner in their honor and delivered his welcoming toast in German. Sadat rose and delivered a long, extemporaneous reply in German. I would learn it was a language he had studied when he was a young officer opposed to British rule of his country.

The second occasion was the Camp David Summit of 1978—President Jimmy Carter, Prime Minister Menachem Begin, and President Sadat—that would lead to the Israeli-Egyptian Peace Treaty. I was national security adviser to Vice President Walter F. Mondale and was privileged to attend the summit throughout. Sadat was a man of great dignity. He was adamant that the Israelis leave the Sinai and quietly, patiently forced acceptance of this position.

Sadat stood firm on his nation's independence and integrity; he also looked to its future. In the late 1970s he groomed Vice President Hosni Mubarak for his future responsibilities. I would participate with the vice president in dinners hosted by the Egyptian ambassador on the occasion of Mubarak's orientation visits to the United States and his talks with U.S. leaders.

If I learned from Sadat, so the reader will learn from this translation of General Fawzi's memoir. In Fawzi's account, Soviet aid revolved around the initial infusion of weapons days into the Six-Day War and five Soviet-Egyptian summit meetings to coordinate, calibrate, and discuss strategy in the region—not just Egypt and Israel, but the far wider Cold War between East and West, between the United States and Soviet Union.

Fawzi offers rare insights that have remained undiscovered to English-language readers until this series published by the U.S. Army magazine, *Infantry*. The extent and tonnage of Soviet military aid are extraordinary and demonstrate the capability of lift by the Russians. Fawzi discusses information sharing with the Soviets to include exchanges on performance of and ways to counter the U.S. A-4 Skyhawk and F-4 Phantom, information derived from action against those aircraft over the skies of North Vietnam.

Today, it is more important than ever to immerse ourselves in direct Arabic sources in order to gain insights for the national security of the United States in the early twenty-first century. General Fawzi allows us to see ourselves and our Israeli ally through his eyes— giving us a clearer understanding of the complexities of the Middle East.

I commend this work to all who are eager for such valuable insights. Commander Aboul-Enein is a serious, accomplished scholar. I know him from years ago when I was serving as college president and he was in the master's program. His commitment to educating from direct Arabic sources has manifested itself in his many publications, including three books published by the Naval Institute Press.

Soviet Aid

The overt U.S. support to Israel led directly to Egypt's embrace of the Soviet Union, according to Fawzi. The Arab frontline states had to have Moscow on their side to confront Israel. Fawzi shares the talking points used in meetings with the Soviets in Moscow:

> The 1967 Six-Day War was a shared loss between Egypt and the USSR, and what impressed Cairo was that Moscow did not use the 1967 defeat to press for ideological concessions. The depth of the 1967 defeat led to an inward look by the Soviet General Staff, which concluded it was Egyptian military bureaucracy and not the quality of Soviet weaponry that led to defeat. On June 9, 1967, days into the Six-Day War, the

Soviets infused Egypt with an initial shipment consisting of 550 airlift sorties of equipment and fifteen ocean-going freighters carrying tons of military hardware. These military shipments included ninety-three MiG-17 and twenty-five MiG-25 fighters to replace Egyptian losses. These MiGs were supplemented by the forty MiG-17s provided by the Algerians during the days after the Six-Day War.

Fawzi continues, "In the initial weeks after the Six-Day War, upward of 50,000 tons were shipped to Egypt by the Soviet Union." Some of the initial infusion of military hardware from 1967 to 1969 came from Warsaw Pact stocks in Czechoslovakia, Hungary, and Yugoslavia.

Fawzi writes of Nasser with admiration, noting "his ability to use the very instance of perceived or real American brinkmanship against the Soviet Union as a means of leveraging or extracting support from Moscow for Egypt's objectives." Nasser assured the Soviet Politburo that Egyptians were reforming their military bureaucracy and that the Egyptian armed forces were being reinvented. The Soviets sought to gain from Egypt's utter dependence on its weapons and gauged that the liberation of Sinai could not take place without a constant and reliable source of military supply and resupply of Soviet weaponry. Nasser was acutely aware of this and discussed with Fawzi this insecurity and dependence on the Russians. Part of Nasser's strategy of getting Iraq's Abdel-Rahman Arif and Algeria's Houari Boumidienne to advocate personally for Egypt in Moscow was to entangle Soviet accession to Egypt's needs with the greater Arab cause. Nasser leveraged a series of Arab summits after the 1967 war to portray himself before Moscow, not only as the representative of Egypt but also as the aspirations of the Arab peoples as a whole. The 1969 revolutions in Libya and Sudan, which were pro-Nasserist, further cemented the perception of Nasser as an Arab leader among the Soviet leadership.

From 1967 to the deployment of Soviet forces in early 1969 to late 1970, there were upward of twelve hundred Soviet military advisers in Egypt. There were a total of five Egyptian-Soviet summits, not including dozens of meetings in Cairo and Moscow conducted at a ministerial level or meetings between the leaders of the Soviet Communist Party and the ASU. Fawzi discusses these summit meetings, beginning with the Nasser-Podgorny summit from June 21 to 23, 1967, in Cairo. The meeting was attended by Marshal Matvei Zakharov, chief of the Soviet General Staff. Also in attendance were Egyptian vice president Zakariyah Moheiddine, ASU leader Ali Sabry, Egyptian foreign minister Mahmoud Riad, and General Fawzi. The summit, coming less than two weeks after the Six-Day War, centered on redefining the Soviet-Egyptian relationship and creating closer military, political, and economic ties between Cairo and Moscow. It discussed an infusion of massive quantities of air force and air defense assets, the reach of the IAF, and technological upgrades for the MiG-21. Podgorny pledged that the Soviets would intervene if Egypt proper were invaded, and there were also discussions of the 1956 Suez Crisis, in which the imperialist powers of Britain and France colluded with Israel in a failed attempt to take the canal. (Missing from Fawzi's memoir is a discussion of how President Dwight Eisenhower blunted France and Britain's plans by leveling economic penalties that led to a pullback of all forces from Egypt.) Podgorny departed Cairo with promises to Egypt of hundreds of millions of dollars of Soviet military aid.

The second Nasser-Podgorny summit took place in Moscow on June 29, 1968. Nasser was joined by Anwar Sadat, Mahmoud Riad, Chief of Staff General Abdel-Moneim Riad, and General Fawzi. During this summit Nasser formally presented Yasser Arafat to the USSR. Nasser wanted to increase the number of Soviet military advisers to the level of a battalion. He wanted a Soviet adviser for every Egyptian military battalion and expressed concerns about Egyptians quickly absorbing the complexity of Soviet military hardware. Nasser extracted hundreds of millions of dollars in Soviet pledges for military aid. Fawzi writes, "Soviet military aid to Egypt in 1969 alone matched what was sent by Moscow from 1955 to 1967."[1]

Seeing leadership's strain on Nasser, Soviet premier Leonid Brezhnev invited him to rest in the resort of Sakhalha. Nasser thanked the Soviet leader, and after opening the International Socialist Conference in Cairo, he returned to the USSR in late July to take up Brezhnev's offer of rest and recuperation. On his return from Moscow, Nasser strategized with Yugoslavia's leader, Marshal Josip Tito. In late 1969 Fawzi prepared Nasser to request from the Soviets help in addressing problems in the EAF and EADF.

For the third summit in Moscow, Nasser sent Anwar Sadat to represent him. This meeting occurred in December 1969, and Fawzi and Foreign Minister Riad accompanied Sadat. The discussions centered on offensive operations in the Sinai and the progress Brezhnev was making on the diplomatic front by pressuring Israel through the United States. The Egyptians and the Soviets talked about the two revolutions that year in Libya and Sudan, which they thought represented a positive development toward their common objectives of pressuring the United States and Israel.

Fawzi's preparation regarding the problems in the EAF and EADF netted an agreement to send sixty Soviet pilots and SA-3 crews to train Egyptians, as well as a thousand Soviet air defense personnel to man defensive missiles in Egypt until October 1970, at which time the Egyptians would be fully trained. Soviet advisers permeated Egyptian formations.[2] Fawzi writes, "They were assigned from company to battalion level. Every air squadron had a minimum of one adviser, each major command two to three advisers, the General Staff three advisers or more, service chiefs two to three advisers." Even Fawzi himself was furnished with a senior-ranking adviser. The Soviet military mission was allocated an entire building in Cairo. Soviet advisers generally served eighteen- to twenty-four-month tours before being relieved. From 1967 to 1970, three Soviet generals headed the Soviet military mission in Egypt. According to Fawzi, they were General Lashinkov,[3] General I. S. Katyshkin,[4] and General Vasily V. Okunev.[5] Twenty Soviet advisers were killed in the War of Attrition, and Fawzi notes with satisfaction that "the Soviet troops and advisers did not attempt to spread their ideology in Egypt. In addition to regular Soviet forces acting as advisers, there would be three hundred contract military technical advisers; that was an agreement between the Egyptian War Ministry and the Soviet Ministry of Trade Affairs." Fawzi writes that these technical advisers "were missile and aircraft experts; the highest-ranking engineer was paid about a hundred dollars per month bonus in addition to the contracted monthly stipend. They were on hand to repair and put together complex weapons systems. Nasser, in an exchange with Brezhnev, tried to convince the Soviet leader to allow his military personnel to enjoy Egypt's cultural sites. However, Brezhnev refused, saying that the Soviet soldier is content to seeing to their duty and had learned of the adverse effects the British had when they [the soldiers] flooded Egyptian tourist and recreation sites."

The fourth summit occurred from January 22 to 25, 1970, in Moscow. This summit saw, in Fawzi's words, "a commitment of thirty-two battalions of SA-3s and a Soviet air defense division to crew them in Egypt." To supplement Egypt's current MiG inventory, eighty-five MiG-21s piloted by Soviets, along with technicians and crews representing three Soviet air divisions, were deployed to Egypt. The Soviets also added fifty Sukhoi-9 jet fighters, ten MiG-21 trainers, four B-15 radars for low-altitude searches, and an upgrade of fifty Egyptian MiG-21s with the latest Y-511 turbojet engines. Fawzi notes that this was the largest single military aid package made by the Soviets to Egypt. The fourth summit was a coup for Nasser and represented a significant shift in the region's balance of forces. On April 18, 1970, IAF jets attempting a strike inside Egypt encountered Soviet pilots, and the Israelis decided to avoid escalating the conflict by downing Soviet-manned planes. Fawzi writes, "The Israelis conducted a mass media campaign about the number of Soviet forces deployed in Egypt, and the United States attempted to pressure the Soviets to cease fueling a Middle East arms race." Fawzi describes a zero-sum tactical effort between Egypt, fielding ever-increasing numbers of air defense systems, and Israel, attempting to prevent this wall of AA missiles and guns from being deployed along the canal. Fawzi writes that Egyptian will triumphed, and Israeli A-4s and F-4s began to fall. In truth, throughout the entire War of Attrition, only twenty-two Israeli planes were downed. After this summit Fawzi focused on bolstering Egypt's EW capabilities to counter effective Israeli jamming and attempts to obtain air corridors into Egypt for deep strikes.

The fifth and final summit occurred June 29 to July 17, 1970, in Moscow and included Nasser, Foreign Minister Riad, Ali Sabry, Mohamed Heikal, and General Fawzi. This was the secret summit between Nasser and Brezhnev, and it involved hours of discussion on the capabilities of the F-4 Phantom, its EW and jamming capabilities, its long-range strike envelope, its loiter times, and lessons from the engagements between the MiG-21 and F-4 over the skies of North Vietnam. Nasser wanted a retaliatory strike option, as the MiG-21 could reach targets only in the Sinai and not Israel proper and the Frog-7 missile had a maximum range of 100 kilometers. Although Fawzi does not provide details, it is likely that Nasser requested Scud-variant ballistic missiles, with a range of 180 kilometers for the Scud-A and 300 kilometers for the Scud-B. The Scud was not delivered to Egypt until the eve of the 1973 Arab-Israeli War. Instead, the Soviets provided the Egyptians with hundreds of millions of dollars in EW equipment and long-range Tu-16 bomber variants, according to Fawzi. However, the war minister does not discuss the planes being outfitted with long-range KS-1 Komet missiles.

Marshal Andrei Grechko and General Fawzi spent hours resolving the tactical problems of crossing the canal, and then they turned to options for protecting the Aswan High Dam, a prestige object, vital source of irrigation and power for Egypt, and legacy project for the Soviets who built the dam. Since the upgraded Tu-16s would be based at Aswan Air Base and Wadi Sidna Air Base, the two military leaders discussed second-strike targets inside Israel. A division of Soviet personnel was deployed to support twenty Tu-16 bombers, and although Fawzi does not discuss which variant, it is likely that he is referring to the Tu-16KS, or "Badger B." In the talks Fawzi noted the Israeli deployment of the ground-to-ground Lance missile, capable of striking SA missile sites along the canal.

The fifth summit also saw agreements reached on EW systems, which arrived in Egypt in August 1970. These were integrated into various SA systems and radars, and among the first areas to get coverage was the Aswan High Dam. The Soviet SA division allowed more Egyptian crews to deploy with their missiles along the canal, as well as along the Red Sea approaches to the canal. The Soviet formations arrived in Egypt in winter dress, and Fawzi had to issue them light summer wear as it was 50 degrees Celsius (more than 120 degrees Fahrenheit) in places, like Aswan, where the Soviets were guarding the canal and manning AA systems. Four MiG-25R reconnaissance jets went to Egypt, piloted by Soviets. In late 1970 mobile bridging equipment arrived in Egypt. According to the agreement reached during the fifth summit, three Soviet frigates, each equipped with batteries of SA-6s and three battalions of amphibious troops, were based at Port Said, extending defensive air coverage over the port's military zone and acting as deterrence to Israeli attacks on the city. The missiles and bombs that were part of the Tu-16s based in Aswan had to be moved by rail to underground storage facilities near the base. Wadi Sidna Air Base in Sudan was also used to base Soviet Tu-16s.

Economic Aid

Fawzi's memoir describes Nasser's belief that developing Egypt's heavy industries was a path toward economic prosperity and social justice. The Soviets constructed the Aswan High Dam and then proceeded to aid Egypt in laying electrical grids and developing its aluminum industries, steel production, and iron manufacturing. The Soviets were also chief importers of Egyptian agricultural products. The financial package for military items that were not outright grants was half of production cost and financed at forty years at an interest rate of 2 percent. The losses of the Egyptian armed forces in the 1956 and 1967 conflicts were grants. The costs for spare parts and maintenance were settled annually between the Egyptian War Ministry and the Soviet Trade Ministry. Egypt restructured Soviet military debt twice, but Fawzi does not discuss terms or when this restructuring occurred.

Final Training and Plans to Liberate the Sinai

The final section of Fawzi's memoir describes a series of military exercises and conferences with his service chiefs and field commanders scheduled for September 1970. These were postponed until early 1971 owing to the unexpected death of Nasser on September 28, 1970. For twelve days from March 14 to 25, 1971, Egyptian leaders and Soviet advisers tested the ability of the armed forces to undertake Plan Granite specifically and Plan 200 generally. Plan Granite involved the following troops supported by the navy and the EAF:

- five infantry divisions
- three mechanized infantry divisions
- two armored divisions
- three artillery divisions
- three reconnaissance battalions
- one amphibious division

The exercise was to occupy the Giddi and Mitla Passes in the center of the Sinai by D plus 4. This force size—about 100,000 troops—was used, refined, and debated from the end of the exercise until General Saad el-Din el-Shazly finalized plans that would initiate the 1973 Yom Kippur War.[6] Shazly planned to cross the canal and establish a presence of 80,000 troops all along the canal no more than fifteen kilometers behind Israeli lines, which was the effective range of his SA missile umbrella. Fawzi's plans were much more ambitious, and the quality of the EAF and the range limitation of Egyptian air defense systems made it doubtful he would have succeeded.

Plan 200, according to Fawzi's conception, envisioned three objectives:

(1) breaching the Bar-Lev line, (2) securing the passes [Giddi, Mitla, and Khatmiya], and finally, (3) fighting armored and mechanized infantry advances with air cover to the international border. Subobjectives included

- destroying Israeli concentration of forces in the center of the Sinai
- crossing the canal and establishing five bridgeheads to push forces to secure the passes in the center of the Sinai
- combining air defense with combat engineers to lay bridges to cross the canal
- breaching the Bar-Lev line using high-pressure water
- concentrating Egyptian forces on the canal over a period of three years (1967–1970)
- having in position a large air defense formation along the canal by 1970
- perfecting the concealment of deployments of Egyptian forces along the canal
- attaining numerical superiority along the entire length of the canal

Exercises were crafted based on the above set of objectives, and in some cases over a hundred judges along with Soviet advisers were used to perfect Egyptian tactics.

On one occasion Fawzi took command of a mass exercise from Operations Center 10, the underground command center built during his tenure. This exercise involved crossing a mock canal with 30,000 troops with the support of the artillery. Fawzi notes, "Over time Israeli forces in the Sinai began to take on a defensive mentality rather than an offensive one." He writes of "the Egyptians analyzing U.S. congressional reports in 1972 and 1973 and concluding that the window of parity achieved by Nasser and Fawzi would close in 1973 with an infusion of $600 million in military aid to Israel in 1972." After Fawzi was removed from office, he discussed American congressional reports with his colleagues and noted that the balance of power would favor Israel in 1973. Therefore, an attack had to happen by 1972 for Egypt to retain the military edge, according to Fawzi's military calculus.

Conclusion: Lessons and Reflections

Fawzi's memoir concludes with reflections on his tenure as war minister (1967–1971). He asserts that Egyptian arms were severely defeated in the Six-Day War not because of the loss of the air force but instead because of the way Egyptian military personnel were trained and led. Poor military training and leadership, coupled with Field Marshal Abdel-Hakim Amer's issuing conflicting orders and calling for a general withdrawal of Egyptian combat forces from the Sinai thirty-six hours into the conflict, led to disastrous Egyptian losses. The Egyptian soldiers were not even given a chance to engage the Israeli soldiers. Fawzi goes on to say that after the 1967 war Israeli forces underestimated Egyptian resolve and that Nasser's commitment to bring about an Israeli withdrawal from the Sinai led him to deepen ties with the Soviets. Fawzi thinks that the War of Attrition was a success and holds out the Rogers Plan to argue the point, writing, "Israel was eager for the U.S.-brokered cease-fire to reduce its losses sustained over a three-year period. Therefore, the attrition of Israeli forces and the wearing down of the Israeli economy had an impact." It is certain Israeli military planners and writers would have a different view, and Fawzi does not take into account the gains the Israelis had from access to energy supplies in the occupied Sinai.

Nasser and Fawzi leveraged Arab outrage to reduce U.S. influence in the region. This maneuver was deliberate, used all elements of Egyptian national power, and was conducted because of America's unwavering support for Israel. The Egyptians wanted Washington to realize that maintaining its posture in the Arab world would remain a challenge unless it had Egyptian cooperation. This strategy in fact took a more tangible expression soon after the 1973 Yom Kippur War, when Arab oil-producing states conducted an oil embargo that affected Western economies.

In addition, Fawzi writes that the closure of the Suez Canal strained the global economy. Fawzi was in the middle of the events in the Suez Canal Zone, which, from 1967 until the start of peace talks between Egypt and Israel in 1977, was a tense area of confrontation no different from Berlin, Cuba, or the Koreas, an area where the superpowers would draw a line of confrontation. His presence in these events is one of many reasons why exposing his perspective and introducing his memoir to America's military personnel for the first time in English matters on several levels.

Fawzi also offers his view on the preparation of the nation, economy, armed forces, subordination of the military to political authority, area of operation, alignment of command and control over the armed forces, and the individual soldier. These are grand concepts debated in America's war colleges, and while our case studies are steeped in the Western tradition, it makes sense in the twenty-first century to introduce our future military leaders to Arab perspectives on these same questions. Reading about their views also sensitizes America's military planners to the evolution of Arab military thinking and the incorporation of Western methods with a regional flavor in overseas matters of military strategy and tactics.

Basic elements of the 1973 Arab-Israeli War can be found even before the loss of the Sinai in the form of Plan Qahir, which was formulated after the 1965 Arab summit. This plan went through various stages of evolution, from defensive to the offensive Plan 200. Fawzi also introduces the regional proclivities toward tactically opening multiple fronts using conventional SF and insurgent guerrilla tactics and toward gradually probing, escalating, and choosing a time to conventionally strike with mass formations. These are lessons to ponder as the United States and her allies confront an Iran that aspires to nuclear capabilities.

Nasser issued orders to begin an offensive to cross the canal the last week of August 1970. He wanted hostilities after the ninetieth day of the Rogers Plan ceasefire, that is, beginning November 7, 1970. This date was three and a half years after Nasser gave the mandate to prepare to take back the Sinai on June 11, 1967. However, Nasser's death and Sadat's accession delayed these plans, and Fawzi became bitter that Sadat did not keep Nasser's military timetable in place. Ultimately, Fawzi was involved in a conspiracy with Ali Sabry to remove Sadat from power, for which he would be tried and incarcerated.

Fawzi sees his legacy as follows:

- He healed the psychological wounds of the 1967 Six-Day War.
- He resolved that liberation of occupied territories could only be attained by military means.
- He restored the morale of the Egyptian armed forces.
- He reduced the wall of fear Israeli forces had built up starting with the 1948 Arab-Israeli War.
- He undertook a massive intelligence collection effort to understand his Israeli adversary.

- He modernized the Egyptian armed forces, incorporating various SA systems, EW, and radar-guided systems. Fawzi refers to this as a renaissance of the Egyptian armed forces.

- He integrated various services within the Egyptian armed forces to attain unity of effort.

Fawzi writes that the "Egyptian people held Nasser responsible for continuing the fight against Israel." According to the war minister's memoir, the Egyptians' outlook created the psychological conditions needed for a popular, or people's, army and aided in the fusing of civilian and military efforts to remove all traces of Israeli aggression. Fawzi also discusses the importance of leveraging the support and even sympathy of the Arab world, the Eastern bloc, Islamic states, and the Nonalignment Movement into various levels of tangible support, from outright military and financial aid to diplomatic pressure. Strategically, Egypt wanted to demonstrate to Israel that remaining in the Sinai would have a cost. Fawzi was concerned with curbing Israel's long arm—its air force—and credits the Egyptians with downing fifty-two planes in the War of Attrition; the Israelis admitted to thirty planes.[7] He also writes, "Countering Israel's strategy of realigning the Middle East map through aggression would be challenged, even at the level of the superpowers." Fawzi ends by saying that his most challenging mission as war minister "was restoring a sense of military tradition, pride, and self-confidence in the individual soldier"—words any military leader of soldiers from any nation can relate to and live by.

★★　**Chapter Sixteen**　★★

Concluding Thoughts

Educating America's Future Military Leaders
on Arab Strategic Thinking

---

*Education is the ability to listen to almost anything without losing
your temper or your self-confidence.*
—ROBERT FROST—

I f this book left you with a desire to read more about the Arab-Israeli conflict, it
is vital that you take a holistic look and approach the conflict from all sides to
gain a true appreciation of warfare in the region. Among the Egyptian generals,
Fawzi is perhaps one of few whose memoir was never before translated or excerpted
in English. The good news is that the late General Saad el-Din el-Shazly (see appendix 2), the armed forces chief of staff and architect of the 1973 canal crossing, wrote
two books that have been translated into English: *The Crossing of the Suez* and *The
Arab Military Option* (both published by American Mideast Research, in 2003 and
1986 respectively). General Abdel-Ghani El-Gamasi, chief of operations during the
1973 war, has also had his memoir translated into English. It is titled *The October
War* and was published by the American University of Cairo Press in 1993.

Nasser's confidant and editor of the newspaper *al-Ahram*, Mohamed
Hassanein Heikal has several books in English, including *Road to Ramadan* (1975,
Quandrangle), *The Sphinx and the Commissar: The Rise and Fall of Soviet Influence
in the Middle East* (1978, Harper & Row), and *The Cairo Documents: The Inside Story
of Nasser and His Relationship with World Leaders, Rebels, and Statesmen* (1973,
Doubleday). Heikal, in *Road to Ramadan*, helps readers explore the question, Did
the Israelis underestimate new methods of employing infantry in the 1973 Yom
Kippur War? His book also contains conversations with Nasser that Fawzi does
not include in his memoir, including one in which General Abdel-Moneim Riad
says to Nasser, "The mere fact that we start an attack at all will be the most important element of surprise!"[1] Heikal also includes a conversation between Nasser and
Soviet premier Nikolai Podgorny, in a meeting after the 1967 Six-Day War, during

which Podgorny became angry that advanced Soviet equipment had landed intact in the hands of the Israelis and therefore the Americans;[2] this exchange is omitted by Fawzi. Heikal credits three men with the reform of the Egyptian armed forces in the aftermath of the Six-Day War: General Fawzi, General Riad, and President Nasser.[3] Although Fawzi expressed bitterness at being relieved of his post by Sadat in 1971 because of his participation in Ali Sabry's attempted soft coup, Heikal makes it clear that Nasser did not intend for Fawzi to fight the war anyway: "He [Fawzi] was not the commander he [Nasser] would choose to fight the war; he wanted a [Bernard Law] Montgomery not a [Erwin] Rommel." Nasser's Montgomery was Abdel-Moneim Riad. Heikal goes onto describe Fawzi as not an imaginative man but a cruel disciplinarian, which was what Egypt needed from 1967 to 1971.[4] In other words, Fawzi would be General George B. McClellan to Riad's and, after his death, Shazly's Ulysses S. Grant.

Shazly, Gamasi, and Heikal are but some of many examples needed when studying warfare. You need to approach your topic from multiple disciplines and perspectives.

Syrian generals' memoirs are much scarcer, but you can read my analysis of the mind and memoir of General Mustafa Tlas in the May/June 2005 edition of the U.S. Army Command and General Staff journal, *Military Review*.[5] Tlas' two-volume memoir represented one of the most difficult assessments I have published, as he writes in a stream-of-consciousness style that is unique among Arab generals writing their autobiographies. Distilling the essence of his strategic thought was a challenge.

I have also written short but deep intellectual biographies of General Saad el-Din el-Shazly and General Abdel-Moneim Riad and published both in *Infantry*, in 2005 and 2004, respectively. These essays are included as appendixes 2 and 3 of this book. Aside from wishing to introduce my fellow American military readers to their thinking, I had the privilege of serving former secretary of defense Donald Rumsfeld as director for North Africa and Egypt for three years (2003–2006). In preparation for this immense responsibility, I felt it was my duty to immerse my mind in Arabic works in the hopes of being a better adviser to Secretary Rumsfeld, Deputy Defense Secretary Paul Wolfowitz, Undersecretary of Defense for Policy Douglas Feith, the late assistant secretary of defense for international security affairs Peter Rodman (d. 2008), and Deputy Undersecretary of Defense for Near East and South Asian Affairs Dr. William J. Luti, who was also my skipper on board USS *Guam* (LPH-9). Captain Luti and I spent many hours on the bridge discussing national security during short breaks navigating the LPH through the Suez Canal. That several Arab-Israeli wars had been fought on the very waters we were travers-ing was not lost to either of us or the 24th Marine Expeditionary Unit, and then

Colonel Natonski, the MEU commander, had me conduct professional military education (PME) on the ship's bow.

On the Israeli side, books can fill an entire bookcase, but Chaim Herzog's military histories of the Arab-Israeli conflict are a great start, and Michael Oren's *Six Days of War* is a must-read.[6] Of note, Oren's volume was turned into a documentary that is worth watching. There are also biographies of Israeli prime ministers and generals that offer additional insights.

While Fawzi concentrates on aligning civil and military efforts toward the liberation of the Sinai and institutes much-needed reforms, such as requiring senior military personnel to justify expenditures before the Council of Ministers, he does not discuss in his memoir how Egypt made up for economic losses from the Six-Day War. The Israeli occupation of the oil fields in the Sinai, coupled with the loss of revenues from the Suez Canal, meant that national funding had to be made up by Soviet aid and infusions of hard currency from Persian Gulf states. Owen Sirrs, in an excellent analytical book titled *Nasser and the Missile Age in the Middle East*, fills the gaps left by Fawzi, discussing not only sources of aid but arguing that between 1967 and 1970 military expenditures accounted for a quarter of Egypt's national budget.[7] I have had the pleasure of working with Sirrs when I was at the Pentagon and enjoyed discussing the region with him.

Fawzi also does not discuss the major event in Egyptian rocket acquisitions from the Soviets, when Nasser successfully argued and received an upgrade from Frog-2 to the Frog-7 (tactical ballistic missile) in 1968. The upgraded missile provided Fawzi with a tactical deep-strike capability against Israeli forces in the Sinai that was never employed during the War of Attrition.[8] The Frog-7 had a maximum range of 92 kilometers but was used as a prestige item and in military parades. It is likely that Fawzi did not want to acknowledge in his memoir the deterrent force of Israeli strategic weapons. His description of massive Soviet military assistance is best described by William Mott IV in his 2001 book, *Soviet Military Assistance: An Empirical Perspective*. Mott writes, "Soviet military assistance to Egypt reached its peak in the early 1970s when Egyptian procurement of Soviet weaponry was about a quarter of all Soviet shipments to countries outside the Warsaw Pact."[9]

Fawzi also does not discuss the details of the 1971 Treaty of Friendship and Cooperation, which President Sadat negotiated with the Soviets. The treaty included a clause claiming for the Soviets the right of intervention. In addition, the war minister does not detail how Sadat's overtures to the United States, which strained Soviet-Egyptian relations, in part caused Fawzi's conspiracy with ASU leader Ali Sabry in his attempted coup against Sadat.

Michael Taylor and John Taylor, in their *Missiles of the World*, include missile systems in Egypt's inventory that Fawzi does not mention in his memoir, despite devoting whole chapters to the architecture of Egypt's missile and AA defenses.[10] It is unclear if Fawzi's omission is purposeful or not. These systems include the Frog-7 unguided surface-to-surface tactical ballistic missile.[11] Also, while Fawzi reported the SA-3 as part of the overall system for closing Israel's air dominance over Egyptian air space, the variant known as "Goa" was not mentioned. Goa caused much concern for the IAF, with its effective slant range of 24 kilometers, or 40,000 feet.[12] The Soviet navy operated the "Kelt" AS-5 air-to-surface missile, with a range of 160 kilometers, from bases in Egypt, making Israeli warships vulnerable to attack from Egyptian shores. Finally, the Soviets provided the Egyptians the "Kennel" AS-1 air-to-surface antiship missile with a maximum 100-kilometer range and upgraded Tu-16 bombers to carry two Kelt missiles underwing.[13]

Reading Taylor and Taylor, you also gain a sense of what was not provided the Egyptians, such as the entire inventory of the Soviet SS-class intercontinental missiles, like the SS-8 "Sasin" and SS-13 "Stark." Sirrs writes that Moscow feared antagonizing the United States and refused to provide Egypt with Scud missiles until 1973, two years after Fawzi left his post as war minister.[14]

A glaring omission from Fawzi's memoir is his side of the story in the 1971 conspiracy involving Ali Sabry, Minister of Interior Sami Sharaf, and former interior minister Sharawi Gom'aa to remove Sadat from power. According to Amons Perlmutter's book, *Egypt: The Praetorian State*, Fawzi was brought into the conspiracy by family ties with Interior Minister Sharaf.[15] In Mohamed Heikal's *Road to Ramadan*, Fawzi is said to have agitated the General Staff, declaring in a May 1971 meeting that there was going to be a sellout to the Americans and that he was resigning. Sadat supporter General Mohammed Sadeq preempted Fawzi, saying, "Mr. Minister since you have resigned maybe you should go have a rest." Without objection or intervention from Fawzi's supporters around the table, Sadat accepted the war minister's resignation that week.[16]

Fawzi and Nasser devoted considerable thought to what constituted a decisive victory, and that was the liberation of the Sinai. When Sadat became leader in 1970, the nature of victory and its attainability was altered, and while Fawzi laid the cornerstones of the 1973 Arab-Israeli War, they would be further refined by Sadat's generals—primarily his chief of staff, General Saad el-Din el-Shazly—into something more realistic. War is not a matter of whim or personality, and this was the tragedy of Sadat's decision to oppose his chief of staff in the midst of the 1973 war and order the advancing of the Egyptian 2nd and 3rd Field Armies to the Giddi and Mitla Passes to relieve Syria from a withering Israeli counteroffensive in the Golan Heights. Out of AA missile range, Egyptian formations were subject to punishing Israeli air strikes and eventually a seam would develop, leading to the envelopment of the Egyptian 3rd Army. It seems that Sadat should have learned the dangers of whim in military affairs from the example of Field Marshal Abdel-Hakim Amer, his relationship with Nasser, and his performance in the 1967 Six-Day War. Why do post-Mubarak Egyptian leaders succumb not only to meddling in military operations but also by doing so through impulse and arbitrary decision making? General Shazly is unique among Egyptian generals for standing up to Sadat and refusing to order an advance of the 2nd and 3rd field armies outside the anti-air protective zone, where they would face certain annihilation by Israeli fighter jets. Shazly was rewarded with ostracism and persecution by Sadat and Mubarak.

The biggest lesson the Israelis can deduce from Fawzi's memoir is that decisive victory has a human element that is dismissed at one's peril. The 1967 Six-Day War ended in such a decisive Israeli victory that Fawzi undertook a complete operational and strategic overhaul of the Egyptian armed forces. The Egyptians' loss so shook the foundations of pan-Arabism and Nasserism that thousands sought refuge in understanding events through the lens of various Islamist political theories. In addition, the 1967 war had geopolitical repercussions, driving more Arab states into the Soviet sphere of influence.

On a tactical level, even if the Egyptians had been provided massive quantities of Soviet weapons in 1955–1956, was it realistic for Moshe Dayan to conclude that they could absorb this weaponry in six months?[17] Could the Egyptians absorb the technology, doctrine, and employment of these weapons systems that quickly? Fawzi writes, in hindsight, that the post-1967 Egyptian army was too illiterate, that a total focus on recruiting a more educated soldier was undertaken, and that this process took years, not six months. More dangerous was the deployment of a mass of Soviet military advisers in Egypt; Fawzi discusses how he had to create infrastructure to house these advisers.

While researching this series, I uncovered Beijing's 1956 offer to provide contingents of Chinese volunteers to Egypt.[18] I found this detail in an out-of-print and obscure publication on Soviet foreign policy released in 1960. Of course, this Chinese offer of intervention in the Middle East was located in a single source and requires further research, but if proven in archives, it would represent the earliest assertion of Chinese power outside of the Pacific region and in the Middle East—made under the chairmanship of Mao Zedong. Today, Chinese government-sponsored firms are a fixture in many nations, and in 2014 China is set to become the leading importer of petroleum products.[19]

Fawzi was imprisoned for several years by Sadat for being part of the 1971 coup attempt. The former war minister appeared several times in the excellent two-part 1998 PBS documentary *The 50-Years War: Israel and the Arabs*, particularly in part 2 of the series, which begins with the 1967 Six-Day War.[20] International relations professor Kirk Beattie interviewed Fawzi for his book *Egypt during the Sadat Years*.

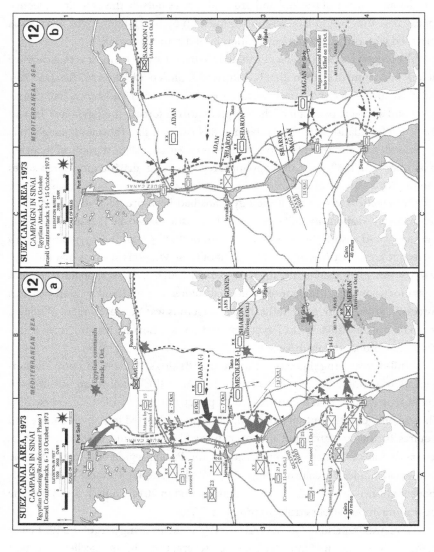

MAP 3. SIDE-BY-SIDE VIEW OF THE EGYPTIAN ATTACK ON OCTOBER 6, 1973, AND THE ISRAELI COUNTERATTACKS ON OCTOBER 14–15 ALONG THE

SUEZ CANAL ZONE   *Courtesy of the Department of History, U.S. Military Academy at West Point. Used with permission.*

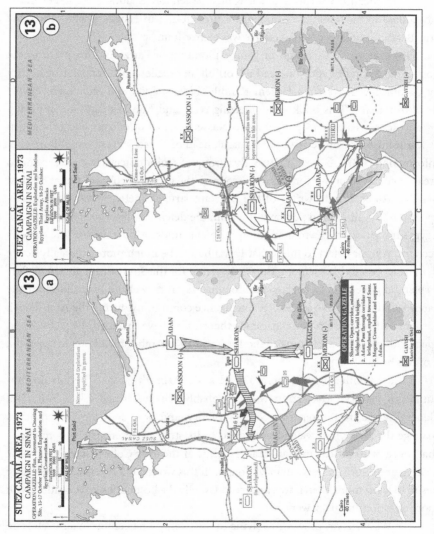

MAP 4. OPERATION GAZELLE, THE SURROUNDING OF THE EGYPTIAN 3RD FIELD ARMY
Courtesy of the Department of History, U.S. Military Academy at West Point. Used with permission.

Beattie describes "an old frail, very polite, sweet, and soft-spoken man who actually wept at the end of the interview as he described how difficult his life had been made, first by Amer, then by Sadat."[21] Beattie makes a compelling argument that being the taskmaster needed to reconstruct Egyptian arms left Fawzi dejected and that it would take another officer or officers to boost morale to the point of pulling off the October 1973 surprise attack against Israeli forces along the Bar-Lev line.[22] Fawzi died in his home at Heliopolis, a Cairo suburb, in February 2000, the same year Beattie's book was published. He was eighty-four.

However, to be thorough in your exploration of Fawzi and his place in the post–Arab Spring Egypt, you need to consult an excellent 2012 revisionist history by Cambridge University's Hazem Kandil: *Soldiers, Spies and Statesmen: Egypt's Road to Revolt*.[23] This book is an amazing read, and Kandil makes a compelling argument that Fawzi was part of a pro-Nasserist cabal of officers and brought in as war minister by his relative Sami Sharaf, head of Nasser's Presidential Bureau of Information (PBI). As early as 1956, this group of senior officials was attempting to create a center of power for Nasser to counter the growing political threat of Field Marshal Amer. Kandil writes of the constant struggle between various security apparatuses built around personalities from the defense to interior minister and of Egypt's transition from a military to a police state under Mubarak. Reading Kandil's account, you may start to think that Fawzi had to be much more politically active than he lets on in his memoir. The CIA's Center for the Study of Intelligence offers a splendid collection of declassified documents on its website that allows for the careful study of the role of the U.S. intelligence community during the Arab-Israeli conflict without hysteria or conspiracy theories.[24] I have included the website and specific documents pertaining to the 1967 and 1973 Arab-Israeli Wars in appendix 1 of this book.

We are familiar with General Douglas MacArthur's quote "There is no substitute for victory." MacArthur would probably cringe if I had asked him, "But General, what are the repercussions of victory, and how does the United States manage the peace in a way advantageous to its strategic interests?" It is my hope that more of America's military leaders while at the War College will spend time writing or exploring Arab military thought. If this work has left you with a burning desire to learn more, then it was a success. Usually the best books leave readers with more questions than answers.

The Western way of war is evolving in the twenty-first century. War itself is no longer only the successful defeat of adversaries, but defeating adversaries in such a way that their dignity is preserved so they can be part of reconstructing the peace. In many ways the U.S. military has been altered by the 1973 Arab-Israeli War and the development of AirLand Battle as a doctrine in the post-Vietnam U.S. Army.

General Stanley McChrystal's 2013 memoir, *My Share of the Burden*, mentions the impact of the 1973 Arab-Israeli War in its fourth chapter, "Renaissance: February 1982–May 1993." The former International Security Assistance Force (ISAF) commander in Afghanistan writes, "With limited budgets in the 1970s, the Army made the decision to pursue five primary weapons systems, highlighted by the M1 Abrams tanks and Apache helicopters, which would transform the force and outclass anything fielded by our potential enemies. In 1982, based on lessons learned from the Arab-Israeli War of 1973, a new doctrine of offensive maneuver called AirLand Battle was adopted that leveraged this enhanced weaponry and technology."[25]

Whatever the phase our nation happens to be in in the Middle East, whether war or peace, an immersion in the language of the region of operation is essential to understand not just the region but also ourselves. This is the main reason for this series, first published in *Infantry* and then compiled and expanded in this Naval Institute book. I urge my fellow Americans to reexplore the Arab-Israeli conflict and write about it in light of the tectonic and unique changes the region is experiencing as we approach the fifth year of the start of the Arab Spring.

There is also hope. As of this writing, Secretary of State John Kerry has jump-started talks in Washington, D.C., between Palestinian Authority leader Mahmoud Abbas and Israeli prime minister Benjamin Netanyahu. This exploration of General Mohamed Fawzi's memoir offers insights into concerns, fears, and countermeasures that need to be understood to bring forth a formula to reconcile Israel with the Palestinians and various Arab states that have become defined by the Palestinian question over seven decades. Regrettably, there can be no rest for the United Stated and its allies, for when the Palestinian question is resolved, we must deal with a balkanized Syria that will never be the same again, a Sinai that has an ever-increasing al-Qaida presence threatening not only the international community but also Egyptian troops, and yet another of a myriad of challenges destabilizing this vital region.

Left unsaid in Fawzi's memoir regarding his preparation of the Egyptian armed forces is whether the Arab-Israeli conflict would escalate regionally with the employment of weapons of mass destruction. Fawzi, intentionally or not, chose to dwell on asymmetric and conventional capabilities. Maybe the thought of weapons of mass destruction was too terrifying for him to contemplate? Maybe an archive held in Cairo will one day unlock the answers? These are questions for future scholars. One thing is certain: thought, education, and the development of realistic policy without hysteria and stereotyping are desperately needed to keep the United States secure in a world changing at the speed of Twitter.

Recommended Reading

Aloni, Shlomo. *Israeli A-4 Skyhawk Units in Combat*. Oxford, UK: Osprey, 2009.

Asher, Daniel. *The Egyptian Strategy for the Yom Kippur War: An Analysis*. Jefferson, NC: McFarland & Co, 2009.

Bar-Siman-Tov, Yaacov. *The Israeli-Egyptian War of Attrition, 1969–1970: A Case-Study of Limited Local War*. New York: Columbia University Press, 1980.

Dupuy, Trevor N. *Elusive Victory: The Arab-Israeli Wars, 1947–1974*. New York: Harper & Row, 1978.

Gamasi, Abdel-Ghani El-. *The October War: Memoirs of Field Marshal El-Gamasi of Egypt*. Cairo: American University of Cairo Press, 1993.

Heikal, Mohamed Hassanein. *The Cairo Documents: The Inside Story of Nasser and His Relationship with World Leaders, Rebels, and Statesmen*. New York: Doubleday, 1973.

———. *The Road to Ramadan*. New York: Quadrangle/New York Times Book, 1975.

———. *The Sphinx and the Commissar: The Rise and Fall of Soviet Influence in the Middle East*. New York: Harper & Row, 1978.

Herzog, Chaim, and Shlomo Gazit. *The Arab-Israeli Wars: War and Peace in the Middle East*, 3rd ed. New York: Vintage Press, 2004.

Kandil, Hazem. *Soldiers, Spies, and Statesmen: Egypt's Road to Revolt*. New York: Verso, 2012.

Lacouture, Jean. *Nasser: A Biography*. New York: Knopf, 1973.

Nutting, Anthony. *Nasser*. New York: Dutton, 1972.

O'Ballance, Edgar. *The Electronic War in the Middle East*. Hamden, CT: Archon Books, 1974.

Oren, Michael B. *Six Days of War: June 1967 and the Making of the Modern Middle East*. New York: Oxford University Press, 2002.

Shazly, Saad el-Din el-. *The Arab Military Option*. San Francisco: American Mideast Research, 1986.

———. *The Crossing of the Suez*, rev. English ed. San Francisco: American Mideast Research, 2003.

Sirrs, Owen L. *A History of the Egyptian Intelligence Service: A History of the Mukhabarat, 1910–2009.* New York: Routledge, 2010.

———. *Nasser and the Missile Age in the Middle East.* New York: Routledge, 2006.

Slaev, Aryeh. *Israel's Intelligence Assessment before the Yom-Kippur War: Disentangling Deception and Distraction.* Portland, OR: Sussex Academic Press, 2010.

Thomas, Gordon. *Gideon's Spies: The Inside Story of Israel's Legendary Secret Service.* New York: St Martin's Press, 2007.

For technical details on AA missile systems that will enhance your understanding of the memoirs of Egyptian generals read the following:

Sandia National Labs. *The Development of Soviet Air Defense Doctrine and Practice.* Albuquerque, NM, 1981.

———. *A Historical Analysis of the Effectiveness of Tactical Air Operations Against and in Support of Armored Forces.* Albuquerque, NM, 1980.

Zaloga, Steven J. *Soviet Air Defense Missiles: Design, Development, and Tactics.* Surrey, UK: Jane's Information Group, 1989.

For an understanding of the role of the U.S. intelligence community in the Arab-Israeli conflict without hysteria and conspiracy theories, consult the declassified archive on the CIA's Center for the Study of Intelligence website (https://www.cia.gov/library/center-for-the-study-of-intelligence) and read the following:

President Nixon and the Role of Intelligence in the 1973 Arab-Israeli War. Washington, DC: Historical Collections, CIA Information Management Services. https://www.cia.gov/library/publications/historical-collection-publications/arab-israeli-war/nixon-arab-isaeli-war.pdf.

Robarge, David S. "CIA Analysis of the 1967 Arab-Israeli War: Getting It Right." *Studies in Intelligence* 49, no. 1. https://www.cia.gov/library/center-for-the-study-of-intelligence/csi-publications/csi-studies/studies/vol49no1/html_files/arab_israeli_war_1.html.

Egyptian General Saad el-Din el-Shazly

Controversial Operational Thinker and Architect
of the 1973 Yom Kippur War*

W hen studying the October 1973 Arab-Israeli War, it is important to read from various sources to gain a better understanding of the conflict. Since there are Western, Israeli, and Arab sources, readers may want to consider the agendas of the author and synthesize a more holistic understanding of this conflict. Egyptian general Saad el-Din el-Shazly's work is an important contribution to understanding the Arab tactical mind. There is a single book by Shazly in English that details his perspectives on the 1973 Yom Kippur War, but it is not as extensive as the Arabic book featured in this review essay. Those wanting to pursue their study of Shazly in English should ask for *The Crossing of the Suez* (San Francisco: American Mideast Research, 1980). You can also request a copy through a website dedicated to General Shazly, www.el-shazly.com, which contains a biography of Shazly as he sees himself in the context of the history of Arab-Israeli conflict.

On May 16, 1971, Egyptian president Anwar Sadat appointed General Shazly armed forces chief of the General Staff. This appointment was significant in Egyptian military history, for it heralded a new shift in the aftermath of the 1967 war toward promoting those with true tactical and strategic abilities, a foundation laid by War Minister Mohamed Fawzi (in office 1967–1971). By the time Shazly assumed his post, he had already tangled with the future Egyptian war minister Field Marshal Ismail Ali in the Congo in 1960 and had alienated several of his peers by instilling in the Egyptian military a competent special forces capability composed of the Saaqa (commandos) and the Mizalaat (paratroops). Shazly would put into practice

---

*Reprinted from the Professional Forum, *Infantry* 94, no. 1 (January/February 2005), and updated to reflect Shazly's passing in 2011 and the changes brought to his legacy since the downfall of the Mubarak regime. This 2005 essay would be used by the Discovery Channel and BBC in the creation of their documentary *20th Century Battlefields*, particularly the episode on the 1973 Arab-Israeli War.

special forces and airborne assault tactics learned in the bitter Egyptian quagmire of the Yemen War, an insurgency that lasted from 1962 to 1967.

During the operational planning phase for the October 1973 war, Shazly had put together all the elements for a successful crossing of the Suez Canal and breach of the Israeli Bar-Lev defensive line. When ordered by President Sadat to go beyond the range of the surface-to-air missile (SAM) air defense umbrella, Shazly became defiant, knowing this was tactical suicide. Egyptian generals—like the late Chief of Operations General Abdel-Ghani El-Gamasi—and Israeli authors have written that Shazly went into complete collapse over the decision. The final straw that led Sadat to relieve Shazly was his insistence on pulling back one or two divisions to counter-attack Ariel Sharon's units that had crossed into Egypt proper along the Ismailiyah road and were clearly a threat to Cairo. The accusation that Shazly went into mental collapse is unfounded and is an example of leaders not wanting to confront facts on the ground and refusing to consider a tactical withdrawal and regrouping of forces.

Shazly went into diplomatic exile as Egypt's ambassador to Portugal. Ultimately, his criticism of Sadat and the Camp David Peace Accords led him to be tried in absentia for illegally publishing his memoir and allegedly leaking military secrets while he was in a more permanent exile in Algeria and Libya. He dabbled with Islamic fundamentalism and the Muslim Brotherhood as a means of under-mining Sadat. In 1979 he wrote *Harb Uktubur: Mudhakiraat Al-Fariq El-Shazly* (The October War: Memoir of General Shazly).[1] It was published in Algeria by the National Establishment for Authors. Ignoring the political aspects of Shazly's career and his dabbling with Islamists, one finds a truly extraordinary book that is the best record of Egyptian tactical-level planning for the 1973 war. Mohamed Fawzi provides a strategic and operational Egyptian perspective; Shazly provides a detailed Arab tactical viewpoint. Shazly's attention to every detail of Operation Badr and his argument with War Minister Ismail Ali and Sadat about going beyond the twelve-kilometer air defense umbrella, which he believed was madness and not within the capability of the Egyptian military, make his book an important Arab viewpoint of the 1973 war. Shazly's memoir and the tactical lessons therein became so influential in Arab military circles that the book went through three printings within four years of initial publication.

This review essay, published in *Infantry Magazine*, will explore aspects of this 491-page book that demonstrate a sophisticated level of tactical analysis of a series of tactical problems and their solutions leading up to D-day, October 6, 1973. The focus is on Shazly's preparation for the conflict. In many ways reading the mem-oir of War Minister Mohamed Fawzi in addition to that of Shazly offers a clearer picture of the Egyptian perspective of the Arab-Israeli conflict. It is fascinating to see how Shazly dismisses the efforts of his relieved superior, Fawzi, who had been implicated in a conspiracy to remove Sadat from power. How much of this dismissal of Fawzi's contribution is political posturing to distance himself from his removed superior and how much is Shazly's attempting to bolster his own role in the planning of the 1973 war is a matter for discussion, debate, and speculation.

Egyptian Military Planning in 1971

Shazly writes, "When I assumed command as Egypt's armed forces chief of staff there was no offensive military plan for the recapture of the Sinai." The two existing plans, Plan 200 and Plan Granite, consisted primarily of commando raids that harassed the Israelis and focused on reconnaissance of the Sinai. Shazly's first order of business was to conduct assessments of Egypt's military capabilities and balance of forces between Egypt and Israel. What came out of this assessment was the following:

- The Egyptian air force (EAF) was weak and could not be relied upon to provide air cover for Egyptian military units operating in the Sinai.

- Israeli pilots had the advantage of a two-to-one ratio in flight-hour training over the Egyptian pilots, and electronic warfare in Egypt's fighter-bombers was nonexistent. Compared to the Israeli air force (IAF), the Egyptian air fleet was a decade behind the times.

- Soviet SAM defenses were respectable but not mobile. Air defense assets were fixed in place, as Egypt did not possess enough light and mobile SA-6 air defense systems. Therefore, Egyptian antiair missile coverage provided only limited air defense capability.

- Antiair guns, such as the ZSU-23, were useless against modern jet fighters, like the F-4 Phantom.

- Egyptian infantry formations were quantitatively superior, but Israel's qualitative edge made the Egyptian-Israeli infantry balance about equal.

- Egypt retained the quantitative edge in artillery. Nevertheless, the Israeli Bar-Lev line undermined Egypt's artillery advantage.

- Egypt's navy was quantitatively superior to Israel's but was useless in the face of Israeli air dominance that extended into the Gulf of Suez and the northern Red Sea. Because of Israeli air dominance, Egyptian frigates could not challenge Israel's coastal patrol craft.

After leading his General Staff through a rigorous analysis process, Shazly concluded that Egypt could only mount and sustain a limited offensive to seize the canal but not liberate the entire Sinai from Israeli occupation. One of the most important aspects of this analysis was that Shazly and his staff would use the EAF in a psychological and demoralizing strike along the Bar-Lev line and in bases in the Sinai.

The Idea for Egyptian SAM Air Defenses

On the basis of their experience during the War of Attrition (1967–1970), the Egyptian General Staff knew that IAF probes into Egyptian air space were characterized by deliberate avoidance of areas known to have high concentrations of SAM sites. Thus, Egyptian air defense planners proposed the creation of thick, fixed forests of SAM batteries that would protect Egyptian ground units advancing a distance of twelve kilometers beyond the eastern shore of the Suez Canal.

Shazly reports that in late summer of 1971, he discussed the General Staff's study with Egyptian war minister Mohammed Sadeq, who took over from General Mohamed Fawzi in May 1971. The study included a detailed examination of Israel's mobilization techniques and need to carry out a decisive and swift victory, as well as of the ability of the Egyptian armed forces to conduct a limited attack to take the eastern banks of the Suez Canal. The plan of attack and capture of the Bar-Lev line was code-named High Minarets, while the plan to attack and capture the Bar-Lev line and also advance ten to fifteen kilometers into the Sinai was code-named Plan 41. According to Shazly's account, a plan was developed, and then shared with the Soviets as a contingency, to take over the Bar-Lev line and push toward the Giddi, Mitla, and Khatmiya Passes, which were well beyond the range of SAM air defenses. The Egyptians did not trust Moscow with their original plans and proposed a more ambitious program to extract more technologically advanced military hardware from the Soviets. When the Egyptians concluded a massive arms deal with Moscow in October 1971, it included a hundred MiG-21s and a limited number of mobile SA-6 antiair missiles. The tactic of proposing a more complex operation to the Soviets seemed to pay off for the Egyptians in Russian military aid.

In late October 1972 Ismail Ali was promoted to war minister, and Shazly briefed him on the plans. Plan 41 by now had evolved into Granite 2, and High Minarets remained the same. During this time Shazly decided to share these plans with a wider audience of Egyptian flag officers to elicit their views on how Israel would likely conduct a counterattack. The director of military intelligence said to expect an Israeli ground response to reinforce the Bar-Lev line within six to eight hours. Shazly and the General Staff disagreed with this intelligence estimate. Rather, they believed that the Israeli mobilization would require ten to twelve hours to accomplish. This led to the tactical discussion of how to delay and undermine Israel's rapid armor response, and the ideas for the "Malyutka" suitcase antitank wire-guided missile (also known by its NATO designation the AT-3 Sagger) took form. These preliminary discussions between Shazly and the flag-level officers shaped the following plan of attack, which would form the nucleus of Operation Badr, formerly known as High Minarets:

- H-hour: Artillery and air strikes along the Bar-Lev line and the Sinai.
- H plus 5–7: Infantry crosses the canal by rubber boats and watercraft as a first assault on the Bar-Lev line.
- H plus 7–9: Bridges are up with an infusion of 30,000 troops along the Bar-Lev line.
- H plus 12: Infantry formations dig in to face the Israeli armored counterstrike.

Egyptian Troop Numbers and Office of Chief of Staff

When Shazly assumed his post as chief of staff in 1971, he commanded a total force of 800,000 troops. Before October 1973 this number would rise to 1,050,000. The Office of the Chief of Staff consisted of 5,000 officers and 20,000 enlisted. Under Shazly the Egyptian General Staff consisted of 40 flag-level officers representing 14 commands.

Shazly writes that he missed the personal contact he had had with officers in the field while serving in the special forces and as commander of the Red Sea Sector. Like many military officers who rise in rank, administration takes a front seat to spending time with troops. However, Shazly felt he should balance reports coming from his commanders with personal contact with field commanders and their staffs. Consequently, he initiated a series of monthly conferences with his forty commanders, who brought with them parts of their staff and battalion commanders. Over time the meetings grew to include more than a hundred senior officers. This solved one of the cardinal sins of the 1967 Six-Day War, when field commanders did not know about Plan Qahir for the defense of the Sinai. From July 1971 to September 1973, Shazly issued more than fifty chief of staff directives, which were distributed to the battalion level. How this was kept secret and Egyptian counterintelligence efforts are not discussed.

With a million-man army, including ten thousand battalion commanders, Shazly oversaw the production of millions of tactical booklets on such topics as desert navigation, air reconnaissance, disengagement and cease-fire, land vehicle navigation, and religion, creed, and victory. There is no indication whether Shazly concerned himself with these booklets eventually falling into Israeli hands or into the hands of other nations.

Among the problems facing him was a 30–40 percent shortage of officers across all ground units. He decided to promote enlisted personnel with college degrees, but many were less than enthusiastic about this promotion, as they felt it would extend their draft—one of the problems of a wholly conscript army. Of note, today's Egyptian armed forces are quite competitive as they represent a social safety net for the soldier and his or her family; however, conscription does remain. Shazly, for the first time in Egyptian military history, had to explain why he needed more officers and assure them that a promotion would not affect their enlistment. He immediately got 15,000 volunteers from the ranks and, using the 1971 to 1973 draft years, was able to acquire another 10,000 officers to add to the 5,000 officers from the regular army. The problems of recruitment extended into the enlisted ranks. As Egypt drafted only 120,000 out of 350,000 eligible draft-age men, this left a shortage of 40,000 troops per year. Shazly had no choice but to lower education and health standards. He also championed the ability of Egyptian women to enlist and become officers serving in the rear echelons.

Numerous Tactical Problems

Planning for the 1973 war revealed numerous tactical problems and subsequently changed, as outlined by Shazly, the Egyptian armed forces in many ways, including establishing amphibious battalions and refocusing on combat engineers as warrior-builders who could lead a frontal assault in conjunction with infantry. Some of the more notable issues are as follows:

The Bar-Lev Sand Barrier: The Bar-Lev line essentially consisted of sand ramparts three to ten meters high to deny a foothold for Egyptian armor when crossing the Sinai. The line included seventeen *maozim* ("strongpoints" in Hebrew) at ten- to thirty-kilometer intervals; each staffed by thirty to ninety soldiers. Each strongpoint was essentially an underground bunker so elaborate it included command and control, fuel storage, and communications centers.

Shazly writes that initially the plan was to get the engineers across the canal. Afterward, they would bore a hole through the sand of the Bar-Lev line, place two hundred kilograms of explosives, and withdraw two hundred meters before detonating the explosive. Egyptian combat engineers reported that this tactic still required a bulldozer to clear twelve hundred square meters of sand and debris. The task also required sixty people and five to six hours to complete the job. The solution came from an unlikely source: a young Egyptian engineer who had worked on the Aswan High Dam project. He argued that pressurized water could clear away sand efficiently. His idea was tested, and orders for hundreds of pressurized water cannon were placed.

The Napalm Pipes: The Israelis had attempted to install a spray that would create a floating sheet of fire along the canal. Although the Israeli effort never worked, the demonstration so impressed the Egyptians that Shazly writes how he and his planners "obsessed over the napalm pipes." Egyptians experimented with methods of blocking the pipes and using fire-retardant chemicals to counter the napalm, plus many other solutions. These napalm pipes were also mentioned in War Minister Fawzi's memoir.

Infantry Kit: It was determined that each infantryman from the initial assault would need enough ammunition and rations to sustain himself until H plus 12 or H plus 18. The soldier's load was further complicated by the necessity of carrying anti-tank weaponry. This included the Malyutka wire-guided tank-buster missile, which usually was employed by a team of two infantrymen, and SA-7 portable infantry antiair missiles. Ultimately, the basic pack an Egyptian infantryman carried was approximately twenty-five to forty kilograms. Rations, which included water, typically weighed four kilograms, clothes and bedding were ten kilograms, and an AK-47 assault rifle and three hundred rounds was fifteen kilograms.

Infantry Night-Vision Equipment: Egyptian troops would be trained to fight at night in an effort to effect tactical surprise on the Israelis, who believed that the Egyptians lacked this capability. So, unlike in the previous Arab-Israeli wars, Egyptian planners equipped their infantry with a variety of night-vision goggles and what Shazly calls "Starlighters" (probably night-vision scopes that rely on a combination of moonlight and starlight). Likewise, antitank infantry teams were equipped with darkened welding glasses to counter what Shazly's book calls "xenon rays," which were emitted by Israeli tanks to blind infantry. The Israelis had evidently employed this tactic during the War of Attrition.

Electric and Gas Golf Carts: Egyptian reconnaissance noted powerful golf carts that the Israelis were using to move around artillery shells and other supplies along the Bar-Lev line. On the basis of this observation, Shazly commissioned a similar cart to carry 150 kilograms of ammunition and supplies up the Bar-Lev incline. Egyptian defense officials raided local Vespa motor scooter agencies to buy the tires necessary for these specially designed military vehicles. More than 2,000 such carts were made, and according to Shazly's memoir, they carried 336 tons of equipment in the first days of the war.

Crossing Brigade: The Egyptian General Staff agonized over the composition of the initial assault force. The generals eventually came up with a figure of 32,000 troops crossing on twelve points in three waves. Specialized crossing battalions made up of military police (to direct traffic), waterborne craft drivers, and mechanics, as well as combat engineers, were established. This unit created forty crossing points for troops of the Egyptian 2nd and 3rd Armies made up of eighteen watercraft, thirty-five-foot bridges (for infantry only), and fifteen bridges (ten heavy for tanks and five light for jeeps and foot crossings).

The task-organized crossing brigade was made up of five hundred officers and a thousand noncommissioned officers. Shazly writes that its main challenge was keeping constant communication among the troops to ensure units linked up on the Sinai side of the canal. This required five hundred walkie-talkies and two hundred portable phones connected by 750 kilometers of wire. Each brigade would be assigned two of the bridges created along the canal.

Medium-Range Missiles: Shazly was aware of an earlier collaboration between Egyptian and German scientists in the 1950s to develop what would become the Al-Qahir and Al-Zafir missiles. When Shazly became chief of staff, he decided to spend time looking into the efficacy of these programs and was the first military leader to order tests of these missiles, which had been in storage. In September 1971 a series of tests were done, and it was determined that the missile was highly inaccurate. Despite this finding, two rocket battalions were created; one code-named Teen (Fig) and the second code-named Zaitun (Olive). Unless one has memorized portions of the Quran, the code names mean nothing. They are a reference to the "Verse of the Fig" (Surat *Al-Teen*, chapter 95:1), which begins, "By the Fig and the Olive, and Mount Sinai." In other words, these code names were specifically meant to refer to the Sinai Peninsula, and these rocket battalions were delegated responsibility for launching medium-range missiles into Israeli positions in the Sinai.

Hovercraft Experiments: Shazly commissioned a British firm to look into creating a small hovercraft that would carry the weight of a single tank across the Great Bitter and Timsah Lakes. A small-scale model and drawings were developed, but the development of the 30-knot craft was never undertaken.

Joint Syrian-Egyptian Studies on the Canal Crossing: Shazly's book describes how "a Syrian major—a combat engineer—with many ideas on how the Egyptians might approach crossing the Suez Canal—spent several months in Egypt studying the problem. Although the major's ideas did not amount to anything actionable," Shazly kept the project going to demonstrate Egyptian-Syrian cooperation to his troops and engineers and to deceive Israel into thinking that Egypt was not getting any closer to solving the problem of assaulting the Bar-Lev line.

Air Defense, the Incessant Problem: Shazly had a healthy respect for Israeli capabilities and envied the enemy's ability to locally manufacture the Gabriel and what he terms the "Loz" air-to-surface missiles. The Egyptians negotiated for six thousand Russians to provide for Egypt's air defense during Shazly's tenure as chief of staff. Shazly also traveled to Pyongyang, and afterward the late North Korean dictator Kim Il Sung provided twenty MiG pilots to aid in providing air defense for Egypt proper in July 1971.

Training and Exercises

One of the major lessons of the 1967 Six-Day War was that despite the lead-up to hostilities, the Egyptian army had not conducted a division-level exercise since 1954. (Fawzi's memoir gives the date of the last division-level exercise as 1956, on the eve of the Suez Crisis.) The Egyptians were not going to make the same mistake again, and Shazly presided over sixteen major exercises called the Tahrir (Liberation) Series. Many of his fifty-three directives were issued as a result of what he observed during these exercises in the field. While Shazly's memoir discounts Fawzi, he actually improved on Fawzi's groundwork in the constant conduct of field exercises and training with new Soviet equipment.

The following is a short list of skills the exercises focused on:

◆ Opening gaps along a sand barrier

◆ Using flame agents while crossing a water barrier

◆ Paddling across a water barrier and assaulting a sand barrier under live fire and flammables

◆ Directing and concentrating fire (for artillery)

◆ Using Soviet-made BMP amphibious infantry fighting vehicles

◆ Fighting at night (division level)

◆ Operating tanks with laser directional finders

◆ Flying Tu-16 bombers

While serving as an attaché in London, Shazly had been very impressed with the professional military education (PME) programs in the British army. He took these ideas and implemented field trips for junior officers and leaders at the battalion level and below to encourage unit cohesion. He also organized hundreds of competitive sporting events between forces, units, and brigades. It is noteworthy that Shazly's book does not mention his education at Fort Benning's Infantry School from 1953 to 1954. It must have deeply affected him, for upon his return he was charged with creating Egypt's paratrooper school, and he organized his country's first paratroop formation, Mizalaat. His daughter, Chahdane, after nagging her father to conduct a jump, became the first Egyptian woman to jump from a military plane with her father.[2]

War Minister Field Marshal Sadeq and General Shazly

When Shazly proposed his limited war theories to War Minister Field Marshal Sadeq, the minister still thought that Shazly's limited attack on the Bar-Lev would be the first stage of the liberation of the entire Sinai, rather than Shazly's more modest goal of establishing a massive beachhead and occupying twelve to fifteen kilometers on the Israeli side of the Suez Canal. This would not be the first time the two would clash, and Shazly's memoir devotes several pages to the subject. What distinguished Shazly from many other generals was his willingness to speak his mind on tactical and operational matters. Here are a few of his disputes with Sadeq:

The T-62 Tank Dispute: The availability of new Soviet T-62 tanks revealed a significant difference in opinion between Shazly and Sadeq on the tactical deployment of Egyptian armor assets. Shazly wanted to concentrate the T-62s into a new tank division that he could deploy along the Sinai front, where they were most needed. Sadeq preferred to spread the tanks among T-55s and T-34s in several armored units. Commander in Chief Sadeq felt that concentrating these tanks in the hands of a single brigadier general was too dangerous for Egypt's internal security. This argument is somewhat reminiscent of the disagreement between German field marshal Erwin Rommel and Field Marshal Gerd Von Runstedt over the division of panzers along the Normandy coast in 1944. Rommel wanted to concentrate his panzers using strategic depth to repel the invasion where it was most crucial. Von Runstedt preferred to spread his panzers along the coastline and repel the invaders from the shore. In hindsight, the T-62, while a maneuverable tank, suffered from a smooth bore that was a liability in combat during the 1973 Yom Kippur War.[3] Comparing Shazly's and Fawzi's recollections, the latter makes more of the significance of convincing Moscow to provide the new T-72 main battle tank. It is likely the Soviets provided many more T-62s than the newly developed T-72.

The Captain Eid Affair: In 1972 a tank commander named Captain Eid was given the mission of intercepting Israeli paratroopers who dropped in and around Cairo. On his own initiative, he decided to exercise his unit in Cairo and stopped his tanks at a downtown mosque so that his troops could pray. As soon as they came out of the mosque, military police surrounded the armored unit, and Captain Eid was rewarded for his initiative by being declared insane (rather than being charged with treason and inciting revolution). Shazly disagreed with the military police's decision to cashier this junior officer, a punitive decision affirmed by War Minister Sadeq, and according to his memoir, he attempted to intervene. But the counter-revolutionary culture in Egypt was too great to save what probably may have been a competent officer. Sadeq was eventually relieved from his post of commander in chief in part because of this incident. Shazly's and Fawzi's memoirs reveal the sclerotic impact preserving the regime had on military initiative, and reading their books provides insights into the problems of having an army dedicated to internal security versus military power projection.

General Ismail Ali

Ismail Ali was an apolitical general, and therefore the perfect choice in a region with a propensity for military coups. He was also a learned infantryman who excelled in his studies at the Frunze Higher Military Academy and who took copious notes as a student. By all accounts he was a Clausewitzian purist who studied the Prussian master through Soviet academies.

Shazly had once gotten into a shouting match with Ismail in 1960, while Shazly commanded Egyptian peacekeepers in the Congo protecting the elected administration of Patrice Lumumba from various rebellions, chiefly in the mineral-rich Katanga region. Ismail Ali—a brigadier at the time—had come to inspect then-colonel Shazly and his unit just as Joseph Mobutu Sese Seko had overthrown and murdered Lumumba, and the Egyptian mission was unraveling. It was a tense environment and made worse by Ismail Ali's failure to appreciate the situation in Leopoldville. Ismail came in with rank to enforce his authority without regard for the government collapse. Now, as Ismail assumed the position of Egypt's war minister, Shazly argued with Sadat that this appointment would create a divisive chain of command owing to Ismail Ali's and Shazly's previous bad experiences with one another. Shazly still did not appreciate Sadat's method of appointing generals, which was in fact meant to create a divide-and-conquer environment in which no one officer could concentrate power in his own hands. Shazly was merely confirming what Sadat was hoping to achieve. In 1969 Ismail became chief of staff, and Shazly was commander of special forces in the Cairo air base of Inchass; there was tension between the two officers. Once again, the two were forced to work with each other in 1972, when Ismail Ali replaced Sadeq as war minister.

Colonel Trevor Dupuy highlights major tactical issues during the October 1973 war in his 1978 seminal book *Elusive Victory: The Arab-Israeli Wars, 1947–1974*.[4] These issues include differences in tactical philosophy between Shazly and Ismail. The first issue was a debate over the breakout beyond the Suez Canal. Ismail sensed that Israeli forces could not simultaneously withstand a Syrian onslaught and an Egyptian offensive into the Giddi and Mitla Passes. Shazly had meticulously planned for the initial takeover of the canal, pushing no more than fifteen kilometers beyond (within range of SAM protection). "Timing is everything," according to Dupuy. Ismail, Depuy argues, "was correct in his assumption that had Egyptian forces attacked between October 7–9, they would have had a chance to secure the passes." I think it is important to pause and understand the importance of these passes. The Sinai is divided into unequal halves by dry mountainous terrain and these passes, and main roads linking east to west go through these passes. The first side to secure the passes will secure the Sinai, and a battalion setting up defensive positions in the hilly and mountainous terrain of the passes can wreak havoc on any opposing force attempting to dislodge the defensive force from the Giddi and Mitla Passes. These passes are of concern today because of the growing militant Islamist insurgency in the Sinai, which constantly challenges Egyptian army units in the peninsula.

Die Cast and Rubicon Crossed

The highest echelon of Syria's high command was led by Defense Minister General Mustafa Tlas, who arrived in the seaport of Alexandria on August 21, 1973. Thirteen Syrian and Egyptian senior officers led by the war minister from each nation spent three days discussing force readiness, military capabilities, and timetables of attack, with the objective of reporting back to their respective political leaders the range of dates for D-day. The date of attack was set for between September 7–11 and October 5–11, 1973.

Sadat conducted his last war counsel with Egyptian military leaders on October 1. That day the respective commanding officers of the 2nd and 3rd Armies were informed of D-day: October 6, with H-hour set at 1400 Cairo time. Shazly's memoir describes the actual point of no return as an exchange between Egyptian naval chief Admiral Fouad Abu-Zikry and himself that day. Shazly gave the order personally to Admiral Zikry to deploy several submarines to blockade the Bab-el-Mandab and Tiran Strait. The Egyptian naval chief told Shazly, "I want to be clear [that] once they deploy with orders, they cannot be recalled until hostilities begin. The sub commanders will commence attacking once they open their orders at sea." Following is a breakdown of when, according to Shazly, commanders were informed of D-day and H-hour:

- October 1—commanders, 2nd and 3rd Armies
- October 3—divisional commanders
- October 4—brigade commanders
- October 5—flight wing and battalion commanders
- October 6, H minus 6 hours—most units and personnel informed

On the evening of October 5, Shazly writes, he left Center Ten Headquarters, turned in early, and returned the next morning. He notes that he had put his faith in God and in what would become the most meticulously and professionally planned military endeavor that the Egyptian military mind had yet conceived.

Shazly's memoir describes the crossing with the details of every hour and unit that crossed over the canal. Since much has been written about the canal crossing, I shall focus on the controversial decision to advance beyond SAM protective range, leading to punishing strikes on Egyptian forces by the IAF. As the 2nd and 3rd Armies advanced, a seam would eventually develop between them and be exploited by the Israelis, leading to their ultimate tactical victory. After October 14, with Sadat and Ismail insisting Shazly extend forces into the passes, the chief of staff made four trips to the Sinai field headquarters. His last trip found the 2nd Army commander in a state of complete collapse, having suffered a heart attack in the field. Both the 2nd and 3rd Army commanders carried out the orders to proceed beyond SAM air coverage but warned Shazly, who already knew, that Ismail's orders were suicidal. Shazly was the first Egyptian general to acknowledge the entrapment of the Egyptian 3rd Army, and he blames this squarely on Sadat and his politically correct sycophant war minister, General Ismail.

Shazly never got over Sadat's orders, which completely destroyed his military gains, first developed as Plan High Minarets. His memoir includes the text of a letter he sent in 1979 requesting Sadat be brought before Parliament to answer for his order, which caused the death of thousands of Egyptian soldiers. He remained a lifelong opponent of Sadat and the Israeli peace plan, and at one point he dabbled with Islamist politics. There are many lessons in his memoir: most important, insight into the nature of Egyptian civil-military affairs, the problems of having a uniformed defense minister, and the way internal political intrigue undermines operation planning for warfare. Shazly's is an important part of a series of books that gives an Arab perspective on warfare and the 1973 war.

In the ultimate irony, one of the leading military architects of the 1973 Arab-Israeli War was written out of the history books by both Sadat and Mubarak. The latter denied Shazly additional pension benefits that come with certain decorations that he had been awarded. Over time Mubarak's role in the final Arab-Israeli war was enhanced by almost Soviet-style mythmaking, including the painting of fictitious scenes of General Mubarak at Sadat's side in the operations room alone. The original photo has several senior officers (minus Mubarak) crowding around Sadat staring at the map table. In a bit of fatalism, Shazly died on February 10, 2011; the next day Mubarak was forcibly removed from three decades of rule. It is not known the extent to which the eighty-eight-year-old Shazly knew about what was happening around him; however, his funeral was used to honor a competent soldier, "The Real Hero of the Crossing." Al Jazeera produced a documentary about Shazly in 2012, an army-built road connecting Cairo to Ismailiyah has been named after him, and finally, the 2013 graduating class of Egypt's military academy was named the Shazly Corps in a ceremony honoring the deceased general and his family, who shared in the victimization felt by many Egyptians under the Mubarak regime.

★★ Appendix 3 ★★

Egyptian General Abdel-Moneim Riad
The Creation of an Adaptive Military Thinker*

Introduction

A rab militaries are notorious for their lack of individual initiative and a rigidity that tends to favor scripted methods of warfare. Some nations, like Egypt, are trying to break away from the rigidity of Soviet-style doctrine and are slowly attempting to adopt combined arms and Western-style tactics. By the late twentieth century, Egypt had at least two generations of officers trained in the United States and furnished with American military hardware, making the Egyptian armed forces very different from the ones in which General Riad served. General Abdel-Fatah al-Sisi, the current war minister and some argue the de facto leader of Egypt, was a graduate of the U.S. Army War College (Class of 2006). He is also the first war minister never to have been involved in Egypt's wars with Israel. Field Marshal Mohamed Tantawi was the last war minister to have served in Egypt's wars with Israel.[1] Arab general staffs, on a more philosophical level, must understand that whether adopting Eastern bloc or Western arms by default, they buy into Eastern or Western doctrine and military methods of fighting. When posed with this question, senior Egyptian generals point to the 1973 Yom Kippur War as an example of using Soviet technology and Egyptian improvisation and tactics in a synthesis that led to a few military surprises during the 1973 Arab-Israeli War. It is hard to argue the success of the opening days of the 1973 Arab-Israeli War, but the Egyptians appear to view the war from the lens of the opening days and not in its entirety. Many Arabic books on the 1973 war focus on the opening successes of Egyptian and Syrian forces but pay scarce attention to lessons learned as Israeli forces tactically achieved the entrapment of the Egyptian 3rd Army. When confronted, it is easy to blame superpower politics for their loss.

Mohammed Al-Gawady, a prolific military author and historian, has conducted quality research and interviewed more than a dozen Egyptian generals,

---

*Reprinted from the Professional Forum, *Infantry* 93, no. 2 (March/April 2004), and updated to reflect current changes in Egypt.

revealing the depth of their tactical and strategic thoughts. He has published several volumes on Egyptian generals who fought, planned, and discussed the 1967 Six-Day War, 1967 reconstruction of the Egyptian armed forces, and 1973 Yom Kippur War. In the late 1990s and early 2000s, Gawady wrote the biographies and analyzed the strategic thoughts of several Egyptian generals, such as the late Abdel-Ghani El-Gamasi (operations director, 1973 war) and Madkoor Aboul-Eez (air marshal after the 1967 war). Egyptians owe this writer a debt of gratitude for preserving the Arab perspective of modern warfare.

This essay will explore Gawady's earliest military biography, that of General Abdel-Moneim Riad (1919–1969), one of Egypt's most adaptive military thinkers.[2] Gawady published this in 1984 as a street pocketbook biography of General Riad, who also has the distinction of being the most senior officer killed in action at the Suez Canal front. Riad is honored with a statue in downtown Cairo, a monument that has seen its share of protests, starting with the 2011 ousting of Mubarak and recently with the 2013 ousting of Mohamed Morsi.

Riad served as commandant of the antiair defense school between 1952 and 1953. While at the antiair school, he focused on education methods and curriculum reform. This included an emphasis on cutting-edge training and improvisation and innovation with the weapons at hand. Riad then assumed command of the 1st Antiair Brigade in Alexandria. As commander of the brigade, he noted that the pilotless planes that were imported and used to train gun crews cost the Egyptian government 50,000 Egyptian pounds. These planes were radio guided and once hit became useless. Riad, now a lieutenant colonel, brought the problems of cost and onetime use to his brother, Dr. Mahmoud Riad, a PhD in electronic engineering who conducted a reverse engineering of the imported plane and worked with his brother to produce a local version for a quarter of the cost. Another innovation Abdel-Moneim Riad brought to Egypt's armed forces during this time was the introduction of radar and electronics to antiair guns. He saw the potential for radar combined with antiair guns to increase accuracy.

The 1956 Suez War

When the combined Israeli, British, and French invasion of Egypt began in 1956 to remove Nasser from power, Riad leapt into his command car and shuttled between Cairo's airfields in an effort to organize defenses and to give orders to fire on jets attacking Egypt's air force assets on the ground. While missiles slammed into the airports and runways were torn by cluster bombs, Riad saw Egyptian aircrews pushing planes into hardened shelters and attempting to disperse the fighter aircraft.

Riad learned much from the Suez campaign, and it would shape his ideas when he became chief of staff eleven years later. While Nasser and War Minister Amer were drunk with political victory, Eisenhower ordered a withdrawal of Anglo-French Israeli forces to forestall a superpower confrontation. Riad understood that the Suez War was a military failure and saw air space in a new light.

The M. V. Frunze Higher Military Academy

Starting in 1958, Colonel Riad attended a yearlong course at the famous Frunze Higher Military Academy, the former Soviet Union's premier school for advanced tactics and strategy. He was among the second group of Arab students to attend the academy. There he absorbed lessons directly from Soviet brigade, divisional, and army commanders who fought in World War II. The Soviets were impressed by his knowledge of Russian (Riad learned Russian, English, French, and German), and his seat was marked by the Frunze instructors for incoming Arab officers to know that here sat the Golden General of the Class of 1959. He learned Russian, German, and French by investing in private tutors as early as 1952. A main criticism of Gawady's biography is it offers no information on Riad's thesis or the battles he took an interest in. Upon Riad's return, he was promoted to flag rank.

Riad then worked at the Egyptian General Staff headquarters as an adviser on air defense. Despite his rank, he attended the latest courses offered by the Egyptian artillery school in missile defense, advanced rocketry, and several other topics to keep current on the latest advances in air defense systems.

General Riad and the Egyptian Military Culture

Riad observed an Egyptian army in disarray with nepotism and military leaders' attempts to profit from their offices without regard for the military readiness of the forces under their command. The Egyptian army began to operate as a business—focusing on making money and losing sight of its real mission, combat. Riad began criticizing what he forecast would be a massive defeat of Egyptian forces; he also threatened to resign his commission. Recognizing he was the only expert in antiair defense, Egyptian leaders could not easily accept his resignation, but they also could not allow him to criticize War Minister Amer and his cronies. A compromise was reached, and Riad was dispatched to Jordan as part of the Unified Arab Command. This decision saved him from the taint of the 1967 Six-Day War and propelled him to later become armed forces chief of staff, when Nasser began looking for a new breed of Egyptian senior officer to reconstruct his tattered forces.

Riad's Unified Command Experience

No record exists of how Riad felt when he was given orders to Jordan, but certainly being selected as armed forces chief of staff was far from his mind. He probably thought the move to Jordan was an exile for speaking out against military decay and corruption. His new post at the Unified Arab Command allowed him to visit several Arab nations, their leaders, and their military officers and to learn of their plans in order to fashion a theory of an Arab-wide air defense network that would guarantee freedom of movement within Arab nations before plans were made for an offensive against Israel.

Between March 1965 and July 1966, Riad attended the Egyptian Higher Military College (known today as the Nasser Higher Military College), where he once again distinguished himself academically before returning to Jordan as a lieutenant general. Riad became convinced at the end of May 1967 that Israel would attack Egypt, and he requested that the Jordanians relieve him so he could go to Egypt and organize air defenses. His request was refused, but one hour before Israeli jets decimated the Egyptian air force, around 0700 on June 5, 1967, Jordanian observers reported a mass formation of Israeli air force jets headed toward Egypt. General Riad was informed, and he sent a signal to Egypt, which, owing to a series of errors and changed codes, never reached the Egyptian General Staff. (The Jordanians were not informed by the Egyptians of the new codes.)

The 1967 War

In late May 1967, days before the outbreak of the 1967 Six-Day War, General Riad met with King Hussein, as tensions built between Egypt and Israel. Riad reviewed the Jordanian troops under his command. Gawady's biography contains no reference to the formations Riad commanded or the sector within the Jordanian front he fought in, but it does mention that Jordanian forces felt attached to Riad, who was a dynamic organizer under fire. On June 11 Nasser accepted responsibility for the crushing defeat and began the process of removing War Minister Field Marshal Amer from office (this process ended with the field marshal's suicide). While Riad was in Jordan, Nasser named him Egypt's new armed forces chief of staff, and he would serve alongside the new war minister General Mohamed Fawzi. Of note, Fawzi's memoir details the relationship between Riad and himself while they were in office. Both men were involved in isolating Field Marshal Amer and managing the threat he posed to Nasser by not resigning after the debacle of the 1967 Six-Day War (see chapter 5).

Riad spent his first days as chief of staff assessing the Suez Canal front to discover the reasons for the rout of the Egyptian army. These reasons were as follows:

- Egypt lacked an effective command and control system.
- Officers fled and did not command their troops.
- There were semiliterate soldiers fighting the twentieth-century war.

General Fawzi, General Ismail Ali (commander of the Suez front from 1967 to 1972), and General Riad took a hard look at the Egyptian armed forces and began to make reconstruction plans on several levels. Gawady's biography of Riad is one of his earlier books and differs from his 1999–2002 books, which explore in depth the discussions between generals and Egyptian presidents Nasser and Sadat. We now know, for instance, that General Ismail Ali had little to do with the reconstruction of Egyptian arms in the aftermath of the 1967 Six-Day War and is now mainly remembered as a sycophant of Sadat in the 1973 Yom Kippur War.

Upon his return from Baghdad, Riad went to inspect the front lines of the Suez front and to motivate Egyptian troops by sharing with them his recent trip to Iraq. An artillery duel broke out during his trip, and he took cover in a foxhole that sustained artillery hits; he died in the field on March 9, 1969.

Strategic Legacy of General Riad

General Riad's idea of breaking down Arab goals into two phases was unveiled by Nasser in an Arab League summit. The first phase was securing military freedom of action within Arab states, particularly with air defense. The second and final objective was to collectively liberate Palestine and lands taken by the Israelis in 1967. These were tall orders strategically; however, the emphasis on air defense would lay the seeds for the massive and overlapping air defense system created by the Egyptians, which decimated Israeli warplanes in the first forty-eight hours of the 1973 war.

In 1953 Colonel Riad challenged a Swiss firm to build an antiair system for Egypt, arguing that technology and jet fighters have changed the way antiair guns can be employed and especially the rate of fire of antiair projectiles. He brought together Swiss and Egyptian engineers who modified the system to Egyptian specifications. This is a lesson to military leaders of the need to push contractors to provide capable weapons systems. Gawady's biography claims that Riad's modifications were employed in North Atlantic Treaty Organization (NATO) countries as well.

Riad also wanted reform in education; it was not enough for an instructor to be a subject matter expert. He invested in a two-month course for military instructors to attend at Egypt's Education Ministry. He wanted people who had the skills to impart knowledge and learn the art of teaching students. Riad was the first general to concern himself with the way Egyptian officers and soldiers learned from Western and former Soviet manuals. He insisted that students not only study the Arabic translations but also make an effort to read the tactical works and operational manuals in the original language.

General Riad also paid attention to the individual soldier. During a lecture to military doctors, he said, "A doctor's place was beside the fighting infantryman, ensuring he [the infantryman] was in top physical condition and treating his battle wounds. Despite the presence of military technology, a military cook [field morale] can make the difference as to defeat or victory." Riad also believed that military commanders are made, not born, through education, opportunity, trust, and experience. He urged Egyptian generals to give their juniors chances to excel and learn from their mistakes. He also believed in soliciting advice from second and third echelons before making a military decision or drafting war plans. These are timeless lessons for any military commander.

NOTES

PREFACE

1. Over an official dinner in 2005 at the Algerian ambassador's residence in Washington, D.C., I was delighted to learn that the Algerian two-star general seated next to me had read my assessment in *Military Review* of the controversial Algerian general Khalid Nezzar's memoir analyzing insurgency tactics used against French colonial rule. We had a candid conversation about the 1990s Algerian civil war and General Nezzar's role in nullifying the electoral gains of the Islamic Salvation Front (FIS) and declaring what in effect was a military junta. Algeria's ambassador, Amine Kherby, could not resist telling us that his residence was once the home of Vice President Lyndon Baines Johnson; in fact, Johnson had spent the night there after the horrible events of 1963 in Dallas. The experience at the ambassador's residence made me reexamine Robert Caro's Pulitzer Prize–winning volumes on Johnson. It was an exchange of ideas shaped by personal experience, something I insist on bringing into my classrooms at the National Defense University and the National Intelligence University in Washington, D.C.

2. Abdel-Fatah al-Sisi, *Democracy in the Middle East* (Carlisle, PA: Army War College, 2006), http://www.scribd.com/doc/158975076/1878–001.

INTRODUCTION

1. Mohamed Fawzi, *Harb Thalathah Sanawat, 1967–1970: Muzakirat al-Fareeq al-Awal Mohamed Fawzi, Wazeer al-Harbiyah al-Asbaq* [The Three Years War, 1967–1970: The Memoir of General Mohamed Fawzi, the Former War Minister], 5th ed. (Cairo: Dar al-Mustaqbal Printing, 1990).

2. David Kimche and Dan Bawley, *The Six Day War: Prologue and Aftermath* (New York: Stein and Day, 1971), 249. In his career Kimche rose to deputy director of Mossad.

3. Anthony Nutting, *Nasser* (New York: Dutton, 1972), 430, 486.

4. Sergei N. Khrushchev, *Nikita Khrushchev and the Creation of a Superpower*, trans. Shirley Benson (University Park: Pennsylvania State University, 2000), 212–213.

CHAPTER 1. Deep Structural Problems Leading to the 1967 Six-Day War Defeat

1. Arthur Goldschmidt, *Biographical Dictionary of Modern Egypt* (Boulder, CO: Lynne Rienner, 2000), 58. Goldschmidt cites Fawzi as being commandant until 1961. Fawzi's memoir says he was commandant until 1962.

2. Gamal Abdel Nasser, *Egypt's Liberation: The Philosophy of the Revolution* (Washington, DC: Public Affairs, 1955).

3. An April 13, 1964, State Department document captured American policy makers' views of the competition with Moscow in the Middle East: "Moscow believes that the British position in Southern Arabia is vulnerable to a combination of border harassment, internal subversion, and pressure in the UN. Khrushchev, we believe, will try to exploit these weaknesses during his visit to Cairo in May, by encouraging Nasser to use the UAR presence in Yemen to support a war, a 'national liberation' struggle." Thomas Hughes, "Indications of Soviet-Arab Pressures against Aden," memorandum to George Ball, April 13, 1964, in *Foreign Relations of the United States, 1964–1968*, ed. Nina Davis Howland and David S. Patterson (Washington, DC: Government Printing Office, 2000), 21:127.

4. In testimony given by General Fawzi to the Committee for the Historical Record convened in the aftermath of the 1967 Six-Day War, Fawzi replied to the following questions:

   Q: *What were the responsibilities of Field Marshal Amer, deputy supreme commander, towards the supreme commander, the president of the republic?*

   Fawzi: *There were no responsibilities.*

   Q: *What were Field Marshal Amer's responsibilities towards the legislature [the National Assembly] at that time?*

   Fawzi: *There were no responsibilities. At the time, no one in the country could question Abd al-Hakim Amer. The president of the republic could not do so, and the National Assembly could not invite him to take the executive seat in the assembly, and answer any questions put to him. This of course never happened. . . . The armed forces were under the command and control of one individual who was answerable to no one.*

   This dialogue captures the essence of Nasser's decision to concentrate military power in the hands of one person. Abdel-Ghani El-Gamasi describes the pre-1967 chain of command as General Fawzi coming third behind Shams Badran and Field Marshal Amer. Badran never rose above the rank of captain, never attended any command and staff colleges, and was appointed war minister below Deputy Commander in Chief Amer solely because he was an Amer sycophant. See Abdel-Ghani El-Gamasi, *Memoirs of Field Marshal El-Gamasi* (Cairo: American University of Cairo Press, 1993), 84–86, for Fawzi's further remarks to the Committee for the Historical Record.

5. Nicholas Katzenbach, circular telegram, October 28, 1966, in *Foreign Relations of the United States, 1964–1968*, 21:34. Excerpt as follows: "Some elements in Egypt seem to believe USG [the U.S. government], particularly 'CIA', actively engaged in joint planning and operations against the UAR regime with Saudi and Jordanians."

CHAPTER 2. The Impact of the Yemen Guerrilla War on Egyptian Military
    Thinking

1. In an exchange between Nasser and his ambassador to Washington, Ahmed Hussein, about the Dulles brothers (John Foster and Allen, who led the State Department and CIA respectively during the Eisenhower administration), Hussein warned, "Remember Guatemala," and Nasser replied, "To hell with Guatemala!" They were referencing the CIA overthrow of Jacobo Arbenz in 1954. See Stephen Kinzer, *The Brothers: John Foster Dulles, Allen Dulles, and Their Secret War* (New York: Henry Holt, 2013), 211–212. Kinzer's book also discusses the Omega Project, a campaign designed under Allen Dulles to undermine Nasser's influence domestically and internationally.

2. When Kennedy was a U.S. senator, he voiced support for nationalist aspirations such as Algerian independence.

3. Frank Leith Jones, *Blowtorch: Robert Komer, Vietnam, and the American Cold War Strategy* (Annapolis, MD: Naval Institute Press, 2013), 51–70.

4. Komer was allegedly a primary architect of a program to discredit Nasser by drawing Egypt deeper into the Yemen War, restricting wheat shipments to place a further strain on the Egyptian economy, and providing a wide range of support to Israel in the hopes of bringing about regime change in Cairo (Hazem Kandil, *Soldiers, Spies and Statesmen: Egypt's Road to Revolt* [New York: Verso, 2012], 73). To appreciate the concerns Johnson and later Nixon had over Nasser's policies and Egypt's impact on the Cold War strategic balance, take time to read some of the selected State Department, National Security Council, and CIA documents provided in notes throughout this book. Also read Frank Leith Jones' excellent book on Robert Komer titled *Blowtorch*, which contains excellent details about how Komer shaped Middle East policy generally and managed Nasser specifically during the Kennedy and Johnson administrations.

5. My mother, unable to obtain a decent education in Saudi Arabia in the late 1950s, attended one of the best private French Catholic schools in Cairo. Among her classmates was the daughter of Patrice Lumumba, Juliana. Nasser had provided asylum and support to the family of the slain Congolese independence leader. My mother's recollections began my interest in Lumumba and the tragedy of the Congo.

6. Owen L. Sirrs, *Nasser and the Missile Age in the Middle East* (New York: Routledge, 2006), 60–61.

7. Jesse Ferris, *Nasser's Gamble: How Intervention in Yemen Caused the Six-Day War and the Decline of Egyptian Power* (Princeton, NJ: Princeton University Press, 2013), 204.

8. Sherman Kent, "Nasser's Problems and Prospects in Yemen," special memorandum, February 18, 1965, in *Foreign Relations of the United States, 1964–1968*, 21:674–675. The following excerpt from this memo sheds light on Nasser's intractable problem in Yemen: "Yet Nasser's efforts to find a way out of the Yemen mess—which Prime Minister Ali Sabry has characterized as 'Egypt's Vietnam'—have thus far been futile."

CHAPTER 3. Mistakes Made in the Preparation of Egyptian Combat Formations for the 1967 Six-Day War

1. Major General Brown and his wife, Susan, were tragically lost to the National Defense University, the Eisenhower School, and the U.S. Air Force on April 19, 2013. General Brown was an avid supporter of my writing and a mentor to me, and Sue was my student, auditing my graduate-level Islam course at the National Defense University. General Brown's foreword was published in *Infantry* a few weeks before his private plane went down in Williamsburg, Virginia. I had a chance to give him the edition of the magazine before his tragic and unexpected death.

2. Moheiddine is mainly remembered as the chief architect of Egypt's security state. He died in 2012 at the age of ninety-four, taking insight into his role in the 1952 revolution and the founding of such entities as the General Intelligence Directorate (GID) to the grave. Kandil, *Soldiers, Spies and Statesmen*, 19.

3. General Rikhye has written that Nasser and Amer disagreed on the translation of the English letter delivered to UNEF. Their disagreement centered on whether to withdraw or redeploy. Nasser wanted UNEF to redeploy to the Sharm el-Sheikh region from the Israeli border and not withdraw. Amer told Nasser that the letter had already been sent. This shows Nasser's concerns about

the language and its implication. See Fawzi's interview about this event in the 1999 PBS documentary *The Fifty Years War: Israel and the Arabs*, directed by David Ash and Dai Richards. See also Michael B. Oren, *Six Days of War: June 1967 and the Making of the Modern Middle East* (New York: Oxford University Press, 2002), 67. Fawzi gave the interview one year before his death and never mentions this detail in his written memoir, published in 1984, a curious omission.

4. Indar Jit Rikhye, *The Sinai Blunder: Withdrawal of the United Nations Emergency Force Leading to the Six Day War of June 1967* (London: Frank Cass, 1980), 16–20. Rikhye's account supplements Fawzi's memoir, filling gaps with, for example, discussion of a May 18, 1967, incident in which Bedouin bandits broke into a Canadian Ordnance Company facility and, in an exchange of fire, killed a Canadian soldier. This was two days after Fawzi delivered his letter requesting the withdrawal of the UNEF and could have been misinterpreted as an escalation by the Egyptians. See Rikhye, *Sinai Blunder*, 27.

5. Ibid., 165.

6. The late Middle East scholar Nadav Safran proposed this argument regarding Nasser's intentions and cited the May 17, 1967, edition of the Egyptian newspaper *al-Ahram*, which published the complete text of Fawzi's letter, laced with hyperbolic commentary. Nadav Safran, *From War to War: The Arab-Israeli Confrontations* (New York: Pegasus, 1969), 286.

7. Rikhye, *Sinai Blunder*, 162.

8. Richard Parker, ed., *The Six Day War: A Retrospective* (Gainesville: University Press of Florida, 1996), 45.

9. Dan Hofstadter, ed., *Egypt and Nasser* (New York: Facts on File, 1973), 3:119–121.

10. John Fricker, "Boeing/McDonnell Douglas F-4 Phantom II Current Operators," *World Air Power Journal* 40 (Spring 2000): 59–60.

11. Lon Nordeen, *Fighters over Israel: The Story of the Israeli Air Force from the War of Independence to the Bekaa Valley* (London: Guild, 1991), 99.

12. "World Air Forces: Israel," *Flight International*, November 16–22, 2004.

13. J. C. Hurewitz, "Superpower Rivalry and the Arab-Israeli Dispute: Involvement or Commitment," in *The USSR and the Middle East*, ed. Michael Confino and Shimon Shamir (Jerusalem: Israel University Press, 1973), 155–156.

14. Ibid., 160.

15. Ibid., 157.

16. Mason Freeman, "The Suez Canal," memorandum to Melvin Laird, May 1, 1971, in *Foreign Relations of the United States, 1969–1976*, ed. Linda W. Qaimmaqami and Edward C. Keefer (Washington, DC: U.S. Government Printing

Office, 2008), 24:100–102. The following excerpts from Freeman's memo add depth to a reading of Fawzi's memoir. As you read, think about the overall general strategic themes and applications of the conclusions and observations of the Pentagon's Joint Staff of the late 1960s versus Egypt's security challenges in the twenty-first century, which include a stable Suez Canal Zone:

> Strategically, a reopened canal, operating as an international water-
> way, would provide the naval forces of all nations with a short
> direct line of communications between the Mediterranean Sea and
> the Red Sea/Indian Ocean/ Persian Gulf. . . . The Soviet Union has
> demonstrated interest in the Indian Ocean area since 1967, when a
> Soviet Pacific Fleet naval task force made its first deployment to the
> area. . . . The principal strategic impact of a reopened canal would
> be to make possible more rapid increases in Soviet military pres-
> ence throughout the Red Sea/Indian Ocean/Persian Gulf area and
> to reduce the cost of Soviet resupply, repair, and military/economic
> aid actions. . . . Access to the Suez Canal would also permit more
> rapid reinforcement of US naval forces stationed in the Persian
> Gulf. . . . On balance, the strategic value of a reopened Suez Canal
> favors the USSR. . . . In view of the interests and strategic advan-
> tages to the Soviets of a reopened canal and the fact the Soviets
> have established a considerable military presence in the United
> Arab Republic (UAR) it appears prudent for the United States to
> explore the possibility of using US support for the reopening of
> the Suez Canal as a lever in seeking UAR agreement to reduce the
> Soviet presence in the UAR. . . . Economically, a reopened Suez
> Canal probably would benefit US NATO Allies, Japan, and coun-
> tries which produce primary products along the Indian Ocean
> littoral. This economic impact could be beneficial to the United
> States. For the Soviets, a reopened canal would provide some eco-
> nomic benefit, but its principal consequence would be strategic.

The memo shows the importance of the Suez Canal in advancing the geostra-
tegic position of the United States and concludes that reopening the canal as part of an agreement for equal access for Israel and Egypt, as well as all nations, would be in the best interest of the United States despite short-term Soviet strategic gains.

Chapter 4. The Collapse of the Egyptian Armed Forces

1. David S. Robarge, "CIA Analysis of the 1967 War: Getting It Right," *Studies in Intelligence* 49, no. 1, https://www.cia.gov/library/center-for-the-study-of -intelligence/csi-publications/csi-studies/studies/vol49no1/html_files/arab _israeli_war_1.html. The article was classified when written and then declassi- fied in 2007 and posted on the CIA website.

2. Bernard Firestone and Robert Vogt, eds., *Lyndon Baines Johnson and the Uses of Power* (Westport, CT: Greenwood Press, 1988), 261–262. See also Michael Bohn, "Hot Line: Even without a Cold War, the Washington-Moscow Link Is Still Up," *Washington Post Magazine*, July 31, 2013, http://www.washing tonpost.com/lifestyle/magazine/hot-line-even-without-a-cold-war-the-wash ington-moscow-link-is-still-up/2013/07/31/5f3305d8-ea34-11e2-8f22 -de4bd2a2bd39_story.html. The Bohn article contains excellent anecdotes, such as a story about Kosygin's first contact with Johnson: when the hotline teletype arrived at the Pentagon, Secretary Robert McNamara had to wake the president to ask for instructions on how to respond. The article reports that nineteen messages were sent between Johnson and Kosygin during the Six- Day War and that the hotline was engaged again by Nixon and Leonid Brezh- nev during the 1973 Yom Kippur War. Of note, the hotline when it sprang into action in 1967 did not extend into the White House, but ended in the Penta- gon; this is why Robert McNamara had to wake the president. See the 2003 Errol Morris documentary of McNamara, *The Fog of War*. A 2003 BBC article on the fortieth anniversary of the Moscow Link, as the hotline was called, recounts that Kosygin, Foreign Minister Andrei Gromyko, and Yuri Andropov of the KGB first went together to communicate on the teletype, not realizing that it was a teletype device, not a telephone. The operator's hands shook as he typed their message; he had never seen all three Soviet leaders in one room, let alone standing over him. See "Cold War Hotline Recalled," BBC News, June 7, 2003, http://news.bbc.co.uk/2/hi/europe/2971558.stm.

3. Harriet Dashiell Schwar and Edward C. Keefer, eds., *Foreign Relations of the United States, 1964–1968* (Washington, DC: Government Printing Office, 2004), 19:366–368, covering June 8, 1967.

4. The following excerpts are from Harold H. Saunders, "The President's Stake in the Middle East," memorandum to Walt Rostow, May 16, 1967, in *Foreign Rela- tions of the United States, 1964–1968*, 21:44: "While we are engaged in Vietnam we want to spare him [President Johnson] the political and the human burden of having to commit American forces in the Middle East too. . . . The 'war of national liberation' as a technique has come to the Middle East on Israel's

borders, and now in South Arabia. His [the president's] friends in the Middle East are asking how we can stand against terrorist attackers in Vietnam and not in Israel or South Arabia. [Egyptian] Foreign Minister Riad told me bluntly 'you are working against us everywhere in the Middle East. You have chosen sides.' No amount of logic or argument will break this suspicion." A National Intelligence Estimate titled "The Eastern Arab World and Its Aftermath" (December 19, 1968, in *Foreign Relations of the United States, 1964–1968*, 21:81) concluded, "The war [June 1967] and its aftermath have greatly reduced U.S. influence in the Arab world and increased that of the USSR. So long as Arab-Israeli tensions remain high, Soviet influence is likely to remain strong particularly among radical Arabs."

CHAPTER 5. Challenges to Civil Authority

1. Oren, *Six Days of War.* I had the great pleasure of meeting Ambassador Oren in a regional studies program organized by the National Defense University's Eisenhower School while I was a student in academic year 2009–2010. I told him how much I admired his book on the Six-Day War. Meeting various ambassadors is one of the great benefits of a National Defense University education.

2. It is not known precisely what Amer swallowed, and the toxicology report has never been made public. Because of the controversy over Amer's death and tenacious legal efforts by his family to understand the truth, a military prosecutor was assigned in September 2012 to investigate the circumstances of his suicide. All surviving files were transferred to the prosecutor. Perhaps the results will finally be made public. ("Military Prosecutor to Investigate Death of Former Egypt Defence Minister Abdel-Hakim Amer," *Ahram Online*, September 6, 2012, http://english.ahram.org.eg/NewsContent/1/64/52162/Egypt /Politics-/Military-prosecutor-to-investigate-death-of-former.aspx.) The late Robin L. Bidwell, in *The Dictionary of Modern Arab History* (New York: Routledge, 1998), 28, indicates that it was a cyanide tablet, as does Jehan Sadat, the widow of Anwar Sadat, in her autobiography, *A Woman of Egypt* (New York: Simon & Schuster, 2002), 240.

3. Cited in Edgar O'Ballance, *The Electronic War in the Middle East* (Hamden, CT: Archon Books, 1974), 25.

4. The two-part Al Jazeera documentary examining the suicide of Field Marshal Abdel-Hakim Amer was produced by Yosri Fouda and aired in 2009 as part of the *Sirri lil Ghaya* (Top Secret) series. The series covers a number of political crimes, conspiracies, and assassinations that altered modern Middle Eastern

history. The installment in this series detailing Amer's death is titled *Mawt al-Rajul al-Thani* (Death of [Egypt's] Second Man).

5. Mohamed Heikal, quoted in Oren, *Six Days of War*, 320.

6. Kandil, *Soldiers, Spies, and Statesmen*.

CHAPTER 6. Starting from Zero

1. Brezhnev gave a speech to the Communist Party of the Soviet Union (CPSU) Central Committee Plenum titled "The Soviet Union's Policy Regarding Israel's Aggression in the Middle East" on June 20, 1967. In it he invoked General Fawzi to absolve the Soviet Union of being complicit in Egypt and Syria's defeat in the Six-Day War: "Major work is being conducted in the army as well. The new Commander in Chief of the UAR armed forces, General Fawzi, issued a command stating that the Soviet Union bears no responsibility for the UAR defeat in the war and that it helped and is continuing to help the United Arab Republic." When reading the Soviet archives alongside Fawzi's memoir, one sees the concern the Soviets had for preserving their superpower prestige around the globe; Nasser capitalized on this concern. See Yaacov Ro'i and Boris Morozov, eds., *The Soviet Union and the June 1967 Six Day War* (Stanford, CA: Stanford University Press, 2008), 328.

2. O'Ballance, *Electronic War in the Middle East*, 33.

3. Oil prices from "Spot Oil Price: West Texas Intermediate," last modified August 14, 2013, http://research.stlouisfed.org/fred2/data/OILPRICE.txt.

4. Daniel Yergin, *The Prize: The Epic Quest for Oil, Money and Power* (New York: Simon & Schuster, 1991). This book, Yergin's masterpiece, is a must-read. In it he details the rise of "the hydrocarbon man," a term he coined. *The Prize* won the 1992 Pulitzer Prize for nonfiction and has been translated into a dozen languages. An excellent documentary based on it was produced by PBS. On a personal note, I carried a well-worn copy of *The Prize* during my deployment on board USS *Guam* (LPH-9) as a newly promoted lieutenant and have read the book more than once, including while I was involved in Operations Southern Watch and Desert Thunder in 1998. A paper prepared by the Department of State Near East Bureau dated February 6, 1967 (in *Foreign Relations of the United States 1964–1968*, 21:41), lucidly captures the concern America's officials had for global dependence on Middle East crude: "Simple statistics on Middle Eastern oil can only be defined as staggering. *The area contains 2/3rds of the Free World's oil reserves, and provides over 1/3rd of its current production. *Production costs are roughly 1/10th those in U.S. *The area supplies over half of Western Europe's oil. *Over 85% of Japan's oil comes from the Persian Gulf.

*Area oil production has increased from 1.3 million barrels per day in 1948 to over 9.5 million b/d at present, for an annual growth rate of 12%." Reading this report, I could not help but reflect on how fracking, shale oil, Russian production, and China's consumption have altered the world's energy calculus; what has not changed is humankind's utter dependence on fossil fuels.

5. Abdel-Magid Farid served as Nasser's secretary general for eleven years and attended many of the president's meetings. He provides a clearer picture of the mind-sets of Nasser and Hussein in his *Nasser: The Final Years* (Reading, UK: Ithaca Press, 1994). In a meeting between King Hussein and Nasser in Cairo on April 6, 1968, Jordanian prime minister Bahjat al-Talhuni asked Nasser whether he was concerned about Israeli retaliation in the aftermath of the "Battle of Karameh," a Palestine Liberation Organization (PLO) raid from Jordanian territory: "What will be the position of the United Arab Republic in the event of an Israeli attack against us?" Nasser replied, "I asked LtGen Fawzi on the day of the attack on al-Karameh to assess the position and to see what we might be able to do militarily. Fawzi told me that he would open fire along the entire front within half an hour of the order being given. Before issuing orders to LtGen Fawzi, I consulted [Egyptian foreign minister] Mahmoud Riad, who advised that a military step of this nature would have far reaching effects on the political front and that it would be better not to embark on it at this time. But if what is meant is the degree of our forces' readiness to cross to the east bank of the Canal, then they still need time to complete their preparations. They also need nearly 20,000 ordinary half-track vehicles, which are going to cost 60 million [Egyptian] pounds." (Farid, *Nasser*, 120.)

CHAPTER 7. Plan Granite

1. Frederick Kempe, *Berlin 1961: Kennedy, Khrushchev, and the Most Dangerous Place on Earth* (New York: Putnam, 2011). After I reviewed this book in my regular book review column in the local Washington, D.C., Navy newspaper, *Waterline*, Admiral James G. Stavridis, USN (Ret.), dean of the Fletcher School, graciously introduced me to the author. This introduction led to Kempe's generous support of my efforts and the foreword for this chapter.

2. O'Ballance, *Electronic War in the Middle East*, 65.

3. While visiting Tripoli, Nasser said to Qadhafi on June 10, 1970, "These days we are also hearing comments about the so-called 'defeated leaderships of 1967.' What do these words mean? What is the significance of reiterating them all over the place? LtGen Fawzi submitted his resignation to me, but I've turned it down. But I've asked him to offer it to the Arab Kings and Presidents at the

forthcoming Tripoli conference. Imagine that these words are not meant for LtGen Fawzi but they are actually aimed at me. I don't think any one of us has forgotten the lesson from the Second World War. Even though the attacking Germans were a few kilometers from Moscow, Stalin and Zhukov stayed put in the capital." Using threatening language, Nasser was asking Qadhafi to cease fanning the flames of discord and reminding him that he was not among the frontline states bordering Israel and bearing the brunt of the conflict. See Farid, *Nasser,* 173.

4. Fawzi's report was noticed by the U.S. State Department and mentioned in Joseph Sisco, "Assessment of Rabat Arab Conference," memorandum to William Rogers, January 6, 1970, in *Foreign Relations of the United States,* 1969–1976 24:56–58. Following is an excerpt from this document: "Rabat Conference ended December 23, 1969, UAR General Fawzi's estimates that it would require at least three years and enormous cost for the Arab armies to reach the point where the Israelis are today; apparently had a sobering effect on Arab leaders. As a result, the assessment of the military situation was realistic and the advocates of an early military solution were largely by-passed. In particular the UAR emerged with greater freedom of action—if Nasser chooses to exercise it. . . . There are those, in fact, who suspect that Nasser wanted General Fawzi's military plan to be rejected in order that he might be left free to seek additional military and economic aid, while remaining open to possibilities for a political settlement." Sisco's memorandum divides the Middle East of that time into East Arab moderates (Saudi Arabia, Kuwait, and Lebanon), Jordan, the militants (Syria, Iraq, and South Yemen), the Maghreb, the Fedayeen, and the UAR. These are camps he saw in his monitoring of developments in the Middle East.

The United States was not unaware of the effect the escalation of hostilities along the Suez Canal was having on regional stability. The secretary of state's reports to the Senate Foreign Relations and House Foreign Affairs Committees provide added depth to the information in Fawzi's memoir: "Diplomatic activity was increasingly overshadowed by intensifying military action, particularly between Israel and the UAR, and by increased Fedayeen activity. In the Spring of 1969, the UAR had declared that the cease-fire observed since the summer of 1967 between Israeli and Egyptian forces was no longer valid; Egypt could no longer passively acquiesce in continued Israeli occupation of Egyptian soil. Heavy artillery exchanges along the Suez Canal led to expanded air activity and finally during the winter and early spring to a series of Israeli air strikes deep into the UAR. In an effort to defuse the military situation and create a climate in which settlement efforts might go forward, the Secretary of State on

March 23, 1970, announced the Administration's decision to hold in abeyance an Israeli request for an additional Phantom and Skyhawk aircraft. . . . Israel's air capacity was sufficient to meet its needs for the time being. At the same time, noting that evidence had just begun to become available of the introduction of Soviet manned SA-3 anti-aircraft missiles in the UAR. The Secretary made clear that we would keep the situation under careful scrutiny and not hesitate to reconsider Israel's request if developments warranted. In addition to the introduction of SA-3s in March, we learned in April that Soviet pilots were flying operational missions over the UAR." William P. Rogers, *United States Foreign Policy, 1969–1970: A Report of the Secretary of State*, Department of State Publication 8575, General Foreign Policy Series 254 (Washington, DC: U.S. Government Printing Office, 1971).

5. Uqbah ibn Nafeeh was born in Mecca in AD 622. His uncle Amr ibn al-A'as, a foe of Prophet Muhammad who converted and went on to conquer Egypt, sent Uqbah to conquer much of present-day Libya and Tunisia. Uqbah died in battle in AD 683 and is considered a chivalric hero in present-day North Africa. Wheelus AFB had been created by the allies in World War II and taken over by the U.S. Air Force afterward.

6. Mohamed Hassanein Heikal, *The Road to Ramadan* (New York: Quadrangle/New York Times Book, 1975), 108.

CHAPTER 8. Formulating a General Strategy for the War of Attrition

1. Lashinkov also assumed the title of commander in chief of the Soviet forces in Egypt.

CHAPTER 9. Redesigning the Egyptian Armed Forces

1. Paul Murphy, ed., *The Soviet Air Forces* (Jefferson, NC: McFarland, 1984).

2. Philip Mosely, *The Kremlin and World Politics: Studies in Soviet Policy and Action* (New York: Vintage Books, 1960), 4.

3. Ibid., 429.

4. W. W. Kulski, *The Soviet Union in World Affairs: A Documented Analysis, 1964–1972* (Syracuse, NY: Syracuse University Press, 1973), 181.

5. Ibid., 454–455.

6. The Battle of Karameh made the reputation of an obscure guerrilla leader named Yasser Arafat (d. 2004). Arafat would propel himself from participating in an obscure guerrilla group to leading the PLO and presiding over the liberation movement for over three decades.

7. Stephen Roth, ed., *The Impact of the Six Day War* (New York: St. Martin's Press, 1988), 132, 141.

CHAPTER 10. Overhauling the Egyptian Armed Forces

1. Raphael Patai, *The Arab Mind*, rev. ed. (New York: Hatherleigh Press, 2007). First published by Scribner's in 1973. Colonel DeAtkine wrote the foreword for the 2002 and 2007 revised editions. He is an esteemed colleague, and we have the pleasure of meeting once or twice a year for a panel discussion on "the Arab mind" at the National Intelligence University.
2. Norvell DeAtkine, "Why Arabs Lose Wars," *Middle East Quarterly* 6, no. 4 (December 1999), http://www.meforum.org/441/why-arabs-lose-wars.
3. It is fairly certain that Fawzi and the other generals were influenced by Carl von Clausewitz (1780–1831) and the Soviet strategist Alexander Svechin (1878–1938). Their other influences are unfortunately left to speculation.
4. Today it is estimated that the Egyptian military runs 30 to 40 percent of the economy, from dairies to cell-phone companies. This system was started by Defense Minister Field Marshal Abdel-Halim Abu Ghazallah (in office from 1981 to 1989), who in a bid to restructure the armed forces sought to decouple more of the military budget from the state by creating companies that would finance ever-larger aspects of the armed forces, particularly morale, welfare, recreation, uniforms, and, likely, secret military projects. In the process Abu Ghazallah improved the condition of the average Egyptian soldier but further entrenched the problem of the armed forces being a state within a state.
5. While the United States was occupied with Vietnam, the Soviet Union developed more robust blue-water naval capabilities, leading to an era of expansion under Admiral Sergei Gorshkov, who turned the Soviet navy into a global power projection force in the later part of the 1970s. This argument was lucidly made by former deputy undersecretary of the Navy Seth Cropsey in his thought-provoking book, *Mayday: The Decline of American Naval Supremacy* (New York: Overlook Press, 2013), 96.

CHAPTER 11. Psychological Recovery, Artillery, Special Forces, and Respect for the Adversary

1. Raphael Israeli, *Man of Defiance: A Political Biography of Anwar Sadat*, with Carol Bardenstein (Totowa, NJ: Barnes and Noble Books, 1985), 81.
2. Ibid., 82.
3. Stacy Perman, *Spies, Inc.: Business Innovation from Israel's Masters of Espionage* (Upper Saddle River, NJ: FT Press, 2004), 64.

4. Balah Island is in the Suez Canal Zone, southeast of Qantarah and northeast of Suez, and is sometimes spelled Ballah Island. It is not to be confused with Balah Island in Assuit Province in Upper Egypt, an island in the middle of the Nile used for Egyptian military training before the 1973 Arab-Israeli War.

CHAPTER 13. Egypt's Air Defense Problem and Egyptian Naval Capabilities

1. Alistair Horne, *A Savage War of Peace: Algeria 1954–1962* (London: MacMillan, 1977).
2. Nutting, *Nasser*.
3. William Taubman, *Khrushchev: The Man and His Era* (New York: W. W. Norton, 2004), 256.
4. O'Ballance, *Electronic War in the Middle East*, 98.
5. Anatoly Kanashchenkov and Alexander Osokin, "Chief Designer Ardalion Rastov," *Military Parade Magazine*, May/June 1998, 126–128.

CHAPTER 14. Egyptian Special Forces Operations

1. The office of prime minister was assumed by Nasser after the 1967 Six-Day War, and he held the office until his death in 1970, after which Foreign Minister Mahmoud Fawzi served as Sadat's first prime minister until September 1971.
2. I have decided to use the terms *First Republic* and *Second Republic* to delineate between the pre– and post–Arab Spring phases of Egypt's political history. My characterization is derived from the labels historically used for political changes in France; the five French Republics represented major shifts in the experiment of the 1789 French Revolution. Whether the July 2013 ousting of the elected Egyptian Islamist president Mohamed Morsi represents a third republic or a corrective revolution remains to be seen.
3. It is useful to merge Fawzi's memoir with State Department archives of the period to reveal a more comprehensive picture of Nixon and his National Security Council's thinking. President Nixon requested two papers on Arab-Israeli problems to be considered by the National Security Council. These papers were drafted by the Interdepartmental Group for Near East and South Asia on January 30, 1969, ten days into Nixon's presidency. Following are excerpts from these documents that add texture to Fawzi's memoir:

> How grave is the Soviet Threat? The Soviet Union continues its effort to reduce western, particularly American positions and influence in the Middle East, and to expand its own. It has established strong but not dominant positions in the UAR, Syria, and Iraq. It

has replaced the bulk of military equipment lost in the [1967] war by those states. It has increased the number of its military advisors substantially. . . . The Soviet Navy has been allowed greater use of Egyptian ports and repair facilities, and a small number of Soviet aircraft [with Egyptian markings] have been conducting recon operations over the Sixth Fleet. . . .

What is the current US position in the Middle East? There are those who see the June 1967 war and its aftermath as having dangerously accelerated the erosion of influence in the Middle East. The trend towards polarization has intensified, driving radical Arab states further into the Soviet orbit and making it increasingly difficult for the Arab moderates to maintain ties with the United States.

See Qaimmaqami and Keefer, *Foreign Relations of the United States, 1969–1976*, 24:4–5.
4. The Reserve Officers School was moved to Isna in the south of Egypt.

CHAPTER 15. Translating Soviet Military Aid into Egyptian Strategic Options

1. On one day alone in February 1970, between eighty and a hundred Soviet cargo ships and tankers were crammed in Alexandria Harbor, and the Soviet 108th Fighter Aviation Brigade, made up of thirty to forty MiG-21s, was tasked with providing aerial escort and cover for Soviet vessels on their approach into Egypt. The unit was based at Janaklis Air Base near Alexandria. See V. V. Zaborskiy, "The Fifth (Mediterranean) Squadron: Air Defense Operations (1970–1972)," *Military Thought* 16, no. 1 (2007): 186–199.
2. General G. U. Dolnikov, a legendary World War II fighter pilot, was designated commander, Soviet Fighter Aviation Force, in Egypt. He had command of Soviet-piloted and -crewed air and air defense units in Egypt. See ibid.
3. General Lashinkov was replaced by General I. S. Katyshkin, who was replaced by General Vasily V. Okunev. The formal title for all three was commander in chief of Soviet forces in Egypt. Arabic-to-Russian translations have seen General Shazly refer to Lashinkov as Lashnekov, and Fawzi referred to Okunev as Okinov. Fawzi refers to his Soviet colleagues by their rank and last name only, wheras Shazly does the same in some parts of his memoir but gives full names in others. It is necessary to consult Russian source materials, like the journal *Military Thought*, to gain a better understanding of the Soviet generals mentioned in Arabic military memoirs. Heikal indicates that General Lashinkov suffered a minor heart attack while in Egypt. See *Road to Ramadan*, 83.

4. I. S. Katyshkin published recollections of his World War II experiences fighting the Germans on the eastern front in a book titled *Sluzhili my v shtabe armeiskom: Voennye Memuary* (Service in the Headquarters of the Army: Military Recollections), part of the Raboche-Krest'ianskaia Krasnaia Armiia (Red Army of Workers and Peasants) Series, which features the personal narratives and biographies of World War II Soviet flag officers. General Katyshkin's recollections were published in 1979 by Russia's largest Moscow-based publisher, Voenizdat (short for Voennoe Izdatelstvo, or "Military Publication"), which was initially created in 1919 to serve the publishing needs of the Soviet military. Fawzi makes no mention of the extraordinary military careers of his Soviet counterparts, and reading his Arabic memoir, I am left wondering whether conversations about eastern front campaigns ever occurred and which battles were discussed. Of note, whereas Fawzi fails to mention his Soviet colleagues' leadership in World War II, General Shazly in his memoir does discuss the Soviets' involvement in certain campaigns of World War II, which he calls the Great Patriotic War, particularly the titanic battles of Kursk and Stalingrad (Saad ed-Din el-Shazly, *The Crossing of the Suez*, rev. English ed. [San Francisco: American Mideast Research, 1980], 102).

5. General Vasily Okunev was instrumental in providing the Egyptians detailed satellite imagery of the Sinai starting in 1971. This imagery enabled Egyptian military planners to better understand the terrain and produce detailed maps (ibid., 115).

6. In October 2011 the first authorized memoir of General Saad el-Din el-Shazly was released in Egypt. General Shazly's memoir had been censored and was among the fruits of the downfall of Egyptian dictator Hosni Mubarak. The operational architect of the 1973 Yom Kippur War, General Shazly was persecuted by both Sadat and Mubarak, and over decades the late general was expunged from Egypt's official military histories. As if on cue, General Shazly passed away on February 10, 2011, the day before Mubarak was forced out of office by Egypt's military leadership.

7. David Nicolle and Tom Cooper, *Arab MiG-19 and MiG-21 Units in Combat* (London: Osprey Press, 2004), 33.

CHAPTER 16. Concluding Thoughts

1. Heikal, *Road to Ramadan*, 45.

2. Ibid., 47.

3. Ibid., 49.

4. Ibid., 48–49.

5. Youssef Aboul-Enein, "Syrian Defense Minister General Mustafa Tlas: Memoirs, Volume Two," *Military Review* 85, no. 3 (May/June 2005): 99–102.

6. Michael Oren, *Six Days of War: June 1967 and the Making of the Modern Middle East* (New York: Oxford University Press, 2002).

7. Sirrs, *Nasser and the Missile Age in the Middle East*, 157.

8. Ibid., 158.

9. William Mott IV, *Soviet Military Assistance: An Empirical Perspective* (Westport, CO: Greenwood Press, 2001), 81.

10. Michael Taylor and John Taylor, *Missiles of the World* (New York: Charles Scribner, 1972), 39.

11. Ibid.

12. Ibid., 45.

13. Ibid., 62.

14. Sirrs, *Nasser and the Missile Age in the Middle East*, 159–160.

15. Amons Perlmutter, *Egypt: The Praetorian State* (Piscataway, NJ: Transaction Books, 1974).

16. Heikal, *Road to Ramadan*, 108

17. Marvin Kalb, *The Road to War: Presidential Commitments Honored and Betrayed* (Washington, DC: Brookings Institution Press, 2013), 204–205.

18. Mosely, *Kremlin and World Politics*, 480. In the top-secret Kissinger transcripts, Nixon's secretary of state told Deng Xiaoping in April 1974: "If we are successful in these disengagement talks [between Egypt and Israel in the Sinai], we can hope to reduce Soviet influence in Syria, as we did in Egypt." See William Burr, ed., *The Kissinger Transcripts: The Top Secret Talks with Beijing and Moscow* (New York: New Press, 1998), 344.

19. "China Likely to Become World's Largest Oil Importer," BBC Business News, August 12, 2013, http://www.bbc.co.uk/news/business-23664989.

20. *The 50-Years War: Israel and the Arabs*, directed by Dai Richards and David Ash (Washington, DC: PBS Home Video, 1998).

21. Kirk Beattie, *Egypt during the Sadat Years* (New York: Palgrave, 2000), 48.

22. Ibid.

23. Kandil, *Soldiers, Spies and Statesmen*. Kandil writes that PBI chief and founder Sami Sharaf, Fawzi's relative, was uncovered as a longtime KGB source. Another PBI chief who was an alleged longtime Israeli source and discussed in Kandil's book, Ashraf Marwan, Nasser's son-in-law, died under mysterious circumstances in 2007, falling from the balcony of his London home. Marwan's espionage role has been a matter of debate since it was publicly revealed in 2002, with one side claiming he was a valuable Israeli spy code-named "The In-Law," "The Angel," "Chotel," "Rashash," and "Babel." The Egyptian side

claims he was a double agent. See Robert Dover, Michael Goodman, and Clau-
dia Hillebrand, eds., *Routledge Companion to Intelligence Studies* (New York:
Routledge, 2013); and Ephraim Kahana and Muhammad Suwaed, *Historical
Dictionary of Middle Eastern Intelligence* (Lanham, MD: Scarecrow Press,
2009), 30.

24. CIA, Center for the Study of Intelligence, https://www.cia.gov/library/center
-for-the-study-of-intelligence.

25. Stanley McChrystal, *My Share of the Task: A Memoir* (New York: Portfolio
/Penguin, 2013).

I had the privilege of meeting General McChrystal at the Pentagon.
He was speaking to West Point cadets before I was to deliver my seminar
on al-Qaida–associated movements. In this encounter I learned General
McChrystal had listened to a recorded version of my seminar "An Analytic
Introduction to the Quran" and found it contributed to his own understanding
of the region. This was among many memorable encounters I have experienced in our military.

Appendix 2. Egyptian General Saad el-Din el-Shazly

1. Saad el-Din el-Shazly, *Harb Uktubur: Mudhakiraat Al-Fariq El-Shazly* (The
October War: Memoir of General Shazly) (Algiers: National Establishment
for Authors, 1979). Shazly was tried and sentenced to life imprisonment in
absentia by an Egyptian court for revealing state secrets by publishing this
book without proper authorization. He had grown to be a tenacious opponent and critic of Anwar Sadat. His sentence was set aside during the Mubarak
regime, and he returned to Egypt after a long exile.

2. Al Jazeera, *Al-General* (The General), aired February and March 2013.

3. Elizabeth Monroe and A. H. Farrar, *The Arab-Israeli War, October 1973: Background and Events*, Adephi Paper #111 (London: International Institute for
Strategic Studies, Winter 1974/1975), 32.

4. Trevor N. Dupuy, *Elusive Victory: The Arab-Israeli Wars, 1947–1974* (New
York: Harper & Row, 1978).

Appendix 3. Egyptian General Abdel-Moneim Riad

1. Field Marshal Tantawi was retired by President Mohamed Morsi in August
2012, after three decades as war minister. Tantawi was a 1956 graduate of
Egypt's military academy, and his replacement, General al-Sisi, was a 1977
graduate, which should provide the reader an appreciation for the generational

differences. Egypt's State Information Service, http://www.sis.gov.eg, features biographies of Egyptian officials.

2. Mohammed al-Gawady, *Al-Shaheed Abdel-Moneim Riad, Samaa Al-Askariyah Al-Misriyah* [The Martyr Abdel-Moneim Riad, Model of the Egyptian Army] (Cairo: Dar al-Ateeba, 1984).

★★★

SELECTED BIBLIOGRAPHY

BOOKS

Beattie, Kirk. *Egypt during the Sadat Years*. New York: Palgrave, 2000.

Confino, Michael, and Shimon Shamir, eds. *The USSR and the Middle East*. Jerusalem: Israel University Press, 1973.

Cropsey, Seth. *Mayday: The Decline of American Naval Supremacy*. New York: Overlook Press, 2013.

Dupuy, Trevor N. *Elusive Victory: The Arab-Israeli Wars, 1947–1974*. New York: Harper & Row, 1978.

Farid, Abdel Magid. *Nasser: The Final Years*. Reading, UK: Ithaca Press, 1994.

Fawzi, Mohamed. *Harb Thalathah Sanawat, 1967–1970: Muzakirat al-Fareeq al-Awal Mohamed Fawzi, Wazeer al-Harbiyah al-Asbaq* [The Three Years War, 1967–1970: The Memoir of General Mohamed Fawzi, the Former War Minister], 5th ed. Cairo: Dar al-Mustaqbal Printing, 1990.

Ferris, Jesse. *Nasser's Gamble: How Intervention in Yemen Caused the Six-Day War and the Decline of Egyptian Power*. Princeton, NJ: Princeton University Press, 2013.

Gamasi, Abdel-Ghani El-. *The October War: Memoirs of Field Marshal El-Gamasi of Egypt*. Cairo: American University of Cairo Press, 1993.

Gawady, Mohammed al-. *Al-Shaheed Abdel-Moneim Riad, Samaa Al-Askariyah Al-Misriyah* [The Martyr Abdel-Moneim Riad, Model of the Egyptian Army]. Cairo: Dar al-Ateeba, 1984.

Goldschmidt, Arthur. *Biographical Dictionary of Modern Egypt*. Boulder, CO: Lynne Rienner, 2000.

Heikal, Mohamed Hassanein. *The Cairo Documents: The Inside Story of Nasser and His Relationship with World Leaders, Rebels, and Statesmen*. New York: Doubleday, 1973.

———. *The Road to Ramadan*. New York: Quadrangle/New York Times Book, 1975.

———. *The Sphinx and the Commissar: The Rise and Fall of Soviet Influence in the Middle East*. New York: Harper & Row, 1978.

Hofstader, Dan, ed. *Egypt and Nasser*, Vol. 3, *1967–72*. New York: Facts on File, 1973.

Horne, Alistair. *A Savage War of Peace: Algeria 1954–1962.* London: MacMillan, 1977.

Howland, Nina Davis, and David S. Patterson, eds. *Foreign Relations of the United States, 1964–1968,* Vol. 21, *Near East Region: Arabian Peninsula.* Washington, DC: Government Printing Office, 2000.

Israeli, Raphael. *Man of Defiance: A Political Biography of Anwar Sadat.* With Carol Bardenstein. Totowa, NJ: Barnes and Noble Books, 1985.

Jones, Frank Leith. *Blowtorch: Robert Komer, Vietnam, and American Cold War Strategy.* Annapolis, MD: Naval Institute Press, 2013.

Kalb, Marvin. *The Road to War: Presidential Commitments Honored and Betrayed.* Washington, DC: Brookings Institution Press, 2013.

Kandil, Hazem. *Soldiers, Spies, and Statesmen: Egypt's Road to Revolt.* New York: Verso, 2012.

Kempe, Frederick. *Berlin 1961: Kennedy, Khrushchev, and the Most Dangerous Place on Earth.* New York: Putnam, 2011.

Khrushchev, Sergei. *Nikita Khrushchev and the Creation of a Superpower.* Translated by Shirley Benson. University Park: Pennsylvania State University, 2000.

Kimche, David, and Dan Bawley. *The Six Day War: Prologue and Aftermath.* New York: Stein and Day, 1971.

Kinzer, Stephen, *The Brothers: John Foster Dulles, Allen Dulles, and Their Secret World War.* New York: Henry Holt and Company, 2013.

Kulski, W. W. *The Soviet Union in World Affairs: A Documented Analysis, 1964–1972.* Syracuse, NY: Syracuse University Press, 1973.

McChrystal, Stanley. *My Share of the Task: A Memoir.* New York: Portfolio/Penguin, 2013.

Mosely, Philip. *The Kremlin and World Politics: Studies in Soviet Policy and Action.* New York: Vintage Books, 1960.

Murphy, Paul, ed. *The Soviet Air Forces.* Jefferson, NC: McFarland, 1984.

Nasser, Gamal Abdel. *Egypt's Liberation: The Philosophy of the Revolution.* Washington, DC: Public Affairs, 1955.

Nicolle, David, and Tom Cooper. *Arab MiG-19 and MiG-21 Units in Combat.* London: Osprey Press, 2004.

Nordeen, Lon. *Fighters over Israel: The Story of the Israeli Air Force from the War of Independence to the Bekaa Valley.* London: Guild, 1991.

Nutting, Anthony. *Nasser.* New York: Dutton, 1972.

O'Ballance, Edgar. *The Electronic War in the Middle East.* Hamden, CT: Archon Books, 1974.

Oren, Michael B. *Six Days of War: June 1967 and the Making of the Modern Middle East.* New York: Oxford University Press, 2002.

Parker, Richard, ed. *The Six Day War: A Retrospective*. Gainesville: University Press of Florida, 1996.

Patai, Raphael. *The Arab Mind*, rev. ed. New York: Hatherleigh Press, 2007.

Perlmutter, Amons. *Egypt: The Praetorian State*. Piscataway, NJ: Transaction Books, 1974.

Perman, Stacy. *Spies, Inc.: Business Innovation from Israel's Masters of Espionage*. Upper Saddle River, NJ: FT Press, 2004.

Qaimmaqami, Linda W., and Edward C. Keefer, eds. *Foreign Relations of the United States 1969–1976*, Vol. 24, *Middle East Region and Arabian Peninsula, 1969–1972, Jordan 1970*. Washington, DC: U.S. Government Printing Office, 2008.

Rikhye, Indar Jit. *The Sinai Blunder: Withdrawal of the United Nations Emergency Force Leading to the Six Day War of June 1967*. London: Frank Cass, 1980.

Ro'i, Yaacov, and Boris Morozov, eds. *The Soviet Union and the June 1967 Six Day War*. Stanford, CA: Stanford University Press, 2008.

Roth, Stephen, ed. *The Impact of the Six Day War*. New York: St Martin's Press, 1988.

Safran, Nadav. *From War to War: The Arab-Israeli Confrontations*. New York: Pegasus, 1969.

Schwar, Harriet Dashiell, and Edward C. Keefer, eds. *Foreign Relations of the United States, 1964–1968*, Vol. 19, *Arab-Israeli Crisis and War, 1967*. Washington, DC: Government Printing Office, 2004.

Shazly, Saad el-Din el-. *The Arab Military Option*. San Francisco: American Mideast Research, 1986.

———. *The Crossing of the Suez*, rev. English ed. San Francisco: American Mideast Research, 2003.

———. *Harb Uktubur: Mudhakiraat Al-Fariq El-Shazly* [The October War: Memoir of General Shazly]. Algiers: National Establishment for Authors, 1979.

Sirrs, Owen L. *Nasser and the Missile Age in the Middle East*. New York: Routledge, 2006.

Taylor, Michael, and John Taylor. *Missiles of the World*. New York: Charles Scribner, 1972.

Yergin, Daniel. *The Prize: The Epic Quest for Oil, Money and Power*. New York: Simon & Schuster, 1991.

ARTICLES AND PAPERS

Aboul-Enein, Youssef. "Syrian Defense Minister General Mustafa Tlas: Memoirs, Volume Two." *Military Review* 85, no. 3 (May/June 2005): 99–102.

DeAtkine, Norville. "Why Arabs Lose Wars." *Middle East Quarterly* 6, no. 4 (December 1999). http://www.meforum.org/441/why-arabs-lose-wars.

Fricker, John. "Boeing/McDonnell Douglas F-4 Phantom II Current Operators." *World Air Power Journal* 40 (Spring 2000): 59–60.

Monroe, Elizabeth, and A. H. Farrar. *The Arab-Israeli War, October 1973: Background and Events*, Adelphi Paper #111. London: International Institute for Strategic Studies, Winter 1974/1975.

Robarge, David S. "CIA Analysis of the 1967 Arab-Israeli War: Getting It Right." *Studies in Intelligence* 49, no. 1. https://www.cia.gov/library/center-for-the -study-of-intelligence/csi-publications/csi-studies/studies/vol49no1/html _files/arab_israeli_war_1.html.

Sisi, Abdel-Fatah al-. *Democracy in the Middle East*. Carlisle, PA: Army War College, 2006. http://www.scribd.com/doc/158975076/1878–001.

INDEX

Names beginning with al and al- are alphabetized under the main element of the name. For example, al-Qaida is alphabetized under Q.

ABOUT THE AUTHOR

YOUSSEF H. ABOUL-ENEIN is a U.S. Navy Medical Service Corps commander and designated Middle East foreign area officer. He currently is adjunct military professor and chair of Islamic Studies at the National Defense University's Dwight D. Eisenhower School for National Security and Resource Strategy (formerly the Industrial College of the Armed Forces, ICAF). Commander Aboul-Enein is also adjunct faculty for Middle East counterterrorism analysis at the National Intelligence University. He currently serves as senior adviser, subject matter expert, warning officer, and instructor on militant Islamist ideology at the Defense Combating Terrorism Center (DCTC) of the Defense Intelligence Agency (DIA) in Washington, D.C. He has been with DCTC since 2006 and took a year off to attend ICAF in the fall of 2010. From 2002 to 2006, Commander Aboul-Enein was country director for North Africa and Egypt, assistant country director for the Arabian Gulf, and special adviser on Islamist militancy at the Office of the Secretary of Defense for International Security Affairs. He advised the secretary of defense and the deputy undersecretary of defense for Near East and South Asian affairs on matters pertaining to the Middle East and represented the Defense Department in interagency meetings and before congressional staffers.

Commander Aboul-Enein holds a BBA from the University of Mississippi, an MBA and MHSA from the University of Arkansas in Little Rock, an MS in strategic intelligence from the National Intelligence University, and an MS in national resource strategy from ICAF. He attained diplomas from the Naval War College (nonresident) Command and Staff College, completing additional studies in international relations and international law; the Marine Corps University (nonresident) Amphibious Warfare School; and the Army War College's (nonresident) Defense Strategy Course. He is rated proficient in the Egyptian, Saudi Peninsular, Levantine, Modern Standard (Upper Level), and Iraqi dialects of Arabic by the Defense Language Institute. Commander Aboul-Enein is author of *Militant Islamist Ideology: Understanding the Global Threat*, which was named among the top 150 most influential books on terrorism and counterterrorism in the May 2012 edition of the journal *Perspectives on Terrorism*. This book was published in paperback in September 2013. He is also the author of *Iraq in Turmoil: Historical Perspectives of Dr. Ali al-Wardi from the Ottoman Empire to King Feisal*, as well as coauthor of *The Secret War for the Middle East*. All of these books were published by the Naval

Institute Press in 2010, 2012, and 2013. He is the recipient of the 2010 National Defense University Foundation Writing Award and a 2010 finalist for the Secretary of Defense National Security Essay Award for his research thesis that focuses on the Nile Basin Conflict in the twenty-first century. His Nile thesis was used by the staff of the U.S. special envoy to the Sudan and was published in the Naval Postgraduate School online journal, *Culture and Conflict*. Commander Aboul-Enein served as a distinguished judge in the 2011 and 2012 Secretary of Defense and Chairman of the Joint Chiefs of Staff National Security Essay Competition. He was also privileged to serve as a distinguished judge for the 2012 and 2013 Galileo Essay Contest for innovative papers within the U.S. intelligence community. Finally, he has lent his expertise on militant Islamist movements to various court proceedings; most recently he testified as an expert government witness in *United States v. PFC Bradley Manning*. Commander Aboul-Enein's deployments include operational tours in Bosnia, Liberia, and the Persian Gulf.